The Complete Works Of Lord Byron: Dramatic Pieces And Poems

Baron George Noël Gordon Byron, J. W. Lake

WORKS

OF

LORD BYRON.

VOL. VI.

THE

COMPLETE WORKS

OF

LORD BYRON

WITH

A BIOGRAPHICAL AND CRITICAL NOTICE

BY J. W. LAKE, ESQ.

VOL. VI.

Dramatic Pieces and Poems.

PARIS

From the Press of Jules Didot senior,

VI, RUE DU PONT-DE-LODI.

PUBLISHED BY BAUDRY, RUE DU COQ-SAINT-HONORÉ,

AND AMYOT, RUE DE LA PAIX.

1825.

CONTENTS

OF

THE SIXTH VOLUME.

HEAVEN AND EARTH, A MYSTERY.

THE DEFORMED TRANSFORMED, A DRAMA.

THE BRIDE OF ABYDOS, A TURKISH TALE.

CONTENTS.

THE CORSAIR, A TALE.

LARA, A TALE.

THE SIEGE OF CORINTH.

THE PRISONER OF CHILLON, A FABLE.

MAZEPPA, A POEM.

THE ISLAND; OR, CHRISTIAN AND HIS COMRADES.

THE LAMENT OF TASSO.

HEAVEN AND EARTH.

A MYSTERY.

FOUNDED ON THE FOLLOWING PASSAGE IN GENESIS,
CHAP. VI.

« And it came to pass ... that the sons of God saw the daughters of men that they were fair; and they took them wives of all which they chose.»

« And woman wailing for her demo ı lover.»—COLERIDGE.

DRAMATIS PERSONÆ.

ANGELS.

SAMIASA.
AZAZIEL.
RAPHAEL, the Archangel.

MEN.

NOAH, and his SONS.
IRAD.

WOMEN.

ANAH.
AHOLIBAMAH.

Chorus of Spirits of the Earth.—Chorus of Mortals.

HEAVEN AND EARTH.

PART I.

SCENE I.—A WOODY AND MOUNTAINOUS DISTRICT NEAR MOUNT ARARAT.—TIME—MIDNIGHT.

Enter ANAH and AHOLIBAMAH.

ANAH.

Our father sleeps: it is the hour when they
Who love us are accustom'd to descend
Through the deep clouds o'er rocky Ararat:—
How my heart beats!

AHOLIBAMAH.

Let us proceed upon
Our invocation.

ANAH.

But the stars are hidden.
I tremble.

AHOLIBAMAH.

So do I, but not with fear
Of aught save their delay.

ANAH.

My sister, though
I love Azaziel more than——oh, too much!
What was I going to say? my heart grows impious.

AHOLIBAMAH.

And where is the impiety of loving
Celestial natures?

ANAH.

But, Aholibamah,
I love our God less since his angel loved me:
This cannot be of good; and though I know not
That I do wrong, I feel a thousand fears
Which are not ominous of right.

AHOLIBAMAH.

Then wed thee
Unto some son of clay, and toil and spin!
There 's Japhet loves thee well, hath loved thee long;
Marry, and bring forth dust!

ANAH.

I should have loved
Azaziel not less were he mortal; yet
I am glad he is not. I cannot outlive him.
And when I think that his immortal wings
Will one day hover o'er the sepulchre
Of the poor child of clay which so adored him,
As he adores the Highest, death becomes
Less terrible; but yet I pity him;
His grief will be of ages, or at least
Mine would be such for him, were I the seraph,
And he the perishable.

AHOLIBAMAH.

Rather say,
That he will single forth some other daughter

Of earth, and love her as he once loved Anah.

ANAH.

And if it should be so, and she so loved him,
Better thus than that he should weep for me.

AHOLIBAMAH.

If I thought thus of Samiasa's love,
All seraph as he is, I 'd spurn him from me.
But to our invocation! 'T is the hour.

ANAH.

Seraph!
From thy sphere!
Whatever star contain thy glory;
In the eternal depths of Heaven
Albeit thou watchest with « the seven, »[1]
Though through space infinite and hoary
Before thy bright wings worlds be driven,
Yet hear!
Oh! think of her who holds thee dear!
And though she nothing is to thee,
Yet think that thou art all to her.
Thou canst not tell,—and never be
Such pangs decreed to aught save me,—
The bitterness of tears.
Eternity is in thine years,
Unborn, undying beauty in thine eyes;
With me thou canst not sympathize,
Except in love, and there thou must
Acknowledge that more loving dust
Ne'er wept beneath the skies.
Thou walk'st thy many worlds, thou see'st
The face of Him who made thee great,
As He hath made me of the least
Of those cast out from Eden's gate:

Yet, seraph, dear!
Oh hear!
For thou hast loved me, and I would not die
Until I know what I must die in knowing,
That thou forget'st in thine eternity
Her whose heart death could not keep from o'erflowing
For thee, immortal essence as thou art!
Great is their love who love in sin and fear;
And such I feel are waging in my heart
A war unworthy: to an Adamite
Forgive, my seraph! that such thoughts appear,
For sorrow is our element;
Delight
An Eden kept afar from sight,
Though sometimes with our visions blent.
The hour is near
Which tells me we are not abandon'd quite.—
Appear! appear!
Seraph!
My own Azaziel! be but here,
And leave the stars to their own light.

AHOLIBAMAH.

Samiasa!
Wheresoe'er
Thou rulest in the upper air—
Or warring with the spirits who may dare
Dispute with Him
Who made all empires' empire; or recalling
Some wandering star which shoots through the abyss,
Whose tenants dying, while their world is falling,
Share the dim destiny of clay in this;
Or joining with the inferior cherubim,

Thou deignest to partake their hymn—
Samiasa!
I call thee, I await thee, and I love thee.
Many worship thee, that will I not:
If that thy spirit down to mine may move thee,
Descend and share my lot!
Though I be form'd of clay,
And thou of beams
More bright than those of day
On Eden's streams,
Thine immortality can not repay
With love more warm than mine
My love. There is a ray
In me, which, though forbidden yet to shine,
I feel was lighted at thy God's and thine.
It may be hidden long: death and decay
Our mother Eve bequeath'd us—but my heart
Defies it: though this life must pass away,
Is *that* a cause for thee and me to part?
Thou art immortal—so am I: I feel—
I feel my immortality o'ersweep
All pains, all tears, all time, all fears, and peal,
Like the eternal thunders of the deep,
Into my ears this truth—« thou livest for ever! »
But if it be in joy
I know not, nor would know;
That secret rests with the Almighty giver
Who folds in clouds the fonts of bliss and woe.
But thee and me He never can destroy;
Change us He may, but not o'erwhelm; we are
Of as eternal essence, and must war
With Him if He will war with us: with *thee*

I can share all things, even immortal sorrow;
For thou hast ventured to share life with *me*,
And shall *I* shrink from thine eternity?
No! though the serpent's sting should pierce me thorough,
And thou thyself wert like the serpent, coil
Around me still! and I will smile
And curse thee not; but hold
Thee in as warm a fold
As——but descend; and prove
A mortal's love
For an immortal. If the skies contain
More joy than thou canst give and take, remain!

ANAH.

Sister! sister! I view them winging
Their bright way through the parted night.

AHOLIBAMAH.

The clouds from off their pinions flinging
As though they bore to-morrow's light.

ANAH.

But if our father see the sight!

AHOLIBAMAH.

He would but deem it was the moon
Rising unto some sorcerer's tune
An hour too soon.

ANAH.

They come! *he* comes!—Azaziel!

AHOLIBAMAH.

Haste
To meet them! Oh! for wings to bear
My spirit, while they hover there,
To Samiasa's breast!

ANAH.

Lo! they have kindled all the west,
Like a returning sunset;—lo!
On Ararat's late secret crest
A mild and many-colour'd bow,
The remnant of their flashing path,
Now shines! and now, behold! it hath
Return'd to night, as rippling foam,
Which the leviathan hath lash'd
From his unfathomable home,
When sporting on the face of the calm deep,
Subsides soon after he again hath dash'd
Down, down, to where the ocean's fountains sleep.

AHOLIBAMAH.

They have touch'd earth! Samiasa!

ANAH.

My Azaziel!

(Exeunt.

SCENE II.

Enter IRAD and JAPHET.

IRAD.

Despond not: wherefore wilt thou wander thus
To add thy silence to the silent night,
And lift thy tearful eye unto the stars?
They cannot aid thee,

JAPHET.

But they soothe me—now
Perhaps she looks upon them as I look.
Methinks a being that is beautiful
Becometh more so as it looks on beauty,

The eternal beauty of undying things.
Oh, Anah!

IRAD.

But she loves thee not.

JAPHET.

Alas!

IRAD.

And proud Aholibamah spurns me also.

JAPHET.

I feel for thee too.

IRAD.

Let her keep her pride,
Mine hath enabled me to bear her scorn;
It may be, time too will avenge it.

JAPHET.

Canst thou
Find joy in such a thought?

IRAD.

Nor joy, nor sorrow.
I loved her well; I would have loved her better,
Had love been met with love: as 't is, I leave her
To brighter destinies, if so she deems them.

JAPHET.

What destinies?

IRAD.

I have some cause to think
She loves another.

JAPHET.

Anah?

IRAD.

No; her sister.

JAPHET.

What other?

IRAD.

That I know not; but her air,
If not her words, tells me she loves another.

JAPHET.

Ay, but not Anah: she but loves her God.

IRAD.

Whate'er she loveth, so she loves thee not,
What can it profit thee?

JAPHET.

True, nothing; but
I love.

IRAD.

And so did I.

JAPHET.

And now thou lov'st not,
Or think'st thou lov'st not, art thou happier?

IRAD.

Yes.

JAPHET.

I pity thee.

IRAD.

Me! why?

JAPHET.

For being happy,
Deprived of that which makes my misery.

IRAD.

I take thy taunt as part of thy distemper,
And would not feel as thou dost, for more shekels
Than all our father's herds would bring if weigh'd

Against the metal of the sons of Cain—
The yellow dust they try to barter with us,
As if such useless and discolour'd trash,
The refuse of the earth, could be received
For milk, and wool, and flesh, and fruits, and all
Our flocks and wilderness afford.—Go, Japhet,
Sigh to the stars as wolves howl to the moon—
I must back to my rest.

JAPHET.

And so would I
If I could rest.

IRAD.

Thou wilt not to our tents, then?

JAPHET.

No, Irad; I will to the cavern, whose
Mouth they say opens from the internal world
To let the inner spirits of the earth
Forth when they walk its surface.

IRAD.

Wherefore so?
What wouldst thou there?

JAPHET.

Soothe further my sad spirit
With gloom as sad: it is a hopeless spot,
And I am hopeless.

IRAD.

But 't is dangerous;
Strange sounds and sights have peopled it with terrors.
I must go with thee.

JAPHET.

Irad, no; believe me
I feel no evil thought and fear no evil.

IRAD.

But evil things will be thy foe the more
As not being of them: turn thy steps aside,
Or let mine be with thine.

JAPHET.

No; neither, Irad;
I must proceed alone.

IRAD.

Then peace be with thee!

(Exit IRAD.

JAPHET (Solus.)

Peace! I have sought it where it should be found,
In love—with love too, which perhaps deserved it;
And, in its stead, a heaviness of heart—
A weakness of the spirit—listless days,
And nights inexorable to sweet sleep—
Have come upon me. Peace! what peace? the calm
Of desolation, and the stillness of
The untrodden forest, only broken by
The sweeping tempest through its groaning boughs;
Such is the sullen or the fitful state
Of my mind overworn. The earth 's grown wicked,
And many signs and portents have proclaim'd
A change at hand, and an o'erwhelming doom
To perishable beings. Oh, my Anah!
When the dread hour denounced shall open wide
The fountains of the deep, how mightest thou
Have lain within this bosom, folded from
The elements; this bosom, which in vain
Hath beat for thee, and then will beat more vainly,
While thine——Oh, God! at least remit to her
Thy wrath! for she is pure amidst the failing

As a star in the clouds, which cannot quench,
Although they obscure it for an hour. My Anah!
How would I have adored thee, but thou wouldst not;
And still would I redeem thee—see thee live
When ocean is earth's grave, and, unopposed
By rock or shallow, the leviathan,
Lord of the shoreless sea and watery world,
Shall wonder at his boundlessness of realm.

(Exit JAPHET.

Enter NOAH and SHEM.

NOAH.

Where is thy brother Japhet?

SHEM.

He went forth,
According to his wont, to meet with Irad,
He said; but, as I fear, to bend his steps
Towards Anah's tents, round which he hovers nightly,
Like a dove round and round its pillaged nest;
Or else he walks the wild up to the cavern
Which opens to the heart of Ararat.

NOAH.

What doth he there? It is an evil spot
Upon an earth all evil; for things worse
Than even wicked men resort there: he
Still loves this daughter of a fated race,
Although he could not wed her if she loved him,
And that she doth not. Oh, the unhappy hearts
Of men! that one of my blood, knowing well
The destiny and evil of these days,
And that the hour approacheth, should indulge
In such forbidden yearnings! Lead the way;
He must be sought for!

SHEM.

Go not forward, father:
I will seek Japhet.

NOAH.

Do not fear for me:
All evil things are powerless on the man
Selected by Jehovah—let us on.

SHEM.

To the tents of the father of the sisters?

NOAH.

No; to the cavern of the Caucasus.

(Exeunt NOAH and SHEM.

SCENE III.—THE MOUNTAINS.—A CAVERN, AND THE ROCKS OF CAUCASUS.

JAPHET (Solus.)

Ye wilds, that look eternal; and thou cave,
Which seem'st unfathomable; and ye mountains,
So varied and so terrible in beauty;
Here, in your rugged majesty of rocks
And toppling trees that twine their roots with stone
In perpendicular places, where the foot
Of man would tremble, could he reach them—yes,
Ye look eternal! Yet, in a few days,
Perhaps even hours, ye will be changed, rent, hurl'd
Before the mass of waters; and yon cave,
Which seems to lead into a lower world,
Shall have its depths search'd by the sweeping wave,
And dolphins gambol in the lion's den!
And man——Oh, men! my fellow-beings! Who
Shall weep above your universal grave,
Save I? Who shall be left to weep? My kinsmen,

Alas! what am I better than ye are,
That I must live beyond ye? Where shall be
The pleasant places where I thought of Anah
While I had hope? or the more savage haunts,
Scarce less beloved, where I despair'd for her?
And can it be!—Shall yon exulting peak,
Whose glittering top is like a distant star,
Lie low beneath the boiling of the deep?
No more to have the morning sun break forth,
And scatter back the mists in floating folds
From its tremendous brow? no more to have
Day's broad orb drop behind its head at even,
Leaving it with a crown of many hues?
No more to be the beacon of the world,
For angels to alight on, as the spot
Nearest the stars? And can those words *no more*
Be meant for thee, for all things, save for us,
And the predestined creeping things reserved
By my sire to Jehovah's bidding? May
He preserve *them*, and *I not* have the power
To snatch the loveliest of earth's daughters from
A doom which even some serpent, with his mate,
Shall 'scape to save his kind to be prolong'd,
To hiss and sting through some emerging world,
Reeking and dank from out the slime, whose ooze
Shall slumber o'er the wreck of this until
The salt morass subside into a sphere
Beneath the sun, and be the monument,
The sole and undistinguish'd sepulchre,
Of yet quick myriads of all life? How much
Breath will be still'd at once! All beauteous world!
So young, so mark'd out for destruction, I

With a cleft heart look on thee day by day,
And night by night, thy number'd days and nights.
I cannot save thee, cannot save even her
Whose love had made me love thee more; but as
A portion of thy dust, I cannot think
Upon thy coming doom without a feeling
Such as—oh God! and canst thou——

(He pauses.

(A rushing sound from the cavern is heard and shouts of laughter—— afterwards a Spirit passes.

JAPHET.

In the name
Of the Most High, what art thou?

SPIRIT (Laughs.)

Ha! ha! ha!

JAPHET.

By all that earth holds holiest, speak!

SPIRIT (Laughs.)

Ha! ha!

JAPHET.

By the approaching deluge! by the earth
Which will be strangled by the ocean! by
The deep which will lay open all her fountains!
The heaven which will convert her clouds to seas,
And the Omnipotent who makes and crushes!
Thou unknown, terrible, and indistinct,
Yet awful thing of shadows, speak to me!
Why dost thou laugh that horrid laugh!

SPIRIT.

Why weep'st thou?

JAPHET.

For earth and all her children.

SPIRIT.

Ha! ha! ha!

(Spirit vanishes.

JAPHET.

How the fiend mocks the tortures of a world,
The coming desolation of an orb,
On which the sun shall rise and warm no life!
How the earth sleeps! and all that in it is
Sleep too upon the very eve of death!
Why should they wake to meet it? What is here,
Which look like death in life, and speak like things
Born ere this dying world? They come like clouds!

(Various Spirits pass from the cavern.

SPIRIT.

Rejoice!
The abhorred race
Which could not keep in Eden their high place,
But listen'd to the voice
Of knowledge without power,
Are nigh the hour
Of death!
Not slow, not single, not by sword, nor sorrow,
Nor years, nor heart-break, nor time's sapping motion,
Shall they drop off. Behold their last to-morrow!
Earth shall be ocean!
And no breath,
Save of the winds, be on the unbounded wave!
Angels shall tire their wings, but find no spot:
Not even a rock from out the liquid grave
Shall lift its point to save,
Or show the place where strong Despair hath died,
After long looking o'er the ocean wide
For the expected ebb which cometh not:

All shall be void,
Destroy'd!
Another element shall be the lord
Of life, and the abhorr'd
Children of dust be quench'd; and of each hue
Of earth nought left but the unbroken blue;
And of the variegated mountain
Shall nought remain
Unchanged, or of the level plain;
Cedar and pine shall lift their tops in vain:
All merged within the universal fountain,
Man, earth, and fire, shall die,
And sea and sky
Look vast and lifeless in the eternal eye.
Upon the foam
Who shall erect a home?

JAPHET (Coming forward.)

My sire!
Earth's seed shall not expire;
Only the evil shall be put away
From day.
Avaunt! ye exulting demons of the waste!
Who howl your hideous joy
When God destroys whom you dare not destroy;
Hence! haste!
Back to your inner caves!
Until the waves
Shall search you in your secret place,
And drive your sullen race
Forth, to be roll'd upon the tossing winds
In restless wretchedness along all space!

SPIRIT.

Son of the saved!
When thou and thine have braved
The wide and warring element;
When the great barrier of the deep is rent,
Shall thou and thine be good or happy?—No!
Thy new world and new race shall be of woe—
Less goodly in their aspect, in their years
Less than the glorious giants, who
Yet walk the world in pride,
The Sons of Heaven by many a mortal bride.
Thine shall be nothing of the past, save tears.
And art thou not ashamed
Thus to survive,
And eat, and drink, and wive?
With a base heart so far subdued and tamed,
As even to hear this wide destruction named,
Without such grief and courage, as should rather
Bid thee await the world-dissolving wave,
Than seek a shelter with thy favour'd father,
And build thy city o'er the drown'd earth's grave?
Who would outlive their kind,
Except the base and blind?
Mine
Hateth thine
As of a different order in the sphere,
But not our own.
There is not one who hath not left a throne
Vacant in Heaven to dwell in darkness here,
Rather than see his mates endure alone.
Go, wretch! and give
A life like thine to other wretches—live!

And when the annihilating waters roar
Above what they have done,
Envy the giant patriarchs then no more,
And scorn thy sire as the surviving one!
Thyself for being his son!

Chorus of Spirits issuing from the cavern.

Rejoice!
No more the human voice
Shall vex our joys in middle air
With prayer;
No more
Shall they adore;
And we, who ne'er for ages have adored
The prayer-exacting Lord,
To whom the omission of a sacrifice
Is vice;
We, we shall view the deep salt sources pour'd
Until one element shall do the work
Of all in chaos; until they,
The creatures proud of their poor clay,
Shall perish, and their bleached bones shall lurk
In caves, in dens, in clefts of mountains, where
The deep shall follow to their latest lair;
Where even the brutes, in their despair,
Shall cease to prey on man and on each other,
And the striped tiger shall lie down to die
Beside the lamb, as though he were his brother;
Till all things shall be as they were,
Silent and uncreated, save the sky:
While a brief truce

Is made with Death, who shall forbear
The little remnant of the past creation,
To generate new nations for his use;
This remnant, floating o'er the undulation
Of the subsiding deluge, from its slime,
When the hot sun hath baked the reeking soil
Into a world, shall give again to Time
New beings—years—diseases—sorrow—crime—
With all companionship of hate and toil,
Until——

JAPHET (interrupting them).

The Eternal will
Shall deign to expound this dream
Of good and evil; and redeem
Unto Himself all times, all things;
And, gather'd under his almighty wings,
Abolish hell!
And to the expiated earth
Restore the beauty of her birth,
Her Eden in an endless paradise,
Where man no more can fall as once he fell,
And even the very demons shall do well!

SPIRIT.

And when shall take effect this wond'rous spell?

JAPHET.

When the Redeemer cometh; first in pain,
And then in glory.

SPIRIT.

Meantime still struggle in the mortal chain,
Till earth wax hoary;
War with yourselves, and Hell, and Heaven, in vain,
Until the clouds look gory

With the blood reeking from each battle plain;
New times, new climes, new arts, new men; but still
The same old tears, old crimes, and oldest ill,
  Shall be amongst your race in different forms;
  But the same moral storms
  Shall oversweep the future, as the waves
  In a few hours the glorious giants' graves.[2]

Chorus of Spirits.

Brethren, rejoice!
  Mortal, farewell!
Hark! hark! already we can hear the voice
  Of growing ocean's gloomy swell;
    The winds, too, plume their piercing wings!
    The clouds have nearly fill'd their springs;
The fountains of the great deep shall be broken,
  And Heaven set wide her windows; while mankind
View, unacknowledged, each tremendous token—
  Still, as they were from the beginning, blind.
We hear the sound they cannot hear,
The mustering thunders of the threatening sphere;
    Yet a few hours their coming is delay'd;
Their flashing banners, folded still on high,
    Yet undisplay'd,
Save to the spirits' all-pervading eye.
  Howl! howl! oh earth!
  Thy death is nearer than thy recent birth:
      Tremble, ye mountains, soon to shrink below
      The ocean's overflow!
The wave shall break upon your cliffs; and shells,
  The little shells of ocean's least things be
Deposed where now the eagle's offspring dwells—

How shall he shriek o'er the remorseless sea!
And call his nestlings up with fruitless yell,
Unanswer'd save by the encroaching swell;—
While man shall long in vain for his broad wings,
The wings which could not save:—
Where could he rest them, while the whole space brings
Nought to his eye beyond the deep, his grave?
Brethren, rejoice!
And loudly lift each superhuman voice—
All die,
Save the slight remnant of Seth's seed—
The seed of Seth,
Exempt for future sorrow's sake from death.
But of the sons of Cain
None shall remain;
And all his goodly daughters
Must lie beneath the desolating waters;
Or, floating upward with their long hair laid
Along the wave, the cruel heavens upbraid,
Which would not spare
Beings even in death so fair.
It is decreed,
All die!
And to the universal human cry
The universal silence shall succeed!
Fly, brethren, fly!
But still rejoice!
We fell!
They fall!
So perish all
These petty foes of heaven who shrink from hell!

(The Spirits disappear, soaring upwards.

JAPHET (Solus.)

God hath proclaim'd the destiny of earth;
My father's ark of safety hath announced it;
The very demons shriek it from their caves;
The scroll[3] of Enoch prophesied it long
In silent books, which, in their silence, say
More to the mind than thunder to the ear:
And yet men listen'd not, nor listen; but
Walk darkling to their doom; which, though so nigh,
Shakes them no more in their dim disbelief,
Than their last cries shall shake the Almighty purpose,
Or deaf obedient ocean, which fulfils it.
No sign yet hangs its banner in the air;
The clouds are few, and of their wonted texture;
The sun will rise upon the earth's last day
As on the fourth day of creation, when
God said unto him, « shine! » and he broke forth
Into the dawn, which lighted not the yet
Unform'd forefather of mankind—but roused
Before the human orison the earlier
Made and far sweeter voices of the birds,
Which in the open firmament of heaven
Have wings like angels, and like them salute
Heaven first each day before the Adamites!
Their matins now draw nigh—the east is kindling—
And they will sing! and day will break! Both near,
So near the awful close! For these must drop
Their out-worn pinions on the deep; and day,
After the bright course of a few brief morrows,—
Ay, day will rise; but upon what? A chaos,
Which was ere day; and which, renew'd, makes time
Nothing! for, without life, what are the hours?

No more to dust than is eternity
Unto Jehovah, who created both.
Without him, even eternity would be
A void: without man, time, as made for man,
Dies with man, and is swallow'd in that deep
Which has no fountain; as his race will be
Devour'd by that which drowns his infant world.—
What have we here? Shapes of both earth and air?
No—*all* of heaven, they are so beautiful.
I cannot trace their features; but their forms,
How lovelily they move along the side
Of the gray mountain, scattering its mist!
And after the swart savage spirits, whose
Infernal immortality pour'd forth
Their impious hymn of triumph, they shall be
Welcome as Eden. It may be they come
To tell me the reprieve of our young world,
For which I have so often pray'd—They come!
Anah! oh God! and with her——

Enter SAMIASA, AZAZIEL, ANAH, and AHOLIBAMAH.

ANAH.

Japhet!

SAMIASA.

Lo!

A son of Adam!

AZAZIEL.

What doth the earth-born here,
While all his race are slumbering?

JAPHET.

Angel! what
Dost thou on earth when thou shouldst be on high?

AZAZIEL.

Know'st thou not, or forget'st thou, that a part
Of our great function is to guard thine earth,

JAPHET.

But all good angels have forsaken earth,
Which is condemn'd; nay, even the evil fly
The approaching chaos. Anah! Anah! my
In vain, and long, and still to be beloved!
Why walk'st thou with this spirit, in those hours
When no good spirit longer lights below?

ANAH.

Japhet, I cannot answer thee; yet, yet
Forgive me——

JAPHET.

May the Heaven, which soon no more
Will pardon, do so! for thou art greatly tempted.

AHOLIBAMAH.

Back to thy tents, insulting son of Noah!
We know thee not.

JAPHET.

The hour may come when thou
May'st know me better; and thy sister know
Me still the same which I have ever been.

SAMIASA.

Son of the patriarch, who hath ever been
Upright before his God, whate'er thy griefs,
And thy words seem of sorrow, mix'd with wrath,
How have Azaziel, or myself, brought on thee
Wrong?

JAPHET.

Wrong! the greatest of all wrongs; but thou

Say'st well, though she be dust, I did not, could not,
Deserve her. Farewell, Anah! I have said
That word so often! but now say it, ne'er
To be repeated. Angel! or whate'er
Thou art, or must be soon, hast thou the power
To save this beautiful—*these* beautiful
Children of Cain?

AZAZIEL.

From what?

JAPHET.

And is it so,
That ye too know not? Angels! angels! ye
Have shared man's sin, and, it may be, now must
Partake his punishment; or at the least
My sorrow.

SAMIASA.

Sorrow! I ne'er thought till now
To hear an Adamite speak riddles to me.

JAPHET.

And hath not the Most High expounded them?
Then ye are lost, as they are lost.

AHOLIBAMAH.

So be it!
If they love as they are loved, they will not shrink
More to be mortal, than I would to dare
An immortality of agonies
With Samiasa!

ANAH.

Sister! sister! speak not
Thus.

AZAZIEL.

Fearest thou, my Anah?

ANAH.

Yes, for thee;
I would resign the greater remnant of
This little life of mine, before one hour
Of thine eternity should know a pang.

JAPHET.

It is for *him*, then! for the seraph thou
Hast left me! That is nothing, if thou hast not
Left thy God too! for unions like to these,
Between a mortal and immortal, cannot
Be happy or be hallow'd. We are sent
Upon the earth to toil and die; and they
Are made to minister on high unto
The Highest; but if he can *save* thee, soon
The hour will come in which celestial aid
Alone can do so.

ANAH.

Ah! he speaks of death.

SAMIASA.

Of death to *us!* and those who are with us!
But that the man seems full of sorrow, I
Could smile.

JAPHET.

I grieve not for myself, nor fear;
I am safe, not for my own deserts, but those
Of a well-doing sire who hath been found
Righteous enough to save his children. Would
His power was greater of redemption! or
That by exchanging my own life for hers,
Who could alone have made mine happy, she,
The last and loveliest of Cain's race, could share
The Ark which shall receive a remnant of
The seed of Seth!

AHOLIBAMAH.

And dost thou think that we,
With Cain's, the eldest born of Adam's, blood
Warm in our veins,—strong Cain! who was begotten
In Paradise,—would mingle with Seth's children?
Seth, the last offspring of old Adam's dotage?
No, not to save all earth, were earth in peril!
Our race hath alway dwelt apart from thine
From the beginning, and shall do so ever.

JAPHET.

I did not speak to thee, Aholibamah!
Too much of the forefather, whom thou vauntest,
Has come down in that haughty blood which springs
From him who shed the first, and that a brother's!
But thou, my Anah! let me call thee mine,
Albeit thou art not; 'tis a word I cannot
Part with, although I must from thee. My Anah!
Thou who dost rather make me dream that Abel
Had left a daughter, whose pure pious race
Survived in thee, so much unlike thou art
The rest of the stern Cainites, save in beauty,
For all of them are fairest in their favour——

AHOLIBAMAH (interrupting him.)

And wouldst thou have her like our father's foe
In mind, in soul? If *I* partook thy thought,
And dream'd that aught of *Abel* was in *her!*—
Get thee hence, son of Noah; thou mak'st strife.

JAPHET.

Offspring of Cain, thy father did so!

AHOLIBAMAH.

But
He slew not Seth; and what hast thou to do

With other deeds between his God and him?

JAPHET.

Thou speakest well: his God hath judged him, and
I had not named his deed, but that thyself
Didst seem to glory in him, nor to shrink
From what he had done.

AHOLIBAMAH.

He was our fathers' father;
The eldest born of man, the strongest, bravest,
And most enduring:—Shall I blush for him,
From whom we had our being? Look upon
Our race; behold their stature and their beauty,
Their courage, strength, and length of days——

JAPHET.

They are number'd.——

AHOLIBAMAH.

Be it so! but while yet their hours endure,
I glory in my brethren and our fathers!

JAPHET.

My sire and race but glory in their God,
Anah! and thou!——

ANAH.

Whate'er our God decrees,
The God of Seth as Cain, I must obey,
And will endeavour patiently to obey:
But could I dare to pray in this dread hour
Of universal vengeance (if such should be),
It would not be to live, alone exempt
Of all my house. My sister! oh, my sister!
What were the world, or other worlds, or all
The brightest future without the sweet past—
Thy love--my father's—all the life, and all

The things which sprung up with me, like the stars,
Making my dim existence radiant with
Soft lights which were not mine? Aholibamah!
Oh! if there should be mercy—seek it, find it:
I abhor death, because that thou must die.

AHOLIBAMAH.

What! hath this dreamer, with his father's ark,
The bugbear he hath built to scare the world,
Shaken *my* sister? Are *we* not the loved
Of seraphs? and if we were not, must we
Cling to a son of Noah for our lives?
Rather than thus——But the enthusiast dreams
The worst of dreams, the fantasies engender'd
By hopeless love and heated vigils. Who
Shall shake these solid mountains, this firm earth,
And bid those clouds and waters take a shape
Distinct from that which we and all our sires
Have seen them wear on their eternal way?
Who shall do this?

JAPHET.

He, whose one word produced them.

AHOLIBAMAH.

Who *heard* that word?

JAPHET.

The universe, which leap'd
To life before it. Ah! smil'st thou still in scorn?
Turn to thy seraphs; if they attest it not,
They are none.

SAMIASA.

Aholibamah, own thy God!

AHOLIBAMAH.

I have ever hail'd Our Maker, Samiasa,

As thine, and mine: a God of love, not sorrow.

JAPHET.

Alas! what else is love but sorrow? Even
He who made earth in love, had soon to grieve
Above its first and best inhabitants.

AHOLIBAMAH.

'T is said so.

JAPHET.

It is even so.

Enter NOAH and SHEM.

NOAH.

Japhet! What
Dost thou here with these children of the wicked?
Dread'st thou not to partake their coming doom?

JAPHET.

Father, it cannot be a sin to seek
To save an earth-born being; and behold,
These are not of the sinful, since they have
The fellowship of angels.

NOAH.

These are they, then,
Who leave the throne of God, to take them wives
From out the race of Cain; the sons of heaven,
Who seek earth's daughters for their beauty?

AZAZIEL.

Patriarch!
Thou hast said it.

NOAH.

Woe, woe, woe to such communion!
Has not God made a barrier between earth
And heaven, and limited each kind to kind?

SAMIASA.

Was not man made in high Jehovah's image?
Did God not love what he had made? And what
Do we but imitate and emulate
His love unto created love?

NOAH.

I am
But man, and was not made to judge mankind,
Far less the sons of God, but as our God
Has deign'd to commune with me, and reveal
His judgments, I reply, that the descent
Of seraphs from their everlasting seat
Unto a perishable and perishing,
Even on the very *eve* of *perishing*, world,
Cannot be good.

AZAZIEL.

What! though it were to save?

NOAH.

Not ye in all your glory can redeem
What He who made you glorious hath condemn'd.
Were your immortal mission safety, 't would
Be general, not for two, though beautiful,
And beautiful they are, but not the less
Condemn'd.

JAPHET.

Oh father! say it not.

NOAH.

Son! son!
If that thou wouldst avoid their doom, forget
That they exist; they soon shall cease to be,
While thou shalt be the sire of a new world,
And better.

JAPHET.

Let me die with *this*, and *them!*

NOAH.

Thou *shouldst* for such a thought, but shalt not; He
Who *can*, redeems thee.

SAMIASA.

And why him and thee,
More than what he, thy son, prefers to both?

NOAH.

Ask him who made thee greater than myself
And mine, but not less subject to his own
Almightiness. And lo! his mildest and
Least to be tempted messenger appears!

Enter RAPHAEL the Archangel.

RAPHAEL.

Spirits!
Whose seat is near the throne,
What do ye here?
Is thus a seraph's duty to be shown
Now that the hour is near
When earth must be alone?
Return!
Adore and burn
In glorious homage with the elected « seven. »
Your place is heaven.

SAMIASA.

Raphael!
The first and fairest of the sons of God,
How long hath this been law,
That earth by angels must be left untrod?

Earth! which oft saw
Jehovah's footsteps not disdain her sod!
The world He loved, and made
For love; and oft have we obey'd
His frequent mission with delighted pinions.
Adoring Him in his least works display'd;
Watching this youngest star of His dominions:
And as the latest birth of His great word,
Eager to keep it worthy of our Lord.
Why is thy brow severe?
And wherefore speak'st thou of destruction near?

RAPHAEL.

Had Samiasa and Azaziel been
In their true place, with the angelic choir,
Written in fire
They would have seen
Jehovah's late decree,
And not inquired their Maker's breath of me:
But ignorance must ever be
A part of sin;
And even the spirits' knowledge shall grow less
As they wax proud within;
For blindness is the first-born of excess.
When all good angels left the world, ye stay'd,
Stung with strange passions, and debased
By mortal feelings for a mortal maid;
But ye are pardon'd thus far, and replaced
With your pure equals: hence! away! away!
Or stay,
And lose eternity by that delay!

AZAZIEL.

And thou! if earth be thus forbidden

In the decree
To us until this moment hidden,
Dost thou not err as we
In being here?

RAPHAEL.

I came to call ye back to your fit sphere,
In the great name and at the word of God!
Dear, dearest in themselves, and scarce less dear
That which I came to do: till now we trod
Together the eternal space, together
Let us still walk the stars. True, earth must die!
Her race, return'd into her womb, must wither,
And much which she inherits; but oh! why
Cannot this earth be made, or be destroy'd
Without involving ever some vast void
In the immortal ranks? immortal still
In their immeasurable forfeiture.
Our brother Satan fell, his burning will
Rather than longer worship dared endure!
But ye, who still are pure!
Seraphs! less mighty than that mightiest one,
Think how he was undone!
And think if tempting man can compensate
For Heaven desired too late?
Long have I warr'd,
Long must I war
With him who deem'd it hard
To be created, and to acknowledge him
Who 'midst the cherubim
Made him as suns to a dependant star,
Leaving the archangels at his right hand dim.
I loved him—beautiful he was: oh Heaven!

Save *His* who made, what beauty and what power
Was ever like to Satan's! Would the hour
In which he fell could ever be forgiven!
The wish is impious: but oh ye!
Yet undestroy'd, be warn'd! Eternity
With him, or with his God, is in your choice:
He hath not tempted you, he cannot tempt
The angels, from his further snares exempt;
But man hath listen'd to his voice,
And ye to woman's—beautiful she is,
The serpent's voice less subtle than her kiss,
The snake but vanquish'd dust; but she will draw
A second host from Heaven, to break Heaven's law.
Yet, yet, oh fly!
Ye cannot die,
But they
Shall pass away,
While ye shall fill with shrieks the upper sky
For perishable clay,
Whose memory in your immortality
Shall long outlast the sun which gave them day:
Think how your essence differeth from theirs
In all but suffering! Why partake
The agony to which they must be heirs—
Born to be plough'd with years, and sown with cares,
And reap'd by Death, lord of the human soil?
Even had their days been left to toil their path
Through time to dust, unshorten'd by God's wrath,
Still they are evil's prey and sorrow's spoil.

AHOLIBAMAH.

Let them fly!
I hear the voice which says that all must die,

Sooner than our white-bearded patriarchs died;
And that on high
An ocean is prepared,
While from below
The deep shall rise to meet heaven's overflow.
Few shall be spared,
It seems; and, of that few, the race of Cain
Must lift their eyes to Adam's God in vain.
Sister! since it is so,
And the Eternal Lord
In vain would be implored
For the remission of one hour of woe,
Let us resign e'en what we have adored,
And meet the wave, as we would meet the sword,
If not unmoved, yet undismay'd,
And wailing less for us than those who shall
Survive in mortal or immortal thrall;
And, when the fatal waters are allay'd,
Weep for the myriads who can weep no more.
Fly, seraphs! to your own eternal shore,
Where winds nor howl nor waters roar.
Our portion is to die,
And yours to live for ever:
But which is best, a dead eternity,
Or living, is but known to the great Giver.
Obey Him, as we shall obey;
I would not keep this life of mine in clay
An hour beyond His will;
Nor see ye lose a portion of His grace,
For all the mercy which Seth's race
Find still.
Fly!

And as your pinions bear ye back to heaven,
Think that my love still mounts with thee on high,
Samiasa!
And if I look up with a tearless eye,
'T is that an angel's bride disdains to weep—
Farewell! Now rise, inexorable deep!

ANAH.

And must we die?
And must I lose thee too,
Azaziel?
Oh, my heart! my heart!
Thy prophecies were true,
And yet thou wert so happy too!
The blow, though not unlook'd for, falls as new;
But yet depart!
Ah, why?
Yet let me not retain thee—fly!
My pangs can be but brief; but thine would be
Eternal, if repulsed from heaven for me.
Too much already hast thou deign'd
To one of Adam's race!
Our doom is sorrow: not to us alone,
But to the spirits who have not disdain'd
To love us, cometh anguish with disgrace.
The first who taught us knowledge hath been hurl'd
From his once archangelic throne
Into some unknown world:
And thou, Azaziel! No—
Thou shalt not suffer woe
For me. Away! nor weep!
Thou canst not weep; but yet
May'st suffer more, not weeping: then forget
Her, whom the surges of the all-strangling deep

Can bring no pang like this. Fly! fly!
Being gone, 't will be less difficult to die.

JAPHET.

Oh say not so!
Father! and thou, archangel, thou!
Surely celestial mercy lurks below
That pure severe serenity of brow:
Let them not meet this sea without a shore,
Save in our ark, or let me be no more!

NOAH.

Peace, child of passion, peace!
If not within thy heart, yet with thy tongue
Do God no wrong!
Live as he wills it—die, when he ordains,
A righteous death, unlike the seed of Cain's.
Cease, or be sorrowful in silence; cease
To weary Heaven's ear with thy selfish plaint.
Wouldst thou have God commit a sin for thee?
Such would it be
To alter his intent
For a mere mortal sorrow. Be a man!
And bear what Adam's race must bear, and can.

JAPHET.

Ay, father! but when they are gone,
And we are all alone,
Floating upon the azure desert, and
The depth beneath us hides our own dear land,
And dearer, silent friends and brethren, all
Buried in its immeasurable breast,
Who, who, our tears, our shrieks, shall then command?
Can we in desolation's peace have rest?
Oh God! be thou a God, and spare

Yet while 't is time!
Renew not Adam's fall:
Mankind were then but twain,
But they are numerous now as are the waves
And the tremendous rain,
Whose drops shall be less thick than would their graves,
Were graves permitted to the seed of Cain.

NOAH.

Silence, vain boy! each word of thine's a crime!
Angel! forgive this stripling's fond despair.

RAPHAEL.

Seraphs! these mortals speak in passion: ye!
Who are, or should be, passionless and pure,
May now return with me

SAMIASA.

It may not be;
We have chosen, and will endure.

RAPHAEL.

Say'st thou?

AZAZIEL.

He hath said it, and I say, amen!

RAPHAEL.

Again!
Then from this hour,
Shorn as ye are of all celestial power,
And aliens from your God,
Farewell!

JAPHET.

Alas! where shall they dwell?
Hark! hark! Deep sounds, and deeper still,
Are howling from the mountain's bosom:
There 's not a breath of wind upon the hill,

Yet quivers every leaf, and drops each blossom:
Earth groans as if beneath a heavy load.

NOAH.

Hark! hark! the sea-birds cry!
In clouds they overspread the lurid sky,
And hover round the mountain, where before
Never a white wing, wetted by the wave,
Yet dared to soar,
Even when the waters wax'd too fierce to brave.
Soon it shall be their only shore,
And then, no more!

JAPHET.

The sun! the sun!
He riseth, but his better light is gone;
And a black circle, bound
His glaring disk around,
Proclaims earth's last of summer days hath shone!
The clouds return into the hues of night,
Save where their brazen-colour'd edges streak
The verge where brighter morns were wont to break.

NOAH.

And lo! yon flash of light,
The distant thunder's harbinger, appears!
It cometh! hence, away,
Leave to the elements their evil prey!
Hence to where our all-hallow'd ark uprears
Its safe and wreckless sides.

JAPHET.

Leave not my Anah to the swallowing tides!
Oh, father, stay!

NOAH.

Must we not leave all life to such? Begone!

JAPHET.

Not I.

NOAH.

Then die
With them!
How dar'st thou look on that prophetic sky,
And seek to save what all things now condemn,
In overwhelming unison
With just Jehovah's wrath?

JAPHET.

Can rage and justice join in the same path?

NOAH.

Blasphemer! dar'st thou murmur even now?

RAPHAEL.

Patriarch, be still a father! smooth thy brow:
Thy son, despite his folly, shall not sink;
He knows not what he says, yet shall not drink
With sobs the salt foam of the swelling waters;
But be, when passion passeth, good as thou,
Nor perish like Heaven's children with man's daughters.

AHOLIBAMAH.

The tempest cometh; heaven and earth unite
For the annihilation of all life.
Unequal is the strife
Between our strength and the Eternal Might!

SAMIASA.

But ours is with thee: we will bear ye far
To some untroubled star,
Where thou and Anah shall partake our lot:
And if thou dost not weep for thy lost earth,
Our forfeit heaven shall also be forgot.

ANAH.

Oh! my dear father's tents, my place of birth!
And mountains, land, and woods, when ye are not,
Who shall dry up my tears?

AZAZIEL.

Thy spirit-lord.
Fear not, though we are shut from heaven,
Yet much is ours, whence we can not be driven.

RAPHAEL.

Rebel! thy words are wicked, as thy deeds
Shall henceforth be but weak: the flaming sword,
Which chased the first-born out of Paradise,
Still flashes in the angelic hands.

AZAZIEL.

It cannot slay us: threaten dust with death,
And talk of weapons unto that which bleeds!
What are thy swords in our immortal eyes?

RAPHAEL.

The moment cometh to approve thy strength;
And learn at length
How vain to war with what thy God commands:
Thy former force was in thy faith.

Enter Mortals, flying for refuge.

Chorus of Mortals.

The heavens and earth are mingling—God! oh God!
What have we done? Yet spare!
Hark! even the forest beasts howl forth their prayer!
The dragon crawls from out his den,
To herd in terror innocent with men;
And the birds scream their agony through air.
Yet, yet, Jehovah! yet withdraw thy rod

Of wrath, and pity thine own world's despair!
Hear not man only but all nature plead!

RAPHAEL.

Farewell, thou earth! ye wretched sons of clay,
I cannot, must not aid you. 'T is decreed!

(Exit RAPHAEL.

JAPHET.

Some clouds sweep on, as vultures for their prey,
While others, fix'd as rocks, await the word
At which their wrathful vials shall be pour'd.
No azure more shall robe the firmament,
Nor spangled stars be glorious: Death hath risen:
In the sun's place a pale and ghastly glare
Hath wound itself around the dying air.

AZAZIEL.

Come, Anah! quit this chaos-founded prison,
To which the elements again repair,
To turn it into what it was: beneath
The shelter of these wings thou shalt be safe,
As was the eagle's nestling once within
Its mother's.—Let the coming chaos chafe
With all its elements! Heed not their din!
A brighter world than this, where thou shalt breathe
Ethereal life, will we explore:
These darken'd clouds are not the only skies.

(AZAZIEL and SAMIASA fly off, and disappear with ANAH and AHOLIBAMAH.

JAPHET.

They are gone! They have disappear'd amidst the roar
Of the forsaken world; and never more,
Whether they live, or die with all earth's life,
Now near its last, can aught restore
Anah unto these eyes.

Chorus of Mortals.

Oh son of Noah! mercy on thy kind!
What, wilt thou leave us all—all—*all* behind?
While safe amidst the elemental strife,
Thou sit'st within thy guarded ark?

A MOTHER (Offering her infant to JAPHET).

Oh let this child embark!
I brought him forth in woe,
But thought it joy
To see him to my bosom clinging so.
Why was he born?
What hath he done—
My unwean'd son—
To move Jehovah's wrath or scorn?
What is there in this milk of mine, that Death
Should stir all heaven and earth up to destroy
My boy,
And roll the waters o'er his placid breath?
Save him, thou seed of Seth!
Or cursed be—with Him who made
Thee and thy race, for which we are betray'd!

JAPHET.

Peace! 't is no hour for curses, but for prayer!

Chorus of Mortals.

For prayer!!!
And where
Shall prayer ascend,
When the swoln clouds unto the mountains bend
And burst,
And gushing oceans every barrier rend,

Until the very deserts know no thirst?
Accursed
Be He, who made thee and thy sire!
We deem our curses vain; we must expire;
But, as we know the worst,
Why should our hymn be raised, our knees be bent
Before the implacable Omnipotent,
Since we must fall the same?
If He hath made earth, let it be His shame,
To make a world for torture:—Lo! they come,
The loathsome waters in their rage!
And with their roar make wholesome nature dumb!
The forest's trees (coeval with the hour
When Paradise upsprung,
Ere Eve gave Adam knowledge for her dower,
Or Adam his first hymn of slavery sung),
So massy, vast, yet green in their old age,
Are overtopp'd,
Their summer blossoms by the surges lopp'd,
Which rise, and rise, and rise.
Vainly we look up to the lowering skies—
They meet the seas,
And shut out God from our beseeching eyes.
Fly, son of Noah, fly, and take thine ease
In thine allotted ocean-tent;
And view, all floating o'er the element,
The corpses of the world of thy young days:
Then to Jehovah raise
Thy song of praise!

A MORTAL.

Blessed are the dead
Who die in the Lord!
And though the waters be o'er earth outspread,

Yet, as *His* word,
Be the decree adored!
He gave me life—He taketh but
The breath which is his own:
And though these eyes should be for ever shut,
Nor longer this weak voice before His throne
Be heard in supplicating tone,
Still blessed be the Lord,
For what is past,
For that which is:
For all are His,
From first to last—
Time—space—eternity—life—death—
The vast known and immeasurable unknown.
He made, and can unmake;
And shall *I*, for a little gasp of breath,
Blasphene and groan?
No; let me die, as I have lived, in faith,
Nor quiver, though the universe may quake!

Chorus of Mortals.

Where shall we fly?
Not to the mountains high;
For now their torrents rush with double roar,
To meet the occean, which, advancing still,
Already grasps each drowning hill,
Nor leaves an unsearch'd cave.

Enter a Woman.

WOMAN.

Oh, save me, save!
Our valley is no more:

My father and my father's tent,
  My brethren and my brethren's herds,
The pleasant trees that o'er our noonday bent
  And sent forth evening songs from sweetest birds,
The little rivulet which freshen'd all
    Our pastures green,
    No more are to be seen.
When to the mountain cliff I climb'd this morn,
    I turn'd to bless the spot,
And not a leaf appear'd about to fall;—
    And now they are not!—
Why was I born?

JAPHET.

To die! in youth to die;
And happier in that doom,
Than to behold the universal tomb
Which I
Am thus condemn'd to weep above in vain.
Why, when all perish, why must I remain?

(The waters rise: men fly in every direction; many are overtaken by the waves; the Chorus of Mortals disperses in search of safety up the mountains; JAPHET remains upon a rock, while the Ark floats towards him in the distance.

NOTES TO HEAVEN AND EARTH.

Note 5, page 5, line 14.

Albeit thou watchest with « the seven, » *etc.*

The Archangels, said to be seven in number.

Note 2, page 23, line 7.

In a few hours the glorious giants' graves.

« And there were Giants in those days, and after; mighty men, which were of old men of renown. »—*Genesis.*

Note 3, page 25, line 5.

The scroll *etc.*

The Book of Enoch, preserved by the Ethiopians, is said by them to be anterior to the flood.

THE

DEFORMED TRANSFORMED.

A DRAMA.

ADVERTISEMENT.

This production is founded partly on the story of a Novel called «The Three Brothers,» published many years ago, from which M. G. Lewis's «Wood Demon» was also taken—and partly on the «Faust» of the great Goëthe. The present publication contains the two first parts only, and the opening chorus of the third. The rest may perhaps appear hereafter.

DRAMATIS PERSONÆ.

MEN.

STRANGER, afterwards CÆSAR.
ARNOLD.
BOURBON.
PHILIBERT.
CELLINI.

WOMEN.

BERTHA.
OLIMPIA.

Spirits, Soldiers, Citizens of Rome, Priests, Peasants, etc.

THE

DEFORMED TRANSFORMED.

PART I.

SCENE I.—A FOREST.

Enter ARNOLD and his mother BERTHA.

BERTHA.

Out, hunchback!

ARNOLD.

I was born so, mother!

BERTHA.

Out!
Thou incubus! Thou night-mare! Of seven sons
The sole abortion!

ARNOLD.

Would that I had been so,
And never seen the light!

BERTHA.

I would so too!
But as thou *hast*—hence, hence—and do thy best.

That back of thine may bear its burthen; 't is
More high, if not so broad as that of others.

ARNOLD.

It *bears* its burthen;—but, my heart! Will it
Sustain that which you lay upon it, mother?
I love, or, at the least, I loved you: nothing
Save you, in nature, can love aught like me.
You nursed me—do not kill me!

BERTHA.

Yes—I nursed thee,
Because thou wert my first-born, and I knew not
If there would be another unlike thee,
That monstrous sport of nature. But get hence,
And gather wood!

ARNOLD.

I will: but when I bring it,
Speak to me kindly. Though my brothers are
So beautiful and lusty, and as free
As the free chase they follow, do not spurn me:
Our milk has been the same.

BERTHA.

As is the hedge-hog's,
Which sucks at midnight from the wholesome dam
Of the young bull, until the milkmaid finds
The nipple next day sore and udder dry.
Call not thy brothers brethren! Call me not
Mother; for if I brought thee forth, it was
As foolish hens at times hatch vipers, by
Sitting upon strange eggs. Out, urchin, out!

(Exit BERTHA.

ARNOLD (Solus.)

Oh mother!——She is gone, and I must do

Her bidding;—wearily but willingly
I would fulfil it, could I only hope
A kind word in return. What shall I do?

(ARNOLD begins to cut wood: in doing this he wounds one of his hands.

My labour for the day is over now.
Accursed be this blood that flows so fast;
For double curses will be my meed now
At home.—What home? I have no home, no kin,
No kind—not made like other creatures, or
To share their sports or pleasures. Must I bleed too
Like them? Oh that each drop which falls to earth
Would rise a snake to sting them, as they have stung me!
Or that the devil, to whom they liken me,
Would aid his likeness! If I must partake
His form, why not his power! Is it because
I have not his will too? For one kind word,
From her who bore me, would still reconcile me
Even to this hateful aspect. Let me wash
The wound.

(ARNOLD goes to a spring, and stoops to wash his hand: he starts back.

They are right; and nature's mirror shows me
What she hath made me. I will not look on it
Again, and scarce dare think on't. Hideous wretch
That I am! The very waters mock me with
My horrid shadow—like a demon placed
Deep in the fountain to scare back the cattle
From drinking therein.

(He pauses.

And shall I live on,
A burthen to the earth, myself, and shame
Unto what brought me into life? Thou blood,
Which flow'st so freely from a scratch, let me

Try if thou wilt not in a fuller stream
Pour forth my woes for ever with thyself
On earth, to which I will restore at once
This hateful compound of her atoms, and
Resolve back to her elements, and take
The shape of any reptile save myself,
And make a world for myriads of new worms!
This knife! now let me prove if it will sever
This withered slip of nature's nightshade—my
Vile form—from the creation, as it hath
The green bough from the forest.

(ARNOLD places the knife in the ground, with the point upwards.

Now 't is set,
And I can fall upon it. Yet one glance
On the fair day, which sees no foul thing like
Myself, and the sweet sun, which warmed me, but
In vain. The birds—how joyously they sing!
So let them, for I would not be lamented:
But let their merriest notes be Arnold's knell;
The falling leaves my monument; the murmur
Of the near fountain my sole elegy.
Now, knife, stand firmly, as I fain would fall!

(As he rushes to throw himself upon the knife, his eye is suddenly caught by the fountain, which seems in motion,

The fountain moves without a wind: but shall
The ripple of a spring change my resolve?
No. Yet it moves again! The waters stir,
Not as with air, but by some subterrane
And rocking power of the internal world.
What 's here? A mist! No more?—

A cloud comes from the fountain. He stands gazing upon it: it is dispelled, and a tall black man comes towards him.

ARNOLD.

What would you? Speak!
Spirit or man?

STRANGER.

As man is both, why not
Say both in one?

ARNOLD.

Your form is man's, and yet
You may be devil.

STRANGER.

So many men are that
Which is so called or thought, that you may add me
To which you please, without much wrong to either.
But come: you wish to kill yourself;—pursue
Your purpose.

ARNOLD.

You have interrupted me.

STRANGER.

What is that resolution which can e'er
Be interrupted? If I be the devil
You deem, a single moment would have made you
Mine, and for ever, by your suicide;
And yet my coming saves you.

ARNOLD.

I said not
You *were* the demon, but that your approach
Was like one.

STRANGER.

Unless you keep company
With him (and you seem scarce used to such high
Society), you can't tell how he approaches;
And for his aspect, look upon the fountain,

And then on me. and judge which of us twain
Look likest what the boors believe to be
Their cloven-footed terror.

ARNOLD.

Do you—dare *you*
To taunt me with my born deformity!

STRANGER.

Were I to taunt a buffalo with this
Cloven foot of thine, or the swift dromedary
With thy sublime of humps, the animals
Would revel in the compliment. And yet
Both beings are more swift, more strong, more mighty
In action and endurance than thyself,
And all the fierce and fair of the same kind
With thee. Thy form is natural: 't was only
Nature's mistaken largess to bestow
The gifts which are of others upon man.

ARNOLD.

Give me the strength then of the buffalo's foot,
When he spurns high the dust, beholding his
Near enemy; or let me have the long
And patient swiftness of the desart-ship,
The helmless dromedary;—and I 'll bear
Thy fiendish sarcasm with a saintly patience.

STRANGER.

I will

ARNOLD (With surprise.)

Thou *canst?*

STRANGER.

Perhaps. Would you aught else?

ARNOLD.

Thou mockest me.

STRANGER.

Not I. Why should I mock
What all are mocking? That 's poor sport methinks.
To talk to thee in human language (for
Thou canst not yet speak mine): the forester
Hunts not the wretched coney, but the boar,
Or wolf, or lion, leaving paltry game
To petty burghers, who leave once a-year
Their walls, to fill their household cauldrons with
Such scullion prey. The meanest gibe at thee,—
Now *I* can mock the mightiest.

ARNOLD.

Then waste not
Thy time on me: I seek thee not

STRANGER.

Your thoughts
Are not far from me. Do not send me back:
I 'm not so easily recalled to do
Good service.

ARNOLD.

What wilt thou do for me?

STRANGER.

Change
Shapes with you, if you will, since yours so irks you;
Or form you to your wish in any shape.

ARNOLD.

Oh! then you are indeed the demon, for
Nought else would wittingly wear mine.

STRANGER.

I 'll show thee
The brightest which the world ere bore, and give thee
Thy choice.

ARNOLD.

On what condition?

STRANGER.

There 's a question!
An hour ago you would have given your soul
To look like other men, and now you pause
To wear the form of heroes.

ARNOLD.

No; I will not.
I must not compromise my soul.

STRANGER.

What soul,
Worth naming so, would dwell in such a carcase?

ARNOLD.

'T is an aspiring one, whate'er the tenement
In which it is mislodged. But name your compact:
Must it be signed in blood?

STRANGER.

Not in your own.

ARNOLD.

Whose blood, then?

STRANGER.

We will talk of that hereafter.
But I 'll be moderate with you, for I see
Great things within you. You shall have no bond
But your own will, no contract save your deeds.
Are you content?

ARNOLD.

I take thee at thy word.

STRANGER.

Now then!—(The Stranger approaches the fountain, and turns to ARNOLD.
A little of your blood.

ARNOLD.

For what?

STRANGER.

To mingle with the magic of the waters,
And make the charm effective.

ARNOLD (Holding out his wounded arm.)

Take it all.

STRANGER.

Not now. A few drops will suffice for this.

(The Stranger takes some of ARNOLD's blood in his hand, and casts it into the fountain.

Shadows of beauty!
Shadows of power!
Rise to your duty—
This is the hour!
Walk lovely and pliant
From the depth of this fountain,
As the cloud-shapen giant
Bestrides the Hartz mountain.
Come as ye were,
That our eyes may behold
The model in air
Of the form I will mould,
Bright as the Iris
When ether is spanned;—
Such *his* desire is, (Pointing to ARNOLD.
Such my command!
Demons heroic—
Demons who wore
The form of the stoic
Or sophist of yore—

Or the shape of each victor,
From Macedon's boy
To each high Roman's picture,
Who breathed to destroy—
Shadows of beauty!
Shadows of power!
Up to your duty—
This is the hour!

(Various phantoms arise from the waters, and pass in succession before the Stranger and ARNOLD.

ARNOLD.

What do I see?

STRANGER.

The black-eyed Roman, with
The eagle's beak between those eyes which ne'er
Beheld a conqueror, or look'd along
The land he made not Rome's, while Rome became
His, and all theirs who heir'd his very name.

ARNOLD.

The phantom's bald; my quest is beauty. Could I
Inherit but his fame with his defects!

STRANGER.

His brow was girt with laurels more than hairs.
You see his aspect—choose it or reject.
I can but promise you his form; his fame
Must be long sought and fought for.

ARNOLD.

I will fight too,
But not as a mock Cæsar. Let him pass;
His aspect may be fair, but suits me not.

STRANGER.

Then you are far more difficult to please

Than Cato's sister, or than Brutus' mother,
Or Cleopatra at sixteen—an age
When love is not less in the eye than heart.
But be it so! Shadow, pass on!

(The phantom of Julius Cæsar disappears.

ARNOLD.

And can it
Be, that the man who shook the earth is gone
And left no footstep?

STRANGER.

There you err. His substance
Left graves enough, and woes enough, and fame
More than enough to track his memory;
But for his shadow, 't is no more than yours,
Except a little longer and less crooked
I' the sun. Behold another! (A second phantom passes.

ARNOLD.

Who is he?

STRANGER.

He was the fairest and the bravest of
Athenians. Look upon him well.

ARNOLD.

He is
More lovely than the last. How beautiful!

STRANGER.

Such was the curled son of Clinias;—would'st thou
Invest thee with his form?

ARNOLD.

Would that I had
Been born with it! But since I may choose further.
I will *look* further.

(The shade of Alcibiades disappears.

STRANGER.

Lo! Behold again!

ARNOLD.

What! that low, swarthy, short-nosed, round-eyed satyr,
With the wide nostrils and Silenus' aspect,
The splay feet and low stature! I had better
Remain that which I am.

STRANGER.

And yet he was
The earth's perfection of all mental beauty,
And personification of all virtue.
But you reject him?

ARNOLD.

If his form could bring me
That which redeemed it—no.

STRANGER.

I have no power
To promise that; but you may try, and find it
Easier in such a form, or in your own.

ARNOLD.

No. I was not born for philosophy,
Though I have that about me which has need on 't.
Let him fleet on.

STRANGER.

Be air, thou hemlock-drinker!

(The shadow of Socrates disappears; another rises.

ARNOLD.

What 's here? whose broad brow and whose curly beard
And manly aspect look like Hercules,
Save that his jocund eye hath more of Bacchus
Than the sad purger of the infernal world,
Leaning dejected on his club of conquest,

As if he knew the worthlessness of those
For whom he 'd fought.

STRANGER.

It was the man who lost
The ancient world for love.

ARNOLD.

I cannot blame him,
Since I have risked my soul because I find not
That which he exchanged the earth for.

STRANGER.

Since so far
You seem congenial, will you wear his features?

ARNOLD.

No. As you leave me choice, I am difficult,
If but to see the heroes I should ne'er
Have seen else on this side of the dim shore
Whence they float back before us.

STRANGER.

Hence, triumvir!
Thy Cleopatra 's waiting.

(The shade of Anthony disappears: another rises.

ARNOLD.

Who is this?
Who truly looketh like a demi-god,
Blooming and bright, with golden hair, and stature,
If not more high than mortal, yet immortal
In all that nameless bearing of his limbs,
Which he wears as the sun his rays—a something
Which shines from him, and yet is but the flashing
Emanation of a thing more glorious still.
Was *he e'er human only?*

STRANGER.

Let the earth speak,
If there be atoms of him left, or even
Of the more solid gold that formed his urn.

ARNOLD.

Who was this glory of mankind?

STRANGER.

The shame
Of Greece in peace, her thunderbolt in war—
Demetrius the Macedonian, and
Taker of cities.

ARNOLD.

Yet one shadow more.

STRANGER (Addressing the shadow.)

Get thee to Lamia's lap!

(The shade of Demetrius Poliorcetes vanishes: another rises.

I 'll fit you still,
Fear not, my hunchback. If the shadows of
That which existed please not your nice taste,
I 'll animate the ideal marble, till
Your soul be reconciled to her new garment.

ARNOLD.

Content! I will fix here.

STRANGER.

I must commend
Your choice. The godlike son of the sea-goddess,
The unshorn boy of Peleus, with his locks
As beautiful and clear as the amber waves
Of rich Pactolus rolled o'er sands of gold,
Softened by intervening chrystal, and
Rippled like flowing waters by the wind,
All vowed to Sperchius as they were—behold them!

And *him*—as he stood by Polixena,
With sanction'd and with soften'd love, before
The altar, gazing on his Trojan bride,
With some remorse within for Hector slain
And Priam weeping, mingled with deep passion
For the sweet downcast virgin, whose young hand
Trembled in *his* who slew her brother. So
He stood i' the temple! Look upon him as
Greece looked her last upon her best, the instant
Ere Paris' arrow flew.

ARNOLD.

I gaze upon him
As if I were his soul, whose form shall soon
Envelope mine.

STRANGER.

You have done well. The greatest
Deformity should only barter with
The extremest beauty, if the proverb 's true
Of mortals, that extremes meet.

ARNOLD.

Come! Be quick!
I am impatient.

STRANGER.

As a youthful beauty
Before her glass. *You both* see what is not,
But dream it is what must be.

ARNOLD.

Must I wait?

STRANGER.

No; that were pity. But a word or two:
His stature is twelve cubits: would you so far
Outstep these times, and be a Titan? Or

(To talk canonically) wax a son
Of Anak?

ARNOLD.

Why not?

STRANGER.

Glorious ambition!
I love thee most in dwarfs! A mortal of
Philistine stature would have gladly pared
His own Goliath down to a slight David;
But thou, my manikin, would'st soar a show
Rather than hero. Thou shalt be indulged,
If such be thy desire; and yet, by being
A little less removed from present men
In figure, thou canst sway them more; for all
Would rise against thee now, as if to hunt
A new-found mammoth; and their cursed engines,
Their culverins and so forth, would find way
Through our friend's armour there, with greater ease
Than the adulterer's arrow through his heel,
Which Thetis had forgotten to baptise
In Styx.

ARNOLD.

Then let it be as thou deem'st best.

STRANGER.

Thou shalt be beauteous as the thing thou see'st,
And strong as what it was, and——

ARNOLD.

I ask not
For valour, since deformity is daring.
It is its essence to o'ertake mankind
By heart and soul, and make itself the equal—
Ay, the superior of the rest. There is

A spur in its halt movements, to become
All that the others cannot, in such things
As still are free to both, to compensate
For stepdame nature's avarice at first.
They woo with fearless deeds the smiles of fortune,
And oft, like Timour, the lame Tartar, win them.

STRANGER.

Well spoken! And thou doubtless wilt remain
Formed as thou art. I may dismiss the mould
Of shadow, which must turn to flesh, to encase
This daring soul, which could achieve no less
Without it?

ARNOLD.

Had no power presented me
The possibility of change, I would
Have done the best which spirit may, to make
Its way, with all deformity's dull, deadly,
Discouraging weight upon me, like a mountain,
In feeling, on my heart as on my shoulders—
An hateful and unsightly mole-hill to
The eyes of happier man. I would have look'd
On beauty, in that sex which is the type
Of all we know or dream of beautiful
Beyond the world they brighten, with a sigh—
Not of love but despair; nor sought to win,
Though to a heart all love, what could not love me
In turn, because of this vile crooked clog
Which makes me lonely. Nay, I could have borne
It all, had not my mother spurn'd me from her.
The she-bear licks her cubs into a sort
Of shape;—my dam beheld my shape was hopeless.
Had she exposed me, like the Spartan, ere

I knew the passionate part of life, I had
Been a clod of the valley,—happier nothing
Than what I am. But even thus, the lowest,
Ugliest, and meanest of mankind, what courage
And perseverance could have done, perchance
Had made me something—as it has made heroes
Of the same mould as mine. You lately saw me
Master of my own life, and quick to quit it;
And he who is so, is the master of
Whatever dreads to die.

STRANGER.

Decide between
What you have been, or will be.

ARNOLD.

I have done so.
You have opened brighter prospects to my eyes,
And sweeter to my heart. As I am now,
I might be fear'd, admired, respected, loved
Of all, save those next to me, of whom I
Would be beloved. As thou showest me
A choice of forms, I take the one I view.
Haste! haste!

STRANGER.

And what shall *I* wear?

ARNOLD.

Surely he
Who can command all forms, will choose the highest,
Something superior even to that which was
Pelides now before us. Perhaps *his*
Who slew him, that of Paris: or—still higher—
The poet's god, clothed in such limbs as are
Themselves a poetry.

STRANGER.

Less will content me;
For I too love a change.

ARNOLD.

Your aspect is
Dusky, but not uncomely.

STRANGER.

If I chose,
I might be whiter; but I have a *penchant*
For black—it is so honest, and besides
Can neither blush with shame nor pale with fear:
But I have worn it long enough of late,
And now I 'll take your figure.

ARNOLD.

Mine!

STRANGER.

Yes. You
Shall change with Thetis' son, and I with Bertha
Your mother's offspring. People have their tastes;
You have yours—I mine.

ARNOLD.

Dispatch! dispatch!

STRANGER.

Even so.

(The Stranger takes some earth and moulds it along the turf. And then addresses the phantom of Achilles.

Beautiful shadow
Of Thetis's boy!
Who sleeps in the meadow
Whose grass grows o'er Troy:

From the red earth, like Adam,[a]
  Thy likeness I shape,
As the being who made him,
  Whose actions I ape.
Thou clay, be all glowing,
  Till the rose in his cheek
Be as fair as, when blowing,
  It wears its first streak!
Ye violets! I scatter,
  Now turn into eyes!
And thou, sunshiny water,
  Of blood take the guise!
Let these hyacinth boughs
  Be his long, flowing hair,
And wave o'er his brows
  As thou wavest in air!
Let his heart be this marble
  I tear from the rock!
But his voice as the warble
  Of birds on yon oak!
Let his flesh be the purest
  Of mould, in which grew
The lily-root surest,
  And drank the best dew!
Let his limbs be the lightest
  Which clay can compound!
And his aspect the brightest
  On earth to be found!
Elements, near me,
  Be mingled and stirr'd,
Know me, and hear me,
  And leap to my word!

Sunbeams, awaken
This earth's animation!
'T is done! He hath taken
His stand in creation!

(ARNOLD falls senseless: his soul passes into the shape of Achilles, which rises from the ground: while the phantom has disappeared, part by part, as the figure was formed from the earth.

ARNOLD (In his new form.)

I love, and I shall be beloved! O life!
At last I feel thee! Glorious spirit!

STRANGER.

Stop!
What shall become of your abandon'd garment,
Yon hump, and lump, and clod of ugliness,
Which late you wore, or were?

ARNOLD.

Who cares! Let wolves
And vultures take it, if they will.

STRANGER.

And if
They do, and are not scared by it, you 'll say
It must be peace-time, and no better fare
Abroad i' the fields.

ARNOLD.

Let us but leave it there,
No matter what becomes on 't.

STRANGER.

That 's ungracious,
If not ungrateful. Whatsoe'er it be,
It hath sustained your soul full many a day.

ARNOLD.

Ay, as the dunghill may conceal a gem,
Which is now set in gold, as jewels should be.

STRANGER.

But if I give another form, it must be
By fair exchange, not robbery. For they
Who make men without women's aid, have long
Had patents for the same, and do not love
Your interlopers. The devil may take men,
Not make them,—though he reap the benefit
Of the original workmanship:—and therefore
Some one must be found to assume the shape
You 've quitted.

ARNOLD.

Who would do so!

STRANGER.

That I know not,
And therefore I must.

ARNOLD.

You!

STRANGER.

I said it ere
You inhabited your present dome of beauty.

ARNOLD.

True. I forget all things in the new joy
Of this immortal change.

STRANGER.

In a few moments
I will be as you were, and you shall see
Yourself for ever by you, as your shadow.

ARNOLD.

I would be spared this.

STRANGER.

But it cannot be.
What! shrink already, being what you are,
From seeing what you were?

ARNOLD.

Do as thou wilt.

STRANGER (To the late form of ARNOLD, extended on the earth.)

Clay! not dead, but soulless!
Though no man would choose thee,
An immortal no less
Deigns not to refuse thee.
Clay thou art; and unto spirit
All clay is of equal merit.

Fire! *without* which nought can live;
Fire! but *in* which nought can live,
Save the fabled salamander.
Or immortal souls which wander,
Praying what doth not forgive,
Howling for a drop of water,
Burning in a quenchless lot:
Fire! the only element
Where nor fish, beast, bird, nor worm,
Save the worm which dieth not,
Can preserve a moment's form,
But must with thyself be blent:
Fire! man's safeguard and his slaughter:
Fire! creation's first-born daughter,
And destruction's threatened son,
When Heaven with the world hath done:
Fire! assist me to renew
Life in what lies in my view

Stiff and cold!
His resurrection rests with me and you!
One little, marshy spark of flame—
And he again shall seem the same;
But I his spirit's place shall hold!

(An ignis-fatuus flits through the wood, and rests on the brow of the body. The Stranger disappears: the body rises.

ARNOLD (In his new form.)

Oh! horrible!

THE STRANGER (In ARNOLD'S late shape.)

What! tremblest thou?

ARNOLD.

Not so—
I merely shudder. Where is fled the shape
Thou lately worest!

STRANGER.

To the world of shadows.
But let us thread the present. Whither wilt thou?

ARNOLD.

Must thou be my companion?

STRANGER.

Wherefore not?
Your betters keep worse company.

ARNOLD.

My betters!

STRANGER.

Oh! you wax proud, I see, of your new form:
I'm glad of that. Ungrateful too! That's well;
You improve apace:—two changes in an instant,
And you are old in the world's ways already.
But bear with me: indeed you'll find me useful

Upon your pilgrimage. But come, pronounce
Where shall we now be errant?

ARNOLD.

Where the world
Is thickest, that I may behold it in
Its workings.

STRANGER.

That 's to say, where there is war
And woman in activity. Let's see!
Spain—Italy—the new Atlantic world—
Afric with all its Moors. In very truth
There is small choice: the whole race are just now
Tugging as usual at each other's hearts.

ARNOLD.

I have heard great things of Rome.

STRANGER.

A goodly choice—
And scarce a better to be found on earth,
Since Sodom was put out. The field is wide too;
For now the Frank, and Hun, and Spanish scion
Of the old Vandals, are at play along
The sunny shores of the world's garden.

ARNOLD.

How
Shall we proceed?

STRANGER.

Like gallants, on good coursers.
What ho! my chargers! Never yet were better,
Since Phaeton was upset into the Po.
Our pages too!

Enter two Pages, with four coal-black Horses.

ARNOLD.

A noble sight!

STRANGER.

And of
A nobler breed. Match me in Barbary,
Or your Kochlani race of Araby,
With these!

ARNOLD.

The mighty steam, which volumes high
From their proud nostrils, burns the very air;
And sparks of flame, like dancing fire-flies, wheel
Around their manes, as common insects swarm
Round common steeds towards sunset.

STRANGER.

Mount, my lord;
They and I are your servitors.

ARNOLD.

And these,
Our dark-eyed pages—what may be their names?

STRANGER.

You shall baptise them.

ARNOLD.

What! in holy water?

STRANGER.

Why not! The deeper sinner, better saint.

ARNOLD.

They are beautiful, and cannot, sure, be demons?

STRANGER.

True; the devil 's always ugly; and your beauty
Is never diabolical.

ARNOLD.

I'll call him
Who bears the golden horn, and wears such bright
And bloooming aspect, *Huon*; for he looks
Like to the lovely boy lost in the forest,
And never found till now. And for the other
And darker, and more thoughtful, who smiles not,
But looks as serious though serene as night,
He shall be *Memnon*, from the Ethiop king
Whose statue turns a harper once a-day,
And you?

STRANGER.

I have ten thousand names, and twice
As many attributes; but as I wear
A human shape, will take a human name.

ARNOLD.

More human than the shape (though it was mine once)
I trust.

STRANGER.

Then call me Cæsar.

ARNOLD.

Why, that name
Belongs to empires, and has been but borne
By the world's lords.

STRANGER.

And therefore fittest for
The devil in disguise—since so you deem me,
Unless you call me pope instead.

ARNOLD.

Well then,
Cæsar thou shalt be. For myself, my name
Shall be plain Arnold still.

6.

CÆSAR.

We 'll add a title—
«Count Arnold:» it hath no ungracious sound,
And will look well upon a billet-doux.

ARNOLD.

Or in an order for a battle-field.

CÆSAR (Sings.)

To horse! to horse! my coal-black steed
Paws the ground and snuffs the air!
There 's not a foal of Arab's breed
More knows whom he must bear!
On the hill he will not tire,
Swifter as it waxes higher;
In the marsh he will not slacken,
On the plain be overtaken;
In the wave he will not sink,
Nor pause at the brook's side to drink;
In the race he will not pant,
In the combat he 'll not faint;
On the stones he will not stumble,
Time nor toil shall make him humble;
In the stall he will not stiffen,
But be winged as a griffin,
Only flying with his feet:
And will not such a voyage be sweet?
Merrily! merrily! never unsound,
Shall our bonny black horses skim over the ground!
From the Alps to the Caucasus, ride we, or fly!
For we 'll leave them behind in the glance of an eye.

(They mount their horses, and disappear.

SCENE II.—A CAMP BEFORE THE WALLS OF ROME.

ARNOLD and CÆSAR.

CÆSAR.

You are well entered now.

ARNOLD.

Ay! but my path
Has been o'er carcases: mine eyes are full
Of blood.

CÆSAR.

Then wipe them and see clearly. Why!
Thou art a conqueror; the chosen knight
And free companion of the gallant Bourbon,
Late Constable of France; and now to be
Lord of the city which hath been earth's lord
Under its emperors, and—changing sex,
Not sceptre, an hermaphrodite of empire—
Lady of the old world.

ARNOLD.

How *old*? What! are there
New worlds?

CÆSAR.

To *you*. You 'll find there are such shortly,
By its rich harvests, new disease, and gold;
From one *half* of the world named a *whole* new one,
Because you know no better than the dull
And dubious notice of your eyes and ears.

ARNOLD.

I 'll trust them.

CÆSAR.

Do! They will deceive you sweetly,

And that is better than the bitter truth.

ARNOLD.

Dog!

CÆSAR.

Man!

ARNOLD.

Devil!

CÆSAR.

Your obedient, humble servant.

ARNOLD.

Say *master* rather. Thou hast lured me on,
Through scenes of blood and lust, till I am here.

CÆSAR.

And where would'st *thou* be?

ARNOLD.

Oh, at peace—in peace!

CÆSAR.

And where is that which is so? From the star
To the winding worm, all life is motion; and
In life *commotion* is the extremest point
Of life. The planet wheels till it becomes
A comet, and destroying as it sweeps
The stars, goes out. The poor worm winds its way,
Living upon the death of other things,
But still, like them, must live and die, the subject
Of something which has made it live and die.
You must obey, what all obey, the rule
Of fixed necessity: against her edict
Rebellion prospers not.

ARNOLD.

And when it prospers——

CÆSAR.

'T is no rebellion.

ARNOLD.

Will it prosper now?

CÆSAR.

The Bourbon hath given orders for the assault,
And by the dawn there will be work.

ARNOLD.

Alas!
And shall the city yield? I see the giant
Abode of the true God, and his true saint,
Saint Peter, rear its dome and cross into
That sky whence Christ ascended from the cross,
Which his blood made a badge of glory and
Of joy (as once of torture unto him,
God and God's Son, man's sole and only refuge).

CÆSAR.

'T is there, and shall be.

ARNOLD.

What?

CÆSAR.

The crucifix
Above, and many altar-shrines below.
Also some culverins upon the walls,
And harquebusses, and what not, besides
The men who are to kindle them to death
Of other men.

ARNOLD.

And those scarce mortal arches,
Pile above pile of everlasting wall,
The theatre where emperors and their subjects

(These subjects *Romans*) stood at gaze upon
The battles of the monarchs of the wild
And wood, the lion and his tusky rebels
Of the then untamed desart, brought to joust
In the arena (as right well they might,
When they had left no human foe unconquered);
Made even the forest pay its tribute of
Life to their amphitheatre, as well
As Dacia men to die the eternal death
For a sole instant's pastime, and « Pass on
To a new gladiator! »—Must it fall?

CÆSAR.

The city or the amphitheatre?
The church, or one, or all? for you confound
Both them and me.

ARNOLD.

To-morrow sounds the assault
With the first cock-crow.

CÆSAR.

Which, if it end with
The evening's first nightingale, will be
Something new in the annals of great sieges:
For men must have their prey after long toil.

ARNOLD.

The sun goes down as calmly, and perhaps
More beautifully, than he did on Rome
On the day Remus leapt her wall.

CÆSAR.

I saw him.

ARNOLD.

You!

CÆSAR.

Yes, sir. You forget I am or was
Spirit, till I took up with your cast shape
And a worse name. I 'm Cæsar and a hunch-back
Now. Well! the first of Cæsars was a bald-head,
And loved his laurels better as a wig
(So history says) than as a glory. Thus
The world runs on, but we 'll be merry still.
I saw your Romulus (simple as I am)
Slay his own twin, quick-born of the same womb,
Because he leapt a ditch ('t was then no wall,
Whate'er it now be); and Rome's earliest cement
Was brother's blood; and if its native blood
Be spilt till the choked Tyber be as red
As e'er 't was yellow, it will never wear
The deep hue of the ocean and the earth,
Which the great robber sons of fratricide
Have made their never-ceasing scene of slaughter
For ages.

ARNOLD.

But what have these done, their far
Remote descendants, who have lived in peace,
The peace of Heaven, and in her sunshine of
Piety?

CÆSAR.

And what had *they* done, whom the old
Romans o'erswept?—Hark!

ARNOLD.

They are soldiers singing
A reckless roundelay, upon the eve
Of many deaths, it may be of their own.

CÆSAR.

And why should they not sing as well as swans?
They are black ones, to be sure.

ARNOLD.

So, you are learned,
I see, too.

CÆSAR.

In my grammar, certes. I
Was educated for a monk of all times,
And once I was well versed in the forgotten
Etruscan letters, and—were I so minded—
Could make their hieroglyphics plainer than
Your alphabet.

ARNOLD.

And wherefore do you not?

CÆSAR.

It answers better to resolve the alphabet
Back into hieroglyphics. Like your statesman,
And prophet, pontiff, doctor, alchymist,
Philosopher, and what not, they have built
More Babels without new dispersion, than
The stammering young ones of the flood's dull ooze,
Who fail'd and fled each other. Why? why, marry,
Because no man could understand his neighbour.
They are wiser now, and will not separate
For nonsense. Nay, it is their brotherhood,
Their Shibboleth, their Koran, Talmud, their
Cabala; their best brick-work wherewithal
They build more—

ARNOLD (Interrupting him.)

Oh, thou everlasting sneerer!

Be silent! How the soldiers' rough strain seems
Softened by distance to a hymn-like cadence!
Listen!

CÆSAR.

Yes. I have heard the angels sing.

ARNOLD.

And demons howl.

CÆSAR.

And man too. Let us listen:
I love all music.

Song of the Soldiers within.

The black bands came over
The Alps and their snow,
With Bourbon, the rover
They past the broad Po.
We have beaten all foemen,
We have captured a king,
We have turned back on no men,
And so let us sing!
Here 's the Bourbon for ever!
Though pennyless all,
We 'll have one more endeavour
At yonder old wall.
With the Bourbon we 'll gather
At day-dawn before
The gates, and together
Or break or climb o'er
The wall: on the ladder,
As mounts each firm foot,
Our shout shall grow gladder,
And death only be mute.

With the Bourbon we 'll mount o'er
The walls of old Rome,
And who then shall count o'er
The spoils of each dome?
Up! up! with the lily!
And down with the keys!
In old Rome, the seven-hilly,
We 'll revel at ease.
Her streets shall be gory,
Her Tyber all red,
And her temples so hoary
Shall clang with our tread.
Oh, the Bourbon! the Bourbon!
The Bourbon for aye!
Of our song bear the burthen!
And fire, fire away!
With Spain for the van-guard,
Our varied host comes?
And next to the Spaniard
Beat Germany's drums;
And Italy's lances
Are couch'd at their mother;
But our leader from France is,
Who warr'd with his brother.
Oh, the Bourbon! the Bourbon!
Sans country or home,
We 'll follow the Bourbon,
To plunder old Rome.

CÆSAR.

An indifferent song
For those within the walls, methinks, to hear.

ARNOLD.

Yes, if they keep to their chorus. But here comes
The general, with his chiefs and men of trust.
A goodly rebel.

Enter the Constable BOURBON, "cum suis," etc. etc. etc.

PHILIBERT.

How now, noble prince,
You are not cheerful!

BOURBON.

Why should I be so?

PHILIBERT.

Upon the eve of conquest, such as ours,
Most men would be so.

BOURBON.

If I were secure!

PHILIBERT.

Doubt not our soldiers. Were the walls of adamant,
They 'd crack them. Hunger is a sharp artillery.

BOURBON.

That they will falter is my least of fears.
That they will be repulsed, with Bourbon for
Their chief, and all their kindled appetites
To marshal them on—were those hoary walls
Mountains, and those who guard them like the gods
Of the old fables, I would trust my Titans;—
But now—

PHILIBERT.

They are but men who war with mortals.

BOURBON.

True: but those walls have girded in great ages,
And sent forth mighty spirits. The past earth

And present phantom of imperious Rome
Is peopled with those warriors; and methinks
They flit along the eternal city's rampart,
And stretch their glorious, gory, shadowy hands,
And beckon me away!

PHILIBERT.

So let them! Wilt thou
Turn back from shadowy menaces of shadows?

BOURBON.

They do not menace me. I could have faced,
Methinks, a Sylla's menace; but they clasp
And raise, and wring their dim and death-like hands,
And with their thin aspen faces and fixed eyes
Fascinate mine. Look there!

PHILIBERT.

I look upon
A lofty battlement.

BOURBON.

And there!

PHILIBERT.

Not even
A guard in sight; they wisely keep below,
Sheltered by the grey parapet, from some
Stray bullet of our lansquenets, who might
Practise in the cool twilight.

BOURBON.

You are blind.

PHILIBERT.

If seeing nothing more than may be seen
Be so.

BOURBON.

A thousand years have manned the walls

With all their heroes,—the last Cato stands
And tears his bowels, rather than survive
The liberty of that I would enslave.
And the first Cæsar with his triumphs flits
From battlement to battlement.

PHILIBERT.

Then conquer
The walls for which he conquered, and be greater!

BOURBON.

True: so I will, or perish.

PHILIBERT.

You can *not*.
In such an enterprise to die is rather
The dawn of an eternal day, than death.

Count ARNOLD and CÆSAR advance.

CÆSAR.

And the mere men—do they too sweat beneath
The noon of this same ever-scorching glory?

BOURBON.

Ah!
Welcome the bitter hunch-back! and his master,
The beauty of our host, and brave as beauteous,
As generous as lovely. We shall find
Work for you both ere morning.

CÆSAR.

You will find,
So please your highness, no less for yourself.

BOURBON.

And if I do, there will not be a labourer
More forward, hunch-back!

CÆSAR.

You may well say so,

For *you* have seen that back—as general,
Placed in the rear in action—but your foes
Have never seen it.

BOURBON.

That 's a fair retort,
For I provoked it:—but the Bourbon's breast
Has been, and ever shall be, far advanced
In danger's face as yours, were you the *devil.*

CÆSAR.

And if I were, I might have saved myself
The toil of coming here.

PHILIBERT.

Why so?

CÆSAR.

One half
Of your brave bands of their own bold accord
Will go to him, the other half be sent,
More swiftly, not less surely.

BOURBON.

Arnold, your
Slight crooked friend 's as snake-like in his words
As his deeds.

CÆSAR.

Your highness much mistakes me.
The first snake was a flatterer—I am none;
And for my deeds, I only sting when stung.

BOURBON.

You are brave, and that 's enough for me; and quick
In speech as sharp in action—and that 's more.
I am not alone a soldier, but the soldiers'
Comrade.

CÆSAR.

They are but bad company, your highness;

And worse even for their friends than foes, as being
More permanent acquaintance.

PHILIBERT.

How now, fellow!
Thou waxest insolent, beyond the privilege
Of a buffoon.

CÆSAR.

You mean I speak the truth.
I 'll lie—it is as easy: then you 'll praise me
For calling you a hero.

BOURBON.

Philibert!
Let him alone; he 's brave, and ever has
Been first with that swart face and mountain shoulder
In field or storm, and patient in starvation;
And for his tongue, the camp is full of licence,
And the sharp stinging of a lively rogue
Is, to my mind, far preferable to
The gross, dull, heavy, gloomy execration
Of a mere famished, sullen, grumbling slave,
Whom nothing can convince save a full meal,
And wine, and sleep, and a few maravedis,
With which he deems him rich.

CÆSAR.

It would be well
If the earth's princes asked no more.

BOURBON.

Be silent!

CÆSAR.

Ay, but not idle. Work yourself with words!
You have few to speak.

PHILIBERT.

What means the audacious

CÆSAR.

To prate, like other prophets.

BOURBON.

Philibert!
Why will you vex him? Have we not enough
To think on? Arnold! I will lead the attack
To-morrow.

ARNOLD.

I have heard as much, my lord.

BOURBON.

And you will follow?

ARNOLD.

Since I must not lead.

BOURBON.

'T is necessary for the further daring
Of our too needy army, that their chief
Plant the first foot upon the foremost ladder's
First step.

CÆSAR.

Upon its topmost, let us hope:
So shall he have his full deserts.

BOURBON.

The world's
Great capital perchance is ours to-morrow.
Through every change the seven-hilled city hath
Retained her sway o'er nations, and the Cæsars
But yielded to the Alarics, the Alarics
Unto the pontiffs. Roman, Goth, or Priest,
Still the world's masters! Civilized, barbarian,
Or saintly, still the walls of Romulus

Have been the circus of an empire. Well!
'T was *their* turn—now 't is ours; and let us hope
That we will fight as well, and rule much better.

CÆSAR.

No doubt, the camp's the school of civic rights.
What would you make of Rome?

BOURBON.

That which it was.

CÆSAR.

In Alaric's time?

BOURBON.

No, slave! In the first Cæsar's,
Whose name you bear, like other curs.

CÆSAR.

And kings.
'T is a great name for bloodhounds.

BOURBON.

There 's a demon
In that fierce rattlesnake thy tongue. Wilt never
Be serious?

CÆSAR.

On the eve of battle, no;—
That were not soldier-like. 'T is for the general
To be more pensive: we adventurers
Must be more cheerful. Wherefore should we think?
Our tutelar deity, in a leader's shape,
Takes care of us. Keep thought aloof from hosts!
If the knaves take to thinking, you will have
To crack those walls alone.

BOURBON.

You may sneer, since
'T is lucky for you that you fight no worse for 't.

CÆSAR.

I thank you for the freedom; 't is the only
Pay I have taken in your highness' service.

BOURBON.

Well, sir, to-morrow you shall pay yourself.
Look on those towers; they hold my treasury.
But, Philibert, we 'll in to council. Arnold,
We would request your presence.

ARNOLD.

Prince, my service
Is yours, as in the field.

BOURBON.

In both we prize it,
And yours will be a post of trust at day-break.

CÆSAR.

And mine?

BOURBON.

To follow glory with the Bourbon.
Good night!

ARNOLD (To CÆSAR.)

Prepare our armour for the assault,
And wait within my tent.

(Exeunt BOURBON, ARNOLD, PHILIBERT, etc.

CÆSAR (Solus.)

Within thy tent!
Think'st thou that I pass from thee with my presence?
Or that this crooked coffer, which contained
Thy principle of life, is aught to me
Except a mask? And these are men, forsooth!
Heroes and chiefs, the flower of Adam's bastards!
This is the consequence of giving matter
The power of thought. It is a stubborn substance,

And thinks chaotically, as it acts,
Ever relapsing into its first elements.
Well! I must play with these poor puppets: 't is
The spirit's pastime in his idler hours.
When I grow weary of it, I have business
Amongst the stars, which these poor creatures deem
Were made for them to look at. 'T were a jest now
To bring one down amongst them, and set fire
Unto their ant-hill: how the pismires then
Would scamper o'er the scalding soil, and, ceasing
From tearing down each others' nests, pipe forth
One universal orison! Ha! ha!

(Exit CÆSAR.

PART II.

SCENE I.—BEFORE THE WALLS OF ROME.—THE ASSAULT; THE ARMY IN MOTION, WITH LADDERS TO SCALE THE WALLS; BOURBON, WITH A WHITE SCARF OVER HIS ARMOUR, FOREMOST.

Chorus of Spirits in the air.

1.

'T is the morn, but dim and dark.
Whither flies the silent lark?
Whither shrinks the clouded sun?
Is the day indeed begun?
Nature's eye is melancholy
O'er the city high and holy:
But without there is a din
Should arouse the saints within,
And revive the heroic ashes
Round which yellow Tyber dashes.
Oh ye seven hills! awaken!
Ere your very base be shaken!

2.

Hearken to the steady stamp!
Mars is in their every tramp!
Not a step is out of tune,
As the tides obey the moon!
On they march, though to self-slaughter,
Regular as rolling water,
Whose high waves o'ersweep the border
Of huge moles, but keep their order,
Breaking only rank by rank.
Hearken to the armour's clank!
Look down o'er each frowning warrior,
How he glares upon the barrier:
Look on each step of each ladder,
As the stripes that streak an adder.

3.

Look upon the bristling wall,
Manned without an interval!
Round and round, and tier on tier,
Cannon's black mouth, shining spear,
Lit match, bell-mouthed musquetoon,
Gaping to be murderous soon.
All the warlike gear of old,
Mixed with what we now behold,
In this strife 'twixt old and new,
Gather like a locust's crew.
Shade of Remus! 'T is a time
Awful as thy brother's crime!
Christians war against Christ's shrine:—
Must its lot be like to thine?

4.

Near—and near—nearer still,
As the earthquake saps the hill,
First with trembling, hollow motion,
Like a scarce-awakened ocean,
Then with stronger shock and louder,
Till the rocks are crushed to powder,—
Onward sweeps the rolling host!
Heroes of the immortal boast!
Mighty chiefs! Eternal shadows!
First flowers of the bloody meadows
Which encŏmpass Rome, the mother
Of a people without brother!
Will you sleep when nations' quarrels
Plough the root up of your laurels?
Ye who wept o'er Carthage burning,
Weep not—*strike!* for Rome is mourning![3]

5.

Onward sweep the varied nations!
Famine long hath dealt their rations.
To the wall, with hate and hunger,
Numerous as wolves, and stronger,
On they sweep. Oh! glorious city,
Must thou be a theme for pity!
Fight, like your first sire, each Roman!
Alaric was a gentle foeman,
Match'd with Bourbon's black banditti!
Rouse thee, thou eternal city!
Rouse thee! Rather give the torch
With thy own hand to thy porch,

Than behold such hosts pollute
Your worst dwelling with their foot.

6.

Ah! behold yon bleeding spectre!
Ilion's children find no Hector;
Priam's offspring loved their brother;
Roma's sire forgot his mother,
When he slew his gallant twin,
With inexpiable sin.
See the giant shadow stride
O'er the ramparts high and wide!
When he first o'erleapt thy wall,
Its foundation mourned thy fall.
Now, though towering like a Babel,
Who to stop his steps are able?
Stalking o'er thy highest dome,
Remus claims his vengeance, Rome!

7.

Now they reach thee in their anger:
Fire, and smoke, and hellish clangor
Are around thee, thou world's wonder!
Death is in thy walls and under.
Now the meeting steel first clashes;
Downward then the ladder crashes,
With its iron load all gleaming,
Lying at its foot blaspheming!
Up again! for every warrior
Slain, another climbs the barrier.
Thicker grows the strife: thy ditches
Europe's mingling gore enriches.

Rome! Although thy wall may perish,
Such manure thy fields will cherish,
Making gay the harvest-home;
But thy hearths, alas! oh, Rome!—
Yet be Rome amidst thine anguish,
Fight as thou wast wont to vanquish!

8.

Yet once more, ye old penates!
Let not your quenched hearths be Ate's!
Yet again, ye shadowy heroes,
Yield not to these stranger Neros!
Though the son who slew his mother,
Shed Rome's blood, he was your brother!
'T was the Roman curbed the Roman;—
Brennus was a baffled foeman.
Yet again, ye saints and martyrs,
Rise! for yours are holier charters.
Mighty gods of temples falling,
Yet in ruin still appalling!
Mightier founders of those altars,
True and christian,—strike the assaulters!
Tyber! Tyber! let thy torrent
Show even nature's self abhorrent.
Let each breathing heart dilated
Turn, as doth the lion baited!
Rome be crush'd to one wide tomb,
But be still the Roman's Rome!

BOURBON, ARNOLD, CÆSAR, and others, arrive at the foot of the wall. ARNOLD is about to plant his ladder.

BOURBON.

Hold, Arnold! I am first.

ARNOLD.

Not so, my lord.

BOURBON.

Hold, sir, I charge you! Follow! I am proud
Of such a follower, but will brook no leader.

(BOURBON plants his ladder, and begins to mount.

Now, boys! On! on!

(A shot strikes him, and BOURBON falls.

CÆSAR.

And off!

ARNOLD.

Eternal Powers!
The host will be appalled.—But vengeance! vengeance!

BOURBON.

'T is nothing—lend me your hand.

(BOURBON takes ARNOLD by the hand and rises; but, as he puts his foot on the step, falls again.

BOURBON.

Arnold! I am sped.
Conceal my fall—all will go well—conceal it!
Fling my cloak o'er what will be dust anon;
Let not the soldiers see it.

ARNOLD.

You must be
Removed; the aid of——

BOURBON.

No, my gallant boy;

Death is upon me. But what is *one* life?
The Bourbon's spirit shall command them still.
Keep them yet ignorant that I am but clay,
Till they are conquerors—then do as you may.

CÆSAR.

Would not your highness choose to kiss the cross?
We have no priest here, but the hilt of sword
May serve instead:—it did the same for Bayard.

BOURBON.

Thou bitter slave! to name *him* at this time!
But I deserve it.

ARNOLD (To CÆSAR.)

Villain, hold your peace!

CÆSAR.

What, when a christian dies? Shall I not offer
A christian « vade in pace?»

ARNOLD.

Silence! Oh!
Those eyes are glazing, which o'erlooked the world,
And saw no equal.

BOURBON.

Arnold, should'st thou see
France——But hark! hark! the assault grows warmer—Oh!
For but an hour, a minute more of life,
To die within the wall! Hence, Arnold, hence!
You lose time—they will conquer Rome without thee.

ARNOLD.

And without *thee!*

BOURBON.

Not so; I' ll lead them still
In spirit. Cover up my dust, and breathe not

That I have ceased to breathe. Away! and be
Victorious!

ARNOLD.

But I must not leave thee thus.

BOURBON.

You must—farewell—Up! up! the world is winning.

BOURBON dies.

CÆSAR (To ARNOLD.)

Come, count, to business.

ARNOLD.

True. I 'll weep hereafter.

ARNOLD covers BOURBON's body with a mantle, and mounts the ladder, crying

The Bourbon! Bourbon! On boys! Rome is ours!

CÆSAR.

Good night, lord constable! thou wert a man.

(CÆSAR follows ARNOLD; they reach the battlement; ARNOLD and CÆSAR are struck down.

CÆSAR.

A precious somerset! Is your countship injured?

ARNOLD.

No. (Remounts the ladder.

CÆSAR.

A rare bloodhound, when his own is heated!
And 't is no boy's play. Now he strikes them down!
His hand is on the battlement—he grasps it
As though it were an altar; now his foot
Is on it, and——What have we here, a Roman?

(A man falls.

The first bird of the covey; he has fallen
On the outside of the nest. Why, how now, fellow?

WOUNDED MAN.

A drop of water!

CÆSAR.

Blood's the only liquid
Nearer than Tyber.

WOUNDED MAN.

I have died for Rome.

(Dies.

CÆSAR.

And so did Bourbon, in another sense.
Oh these immortal men! and their great motives!
But I must after my young charge. He is
By this time i' the forum. Charge! charge!

(CÆSAR mounts the ladder; the scene closes.

SCENE II.—COMBATS BETWEEN THE BESIEGERS AND BESIEGED IN THE STREETS. INHABITANTS FLYING IN CONFUSION.

Enter CÆSAR.

CÆSAR.

I cannot find my hero; he is mixed
With the heroic crowd that now pursue
The fugitives, or battle with the desperate.
What have we here? A cardinal or two
That do not seem in love with martyrdom.
How the old red-shanks scamper! Could they doff
Their hose, as they have doff'd their hats, 't would be
A blessing, as a mark the less for plunder.
But let them fly, the crimson kennels now
Will not much stain their stockings, since the mire
Is of the self-same purple hue.

Enter a party fighting—ARNOLD at the head of the besiegers.

He comes,
Hand in hand with the mild twins—Gore and glory.
Holla! hold, count!

ARNOLD.

Away! they must not rally.

CÆSAR.

I tell thee, be not rash; a golden bridge
Is for a flying enemy. I gave thee
A form of beauty, and an
Exemption from some maladies of body,
But not of mind, which is not mine to give.
But though I gave the form of Thetis' son,
I dipt thee not in Styx; and 'gainst a foe
I would not warrant thy chivalric heart
More than Pelides' heel; why then be cautious,
And know thyself a mortal still.

ARNOLD

And who
With aught of soul would combat if he were
Invulnerable? That were pretty sport.
Think'st thou I beat for hares when lions roar?

(ARNOLD rushes into the combat.

CÆSAR.

A precious sample of humanity!
Well, his blood's up, and if a little's shed,
'T will serve to curb his fever.

(ARNOLD engages with a Roman, who retires towards a portico.

ARNOLD.

Yield thee, slave!
I promise quarter.

ROMAN.

That's soon said.

ARNOLD.

And done—
My word is known.

ROMAN.

So shall be my deeds.

(They re-engage. CÆSAR comes forward.

CÆSAR.

Why, Arnold! Hold thine own; thou hast in hand
A famous artizan, a cunning sculptor;
Also a dealer in the sword and dagger.
Not so, my musqueteer; 't was he who slew
The Bourbon from the wall.

ARNOLD.

Ay, did he so?
Then he hath carved his monument.

ROMAN.

I yet
May live to carve your betters.

CÆSAR.

Well said, my man of marble! Benvenuto,
Thou hast some practice in both ways; and he
Who slays Cellini, will have work'd as hard
As e'er thou didst upon Carrara's blocks.

ARNOLD disarms and wounds CELLINI, but slightly; the latter draws a pistol and fires; then retires and disappears through the portico.

CÆSAR.

How farest thou? Thou hast a taste, methinks,
Of red Bellona's banquet.

ARNOLD (Staggers.)

'T is a scratch.

Lend me thy scarf. He shall not 'scape me thus.

CÆSAR.

Where is it?

ARNOLD.

In the shoulder, not the sword-arm—
And that 's enough. I am thirsty: would I had
A helm of water!

CÆSAR.

That 's a liquid now
In requisition, but by no means easiest
To come at.

ARNOLD.

And my thirst increases; but
I 'll find a way to quench it.

CÆSAR.

Or be quenched
Thyself?

ARNOLD.

The chance is even; we will throw
The dice thereon. But I lose time in prating;
Prithee be quick.

(CÆSAR binds on the scarf.

And what do'st thou so idly?
Why dost not strike?

CÆSAR.

Your old philosophers
Beheld mankind, as mere spectators of
The Olympic games. When I behold a prize
Worth wrestling for, I may be found a Milo.

ARNOLD.

Ay, 'gainst an oak.

CÆSAR.

A forest when it suits me.
I combat with a mass, or not at all.
Meantime, pursue thy sport as I do mine:
Which is just now to gaze, since all these labourers
Will reap my harvest gratis.

ARNOLD.

Thou art still
A fiend!

CÆSAR.

And thou—a man.

ARNOLD.

Why, such I fain would show me.

CÆSAR.

True—as men are.

ARNOLD.

And what is that?

CÆSAR.

Thou feelest and thou seest.

(Exit ARNOLD, joining in the combat which still continues between detached parties. The scene closes.

SCENE III.—ST. PETER'S.—THE INTERIOR OF THE CHURCH.—THE POPE AT THE ALTAR.—PRIESTS, ETC. CROWDING IN CONFUSION, AND CITIZENS FLYING FOR REFUGE, PURSUED BY SOLDIERY.—ENTER CÆSAR.

A SPANISH SOLDIER.

Down with them, comrades! seize upon those lamps!
Cleave yon bald-pated shaveling to the chine!
His rosary's of gold!

LUTHERAN SOLDIER.

Revenge! Revenge!
Plunder hereafter, but for vengeance now—
Yonder stands Anti-Christ!

CÆSAR (Interposing.)

How now, schismatic!
What woulds't thou?

LUTHERAN SOLDIER.

In the holy name of Christ,
Destroy proud Anti-Christ. I am a christian.

CÆSAR.

Yea, a disciple that would make the founder
Of your belief renounce it, could he see
Such proselytes. Best stint thyself to plunder.

LUTHERAN SOLDIER.

I say he is the devil.

CÆSAR.

Hush! keep that secret,
Lest he should recognise you for his own.

LUTHERAN SOLDIER.

Why would you save him? I repeat he is
The devil, or the devil's vicar upon earth.

CÆSAR.

And that 's the reason; would you make a quarrel
With your best friends? You had far best be quiet;
His hour is not yet come

LUTHERAN SOLDIER.

That shall be seen!

(The Lutheran soldier rushes forward; a shot strikes him from one of the Pope's guards, and he falls at the foot of the alter.

CÆSAR (To the Lutheran.)

I told you so.

LUTHERAN SOLDIER.

And will you not avenge me?

CÆSAR.

Not I! You know that « vengeance is the Lord's: »
You see he loves no interlopers.

LUTHERAN (Dying.)

Oh!
Had I but slain him, I had gone on high,
Crown'd with eternal glory! Heaven forgive
My feebleness of arm that reach'd him not,
And take thy servant to thy mercy. 'T is
A glorious triumph still; proud Babylon 's
No more; the harlot of the seven hills
Hath changed her scarlet raiment for sackcloth
And ashes!

(The Lutheran dies.

CÆSAR.

Yes, thine own amidst the rest.
Well done, old Babel!

(The guards defend themselves desperately, while the pontiff escapes, by a private passage, to the Vatican, and the Castle of Saint Angelo.

Ha! right nobly battled!
Now, priest! now, soldier! the two great professions
Together by the ears and hearts! I have not
Seen a more comic pantomime since Titus
Took Jewry. But the Romans had the best then;
Now they must take their turn.

SOLDIERS.

He hath escaped!
Follow!

ANOTHER SOLDIER.

They have barred the narrow passage up,

And it is clogged with dead even to the door.

CÆSAR.

I am glad he hath escaped: he may thank me for 't
In part. I would not have his bulls abolished—
'T were worth one half our empire: his indulgences
Demand some in return;—no, no, he must not
Fall;—and besides, his now escape may furnish
A future miracle, in future proof
Of his infallibility.

(To the Spanish soldiery.

Well, cut-throats!
What do you pause for? If you make not haste,
There will not be a link of pious gold left.
And *you* too, catholics! Would ye return
From such a pilgrimage without a relic?
The very Lutherans have more true devotion:
See how they strip the shrines!

SOLDIERS.

By holy Peter!
He speaks the truth; the heretics will bear
The best away.

CÆSAR.

And that were shame! Go to!
Assist in their conversion.

(The soldiers disperse; many quit the church, others enter.

They are gone,
And others come: so flows the wave on wave
Of what these creatures call eternity,
Deeming themselves the breakers of the ocean,
While they are but its bubbles, ignorant
That foam is their foundation. So, another!

Enter OLIMPIA, flying from the pursuit—She springs upon the altar.

SOLDIER.

She 's mine.

ANOTHER SOLDIER (Opposing the former.)

You lie, I tracked her first; and, were she
The Pope's niece, I 'll not yield her. (They fight.

THIRD SOLDIER (Advancing towards OLIMPIA.)

You may settle
Your claims; I 'll make mine good.

OLIMPIA.

Infernal slave!
You touch me not alive.

THIRD SOLDIER.

Alive or dead!

OLIMPIA (Embracing a massive crucifix.)

Respect your God!

THIRD SOLDIER.

Yes, when he shines in gold.
Girl, you but grasp your dowry.

(As he advances, OLIMPIA, with a strong and sudden effort, casts down the crucifix; it strikes the soldier, who falls.

THIRD SOLDIER.

Oh, great God!

OLIMPIA.

Ah! now you recognise him.

THIRD SOLDIER.

My brain 's crush'd!
Comrades, help ho! All 's darkness! (He dies.

OTHER SOLDIERS (Coming up.)

Slay her, although she had a thousand lives:
She has killed our comrade.

OLIMPIA.

Welcome such a death!
You have no life to give, which the worst slave
Would take. Great God! through thy redeeming Son,
And thy Son's Mother, now receive me as
I would approach thee, worthy her, and him, and thee!

Enter ARNOLD.

ARNOLD.

What do I see! Accursed jackals!
Forbear!

CÆSAR (Aside, and laughing.)

Ha! ha! here 's equity! The dogs
Have as much right as he. But to the issue!

SOLDIERS.

Count, she hath slain our comrade.

ARNOLD.

With what weapon?

SOLDIER.

The cross, beneath which he is crush'd; behold him
Lie there, more like a worm than man; she cast it
Upon his head.

ARNOLD.

Even so; there is a woman
Worthy a brave man's liking. Were ye such,
Ye would have honour'd her. But get ye hence,
And thank your meanness, other god you have none,
For your existence. Had you touch'd a hair
Of those dishevelled locks, I would have thinn'd
Your ranks more than the enemy. Away!
Ye jackals! gnaw the bones the lion leaves,
But not even these till he permits.

A SOLDIER (Murmuring.)

'The lion

Might conquer for himself then.

ARNOLD (Cuts him down.)

Mutineer!

Rebel in hell—you shall obey on earth!

(The soldiers assault ARNOLD.

Come on! I 'm glad on 't! I will show you, slaves,
How you should be commanded, and who led you
First o'er the wall you were as shy to scale,
Until I waved my banners from its height,
As you are bold within it.

(ARNOLD mows down the foremost; the rest throw down their arms.

SOLDIERS.

Mercy! mercy!

ARNOLD.

Then learn to grant it. Have I taught you *who*
Lead you o'er Rome's eternal battlements?

SOLDIERS.

We saw it, and we know it; yet forgive
A moment's error in the heat of conquest—
The conquest which you led to.

ARNOLD.

Get you hence!

Hence to your quarters! you will find them fixed
In the Colonna palace!

OLIMPIA (Aside.)

In my father's

House!

ARNOLD (To the soldiers.)

Leave your arms; ye have no further need
Of such: the city 's render'd. And mark well

You keep your hands clean, or I 'll find out a stream,
As red as Tyber now runs, for your baptism.

SOLDIERS (Deposing their arms, and departing.)

We obey!

ARNOLD (To OLIMPIA.)

Lady! you are safe.

OLIMPIA.

I should be so,
Had I a knife even; but it matters not—
Death hath a thousand gates; and on the marble,
Even at the altar foot, whence I look down
Upon destruction, shall my head be dash'd,
Ere thou ascend it. God forgive thee, man!

ARNOLD.

I wish to merit his forgiveness, and
Thine own, although I have not injured thee.

OLIMPIA.

No! Thou hast only sack'd my native land—
No injury!—and made my father's house
A den of thieves—No injury!—this temple—
Slippery with Roman and holy gore—
No injury! And now thou would'st preserve me,
To be—but that shall never be!

(She raises her eyes to heaven, folds her robe round her, and prepares to dash herself down on the side of the altar opposite to that where ARNOLD stands.

ARNOLD.

Hold! hold!
I swear.

OLIMPIA.

Spare thine already forfeit soul

A perjury for which even hell would loathe thee.
I know thee.

ARNOLD.

No, thou know'st me not; I am not
Of those men, though——

OLIMPIA.

I judge thee by thy mates;
It is for God to judge thee as thou art.
I see thee purple with the blood of Rome;
Take mine, 't is all thou e'er shalt have of me!
And here, upon the marble of this temple,
Where the baptismal font baptised me God's,
I offer him a blood less holy
But not less pure (pure as it left me then,
A redeemed infant) than the holy water
The saints have sanctified!

(OLIMPIA waves her hand to ARNOLD with disdain, and dashes herself on the pavement from the altar.

ARNOLD.

Eternal God!
I feel thee now! Help! help! She 's gone.

CÆSAR (Approaches.)

I am here.

ARNOLD.

Thou! but oh, save her!

CÆSAR (Assisting him to raise OLIMPIA.)

She hath done it well;
The leap was serious!

ARNOLD.

Oh! she is lifeless!

CÆSAR.

If

She be so, I have nought to do with that:
The resurrection is beyond me.

ARNOLD.

Slave!

CÆSAR.

Ay, slave or master, 't is all one: methinks
Good words however are as well at times.

ARNOLD.

Words!—Canst thou aid her?

CÆSAR.

I will try. A sprinkling
Of that same holy water may be useful.

(He brings some in his helmet from the font.

ARNOLD.

'T is mixed with blood.

CÆSAR.

There is no cleaner now
In Rome.

ARNOLD.

How pale! how beautiful! how lifeless!
Alive or dead, thou essence of all beauty,
I love but thee!

CÆSAR.

Even so Achilles loved
Penthesilea; with his form it seems
You have his heart, and yet it was no soft one.

ARNOLD.

She breathes! But no, 't was nothing, or the last
Faint flutter life disputes with death.

CÆSAR.

She breathes.

ARNOLD.

Thou say'st it? Then 't is truth.

CÆSAR.

You do me right—
The devil speaks truth much oftener than he 's deem'd:
He hath an ignorant audience.

ARNOLD (Without attending to him.)

Yes! her heart beats.
Alas! that the first beat of the only heart
I ever wish'd to beat with mine, should vibrate
To an assassin's pulse.

CÆSAR.

A sage reflexion,
But somewhat late i' the day. Where shall we bear her?
I say she lives.

ARNOLD.

And will she live?

CÆSAR.

As much
As dust can.

ARNOLD.

Then she is dead!

CÆSAR.

Bah! bah! You are so,
And do not know it. She will come to life—
Such as you think so, such as you now are;
But we must work by human means.

ARNOLD.

We will
Convey her unto the Colonna palace,
Where I have pitch'd my banner.

CÆSAR.

Come then! raise her up!

ARNOLD.

Softly!

CÆSAR.

As softly as they bear the dead,
Perhaps because they cannot feel the jolting.

ARNOLD.

But doth she live indeed?

CÆSAR.

Nay, never fear!
But, if you rue it after, blame not me.

ARNOLD.

Let her but live!

CÆSAR.

The spirit of her life
Is yet within her breast, and may revive.
Count! count! I am your servant in all things,
And this is a new office:—'t is not oft
I am employ'd in such; but you perceive
How stanch a friend is what you call a fiend.
On earth you 've often only fiends for friends;
Now *I* desert not mine. Soft! bear her hence,
The beautiful half-clay, and nearly spirit!
I am almost enamour'd of her, as
Of old the angels of her earliest sex.

ARNOLD.

Thou!

CÆSAR.

I. But fear not. I 'll not be your rival.

ARNOLD.

Rival!

CÆSAR.

I could be one right formidable;
But since I slew the seven husbands of
Tobias' future bride (and after all
'T was sucked out by some incense), I have laid
Aside intrigue: 't is rarely worth the trouble
Of gaining, or—what is more difficult—
Getting rid of your prize again; for there 's
The rub! at least to mortals.

ARNOLD.

Prithee, peace!
Softly! methinks her lips move, her eyes open!

CÆSAR.

Like stars, no doubt; for that 's a metaphor
For Lucifer and Venus.

ARNOLD.

To the palace
Colonna, as I told you!

CÆSAR.

Oh! I know
My way through Rome.

ARNOLD.

Now onward, onward! Gently!

Exeunt, bearing OLIMPIA.—The scene closes.

PART III.

SCENE I.—A CASTLE IN THE APENNINES, SURROUNDED BY A WILD BUT SMILING COUNTRY.—CHORUS OF PEASANTS SINGING BEFORE THE GATES.

Chorus.

1.

The wars are over,
  The spring is come;
The bride and her lover
  Have sought their home:
They are happy, we rejoice;
Let their hearts have an echo in every voice!

2.

The spring is come; the violet's gone,
The first-born child of the early sun;
With us she is but a winter's flower,
The snow on the hills cannot blast her bower,

And she lifts up her dewy eye of blue
To the youngest sky of the self-same hue.

3.

And when the spring comes with her host
Of flowers, that flower beloved the most
Shrinks from the crowd that may confuse
Her heavenly odour and virgin hues.

4.

Pluck the others, but still remember
Their herald out of dim December—
The morning star of all the flowers,
The pledge of daylight's lengthen'd hours;
Nor, midst the roses, e'er forget
The virgin, virgin violet.

Enter CÆSAR.

CÆSAR (Singing.)

The wars are all over,
Our swords are all idle,
The steed bites the bridle,
The casque's on the wall.
There's rest for the rover;
But his armour is rusty,
And the veteran grows crusty,
As he yawns in the hall.
He drinks—but what's drinking?
A mere pause from thinking!
No bugle awakes him with life and death call.

Chorus.

But the hound bayeth loudly,
The boar 's in the wood
And the falcon longs proudly
To spring from her hood:
On the wrist of the noble
She sits like a crest,
And the air is in trouble
With birds from their nest.

CÆSAR.

Oh! shadow of glory!
Dim image of war!
But the chace hath no story,
Her hero no star,
Since Nimrod, the founder
Of empire and chace,
Who made the woods wonder
And quake for their race.
When the lion was young,
In the pride of his might,
Then 't was sport for the strong
To embrace him in fight;
To go forth, with a pine
For a spear, 'gainst the mammoth,
Or strike through the ravine
At the foaming behemoth;
While man was in stature
As towers in our time,
The first born of nature,
And, like her, sublime!

Chorus.

But the wars are over,
The spring is come;
The bride and her lover
Have sought their home;
They are happy, and we rejoice;
Let their hearts have an echo from every voice!

(Exeunt the peasantry, singing.

NOTES TO THE DEFORMED TRANSFORMED.

Note 1, page 65, line 19.

Bestrides the Hartz mountain, *etc.*

This is a well-known German superstition—a gigantic shadow produced by reflection on the Brocken.

Note 2, page 76, line 1.

From the red earth, like Adam, *etc.*

Adam means *red earth*, from which the first man was formed.

Note 3, page 104, line 16.

Weep not—*strike!* for Rome is mourning!

Scipio, the second Africanus, is said to have repeated a verse of Homer and wept o'er the burning of Carthage. He had better have granted it a capitulation.

9.

THE

BRIDE OF ABYDOS.

A TURKISH TALE.

« Had we never loved so kindly,
Had we never loved so blindly,
Never met or never parted,
We had ne'er been broken-hearted. »

Burns.

TO

THE RIGHT HONOURABLE

LORD HOLLAND,

THIS TALE

IS INSCRIBED, WITH

EVERY SENTIMENT OF REGARD

AND RESPECT,

BY HIS GRATEFULLY OBLIGED

AND SINCERE FRIEND,

BYRON.

THE

BRIDE OF ABYDOS.

CANTO I.

I.

KNOW ye the land where the cypress and myrtle
  Are emblems of deeds that are done in their clime,
Where the rage of the vulture, the love of the turtle,
  Now melt into sorrow, now madden to crime?
Know ye the land of the cedar and vine,
Where the flowers ever blossom, the beams ever shine;
Where the light wings of zephyr, oppress'd with perfume,
Wax faint o'er the gardens of Gúl[1] in her bloom;
Where the citron and olive are fairest of fruit,
And the voice of the nightingale never is mute;
Where the tints of the earth, and the hues of the sky,
In colour though varied, in beauty may vie,
And the purple of ocean is deepest in die;
Where the virgins are soft as the roses they twine,
And all, save the spirit of man, is divine?

'T is the clime of the east; 't is the land of the sun—
Can he smile on such deeds as his children have done?[2]
Oh! wild as the accents of lovers' farewell
Are the hearts which they bear, and the tales which they tell.

II.

Begirt with many a gallant slave,
Apparell'd as becomes the brave,
Awaiting each his lord's behest
To guide his steps, or guard his rest,
Old Giaffir sate in his divan:
  Deep thought was in his aged eye;
And though the face of mussulman
  Not oft betrays to standers by
The mind within, well skill'd to hide
All but unconquerable pride,
His pensive cheek and pondering brow
Did more than he was wont avow.

III.

« Let the chamber be clear'd. »—The train disappear'd—
  « Now call me the chief of the haram-guard. »
With Giaffir is none but his only son,
  And the Nubian awaiting the sire's award.
  « Haroun—when all the crowd that wait
  Are pass'd beyond the outer gate,
  (Woe to the head whose eye beheld
  My child Zuleika's face unveil'd!)
  Hence, lead my daughter from her tower;
  Her fate is fix'd this very hour:
  Yet not to her repeat my thought;
  By me alone be duty taught! »

« Pacha! to hear is to obey. »
No more must slave to despot say—
Then to the tower had ta'en his way,
But here young Selim silence brake,
   First lowly rendering reverence meet;
And downcast look'd, and gently spake,
   Still standing at the pacha's feet:
For son of moslem must expire,
Ere dare to sit before his sire!

« Father! for fear that thou should'st chide
My sister, or her sable guide,
Know—for the fault, if fault there be,
Was mine, then fall thy frowns on me—
So lovelily the morning shone,
   That—let the old and weary sleep—
I could not; and to view alone
   The fairest scenes of land and deep,
With none to listen and reply
To thoughts with which my heart beat high
Were irksome—for whate'er my mood,
In sooth I love not solitude;
I on Zuleika's slumber broke,
   And, as thou knowest that for me
   Soon turns the haram's grating key,
Before the guardian slaves awoke
We to the cypress groves had flown,
And made earth, main, and heaven our own!
There linger'd we, beguiled too long
With Mejnoun's tale or Sadi's song;[3]
Till I, who heard the deep tambour[4]
Beat thy divan's approaching hour,

To thee and to my duty true,
Warn'd by the sound, to greet thee flew:
But there Zuleika wanders yet—
Nay, father, rage not—nor forget
That none can pierce that secret bower
But those who watch the women's tower.»

IV.

« Son of a slave»—the pacha said—
« From unbelieving mother bred,
Vain were a father's hope to see
Aught that beseems a man in thee.
Thou, when thine arm should bend the bow,
And hurl the dart, and curb the steed,
Thou, Greek in soul if not in creed,
Must pore where babbling waters flow,
And watch unfolding roses blow,
Would that yon orb, whose matin glow
Thy listless eyes so much admire,
Would lend thee something of his fire!
Thou, who would'st see this battlement
By christian cannon piecemeal rent;
Nay, tamely view old Stambol's wall
Before the dogs of Moscow fall,
Nor strike one stroke for life and death
Against the curs of Nazareth!
Go—let thy less than woman's hand
Assume the distaff—not the brand.
But, Haroun!—to my daughter speed:
And hark—of thine own head take heed—
If thus Zuleika oft takes wing—
Thou see'st yon bow—it hath a string!»

V.

No sound from Selim's lip was heard,
At least that met old Giaffir's ear,
But every frown and every word
Pierced keener than a christian's sword.
« Son of a slave!—reproach'd with fear!
Those gibes had cost another dear.
Son of a slave!—and *who* my sire?»
Thus held his thoughts their dark career,
And glances e'en of more than ire
Flash forth, then faintly disappear.
Old Giaffir gazed upon his son
And started; for within his eye
He read how much his wrath had done;
He saw rebellion there begun:
« Come hither, boy—what, no reply?
I mark thee—and I know thee too;
But there be deeds thou dar'st not do:
But if thy beard had manlier length,
And if thy hand had skill and strength,
I 'd joy to see thee break a lance,
Albeit against my own perchance.»

As sneeringly these accents fell,
On Selim's eye he fiercely gazed:
That eye return'd him glance for glance,
And proudly to his sire's was raised,
Till Giaffir's quail'd and shrunk askance—
And why—he felt, but durst not tell.
« Much I misdoubt this wayward boy
Will one day work me more annoy:

I never loved him from his birth,
And—but his arm is little worth,
And scarcely in the chase could cope
With timid fawn or antelope,
Far less would venture into strife
Where man contends for fame and life—
I would not trust that look or tone:
No—nor the blood so near my own.
That blood—he hath not heard—no more—
I 'll watch him closer than before.
He is an Arab[5] to my sight,
Or christian crouching in the fight—
But hark!—I hear Zuleika's voice;
  Like houris' hymn it meets mine ear:
She is the offspring of my choice;
  Oh! more than e'en her mother dear,
With all to hope, and nought to fear—
My peri! ever welcome here!
Sweet, as the desert fountain's wave
To lips just cool'd in time to save—
  Such to my longing sight art thou;
Nor can they waft to Mecca's shrine
More thanks for life, than I for thine,
  Who blest thy birth, and bless thee now.»

VI.

Fair, as the first that fell of womankind,
  When on that dread yet lovely serpent smiling,
Whose image then was stamp'd upon her mind—
  But once beguiled—and ever more beguiling;
Dazzling, as that, oh! too transcendant vision
  To sorrow's phantom-peopled slumber given,

When heart meets heart again in dreams Elysian,
   And paints the lost on earth revived in heaven;
Soft, as the memory of buried love;
Pure, as the prayer which childhood wafts above;
Was she—the daughter of that rude old chief,
Who met the maid with tears—but not of grief.

Who hath not proved how feebly words essay
To fix one spark of beauty's heavenly ray?
Who doth not feel, until his failing sight
Faints into dimness with its own delight,
His changing cheek, his sinking heart confess
The might—the majesty of loveliness?
Such was Zuleika—such around her shone
The nameless charms unmark'd by her alone;
The light of love, the purity of grace,
The mind, the music breathing from her face,[6]
The heart whose softness harmonized the whole—
And, oh! that eye was in itself a soul!

Her graceful arms in meekness bending
   Across her gently-budding breast;
At one kind word those arms extending
   To clasp the neck of him who blest
   His child caressing and carest,
   Zuleika came—and Giaffir felt
   His purpose half within him melt:
   Not that against her fancied weal
   His heart though stern could ever feel;
   Affection chain'd her to that heart;
   Ambition tore the links apart.

VII.

«Zuleika! child of gentleness!
How dear this very day must tell,
When I forget my own distress,
In losing what I love so well,
To bid thee with another dwell:
Another! and a braver man
Was never seen in battle's van.
We moslem reck not much of blood;
But yet the line of Carasman [7]
Unchanged, unchangeable hath stood
First of the bold Timariot bands
That won and well can keep their lands.
Enough that he who comes to woo
Is kinsman of the Bey Oglou;
His years need scarce a thought employ;
I would not have thee wed a boy.
And thou shalt have a noble dower:
And his and my united power
Will laugh to scorn the death-firman,
Which others tremble but to scan,
And teach the messenger [8] what fate
The bearer of such boon may wait.
And now thou know'st thy father's will;
All that thy sex hath need to know:
'T was mine to teach obedience still—
The way to love thy lord may show.»

VIII.

In silence bow'd the virgin's head;
And if her eye was fill'd with tears

That stifled feeling dare not shed,
And changed her cheek from pale to red,
And red to pale, as through her ears
Those winged words like arrows sped,
What could such be but maiden fears?
So bright the tear in beauty's eye,
Love half regrets to kiss it dry;
So sweet the blush of bashfulness,
Even pity scarce can wish it less!
Whate'er it was the sire forgot;
Or if remember'd, mark'd it not;
Thrice clapp'd his hands, and call'd his steed,[9]
Resign'd his gem-adorn'd chibouque,[10]
And mounting featly for the mead,
With Maugrabee[11] and Mamaluke,
His way amid his delis took,[12]
To witness many an active deed
With sabre keen, or blunt jereed.
The Kislar only and his Moors
Watch well the haram's massy doors.

IX.

His head was leant upon his hand,
His eye look'd o'er the dark blue water
That swiftly glides and gently swells
Between the winding Dardanelles;
But yet he saw nor sea nor strand,
Nor even his pacha's turban'd band
Mix in the game of mimic slaughter,
Careering cleave the folded felt[13]
With sabre stroke right sharply dealt;

Nor mark'd the javelin-darting crowd,
Nor heard their ollahs [14] wild and loud—
He thought but of old Giaffir's daughter!

X.

No word from Selim's bosom broke;
One sigh Zuleika's thought bespoke:
Still gazed he through the lattice grate,
Pale, mute, and mournfully sedate.
To him Zuleika's eye was turn'd,
But little from his aspect learn'd:
Equal her grief, yet not the same;
Her heart confess'd a gentler flame;
But yet that heart alarm'd or weak,
She knew not why, forbade to speak.
Yet speak she must—but when essay?
« How strange he thus should turn away!
Not thus we e'er before have met;
Not thus shall be our parting yet.»
Thrice paced she slowly through the room,
And watch'd his eye—it still was fix'd:
She snatch'd the urn wherein was mix'd
The Persian atar-gul's [15] perfume,
And sprinkled all its odours o'er
The pictured roof [16] and marble floor:
The drops, that through his glittering vest
The playful girl's appeal addrest,
Unheeded o'er his bosom flew,
As if that breast were marble too.
«What, sullen yet? it must not be—
Oh! gentle Selim, this from thee!»

She saw in curious order set
The fairest flowers of eastern land—
« He loved them once; may touch them yet.
If offer'd by Zuleika's hand. »
The childish thought was hardly breathed
Before the rose was pluck'd and wreathed;
The next fond moment saw her seat
Her fairy form at Selim's feet:
« This rose to calm my brother's cares
A message from the bulbul[17] bears;
It says to night he will prolong
For Selim's ear his sweetest song;
And though his note is somewhat sad,
He 'll try for once a strain more glad,
With some faint hope his alter'd lay
May sing these gloomy thoughts away.

XI.

« What! not receive my foolish flower?
Nay then I am indeed unblest:
On me can thus thy forehead lower?
And know'st thou not who loves thee best?
Oh, Selim dear! Oh, more than dearest!
Say, is it me thou hat'st or fearest?
Come, lay thy head upon my breast,
And I will kiss thee into rest,
Since words of mine, and songs must fail,
E'en from my fabled nightingale.
I knew our sire at times was stern,
But this from thee had yet to learn:
Too well I know he loves thee not;
But is Zuleika's love forgot?

Ah! deem I right? the pacha's plan—
This kinsman Bey of Carasman
Perhaps may prove some foe of thine.
If so, I swear by Mecca's shrine,
If shrines that ne'er approach allow
To woman's step admit her vow,
Without thy free consent, command,
The sultan should not have my hand!
Think'st thou that I could bear to part
With thee and learn to halve my heart?
Ah! were I sever'd from thy side,
Where were thy friend—and who my guide?
Years have not seen, time shall not see
The hour that tears my soul from thee:
E'en Azrael,[18] from his deadly quiver
  When flies that shaft, and fly it must,
That parts all else, shall doom for ever
  Our hearts to undivided dust!»

XII.

He lived—he breathed—he moved—he felt;
He raised the maid from where she knelt;
His trance was gone—his keen eye shone
With thoughts that long in darkness dwelt;
With thoughts that burn—in rays that melt.
  As the stream late conceal'd
    By the fringe of its willows,
  When it rushes reveal'd
    In the light of its billows;
  As the bolt bursts on high
    From the black cloud that bound it,
  Flash'd the soul of that eye
    Through the long lashes round it.

A war-horse at the trumpet's sound,
A lion roused by heedless hound,
A tyrant waked to sudden strife
By graze of ill-directed knife,
Starts not to more convulsive life
Than he, who heard that vow, display'd,
And all, before repress'd, betray'd:
« Now thou art mine, for ever mine,
With life to keep, and scarce with life resign;
Now thou art mine, that sacred oath,
Though sworn by one, hath bound us both.
Yes, fondly, wisely hast thou done;
That vow hath saved more heads than one:
But blench not thou—thy simplest tress
Claims more from me than tenderness;
I would not wrong the slenderest hair
That clusters round thy forehead fair,
For all the treasures buried far
Within the caves of Istakar.[19]
This morning clouds upon me lower'd,
Reproaches on my head were shower'd,
And Giaffir almost call'd me coward!
Now I have motive to be brave;
The son of his neglected slave,
Nay, start not, 't was the term he gave,
May show, though little apt to vaunt,
A heart his words nor deeds can daunt.
His son indeed!—yet, thanks to thee,
Perchance I am, at least shall be;
But let our plighted secret vow
Be only known to us as now.
I know the wretch who dares demand
From Giaffir thy reluctant hand;

More ill-got wealth, a meaner soul
Holds not a musselim's[20] controul:
Was he not bred in Egripo?[21]
A viler race let Israel show!
But let that pass—to none be told
Our oath; the rest shall time unfold.
« To me and mine leave Osman Bey;
I 've partisans for peril's day:
Think not I am what I appear;
I 've arms, and friends, and vengeance near.»

XIII.

«Think not thou art what thou appearest!
My Selim, thou art sadly changed:
This morn I saw thee gentlest, dearest;
But now thou 'rt from thyself estranged.
My love thou surely knew'st before,
It ne'er was less, nor can be more.
To see thee, hear thee, near thee stay,
And hate the night I know not why,
Save that we meet not but by day;
With thee to live, with thee to die,
I dare not to my hope deny:
Thy cheek, thine eyes, thy lips to kiss,
Like this—and this—no more than this;
For, Alla! sure thy lips are flame:
What fever in thy veins is flushing?
My own have nearly caught the same,
At least I feel my cheek too blushing.
To soothe thy sickness, watch thy health,
Partake, but never waste thy wealth,

Or stand with smiles unmurmuring by,
And lighten half thy poverty;
Do all but close thy dying eye,
For that I could not live to try;
To these alone my thoughts aspire:
More can I do? or thou require?
But, Selim, thou must answer why
We need so much of mystery?
The cause I cannot dream nor tell,
But be it, since thou say'st 't is well;
Yet what thou mean'st by 'arms' and 'friends,'
Beyond my weaker sense extends.
I meant that Giaffir should have heard
  The very vow I plighted thee;
His wrath would not revoke my word:
  But surely he would leave me free.
  Can this fond wish seem strange in me,
To be what I have ever been?
What other hath Zuleika seen
From simple childhood's earliest hour?
  What other can she seek to see
Than thee, companion of her bower,
  The partner of her infancy?
These cherish'd thoughts with life begun,
  Say, why must I no more avow?
What change is wrought to make me shun
  The truth; my pride, and thine till now?
To meet the gaze of stranger's eyes
Our law, our creed, our God denies;
Nor shall one wandering thought of mine
At such, our Prophet's will, repine:

No! happier made by that decree!
He left me all in leaving thee.
Deep were my anguish, thus compell'd
To wed with one I ne'er beheld:
This wherefore should I not reveal?
Why wilt thou urge me to conceal?
I know the pacha's haughty mood
To thee hath never boded good;
And he so often storms at nought,
Alla! forbid that e'er he ought!
And why I know not, but within
My heart concealment weighs like sin.
If then such secrecy be crime,
  And such it feels while lurking here;
Oh, Selim! tell me yet in time,
  Nor leave me thus to thoughts of fear.
Ah! yonder see the tchocadar,[12]
My father leaves the mimic war;
I tremble now to meet his eye—
Say, Selim, canst thou tell me why?»

XIV.

« Zuleika—to thy tower's retreat
Betake thee—Giaffir I can greet:
And now with him I fain must prate
Of firmans, imposts, levies, state.
There's fearful news from Danube's banks,
Our vizier nobly thins his ranks,
For which the Giaour may give him thanks!
Our sultan hath a shorter way
Such costly triumph to repay.

But, mark me, when the twilight drum
  Hath warn'd the troops to food and sleep,
Unto thy cell will Selim come:
  Then softly from the haram creep,
  Where we may wander by the deep:
  Our garden-battlements are steep;
Nor these will rash intruder climb
To list our words, or stint our time;
And if he doth, I want not steel
Which some have felt, and more may feel.
Then shalt thou learn of Selim more
Than thou hast heard or thought before;
Trust me, Zuleika—fear not me!
Thou know'st I hold a haram-key.»

«Fear thee, my Selim! ne'er till now
Did word like this——»

«Delay not thou;
I keep the key—and Haroun's guard
Have *some*, and hope of *more* reward.
To-night, Zuleika, thou shalt hear
My tale, my purpose, and my fear:
I am not, love! what I appear.»

NOTES TO CANTO I.

Note 1, page 137, line 9.

Wax faint o'er the gardens of gul in her bloom; *etc.*

« Gul, » the rose.

Note 2, page 138, line 2.

Can he smile on such deeds as his children have done?

« Souls made of fire, and children of the sun,
With whom revenge is virtue. »

YOUNG's *Revenge*.

Note 3, page 139, line 29.

With Mejnoun's tale, or Sadi's song; *etc.*

Mejnoun and Leila, the Romeo and Juliet of the east. Sadi, the moral poet of Persia.

Note 4, page 139, line 30.

Till I, who heard the deep tambour *etc.*

Tambour, Turkish drum, which sounds at sunrise, noon, and twilight.

Note 5, page 142, line 11.

He is an Arab to my sight, *etc.*

The Turks abhor the Arabs (who return the compliment a hundred-fold) even more than they hate the Christians.

Note 6, page 143, line 16.

The mind, the music breathing from her face, *etc.*

This expression has met with objections. I will not refer to «Him who hath not music in his soul,» but merely request the reader to recollect, for ten seconds, the features of the woman whom he believes to be the most beautiful; and if he then does not comprehend fully what is feebly expressed in the above line, I shall be sorry for us both. For an eloquent passage in the latest work of the first female writer of this, perhaps of any, age, on the analogy (and the immediate comparison excited by that analogy) between «painting and music,» see vol. iii. cap. 10. DE L'ALLEMAGNE. And is not this connexion still stronger with the original than the copy? With the colouring of nature than of art? After all, this is rather to be felt than described; still I think there are some who will understand it, at least they would have done had they beheld the countenance whose speaking harmony suggested the idea; for this passage is not drawn from imagination, but memory, that mirror which affliction dashes to the earth, and looking down upon the fragments, only beholds the reflection multiplied!

Note 7, page 144, line 10.

But yet the line of Carasman *etc.*

Carasman Oglou, or Kara Osman Oglou, is the principal landholder in Turkey; he governs Magnesia: those who, by a kind of feudal tenure, possess land on condition of service, are called Timariots: they serve as spahis, according to the extent of territory, and bring a certain number into the field, generally cavalry.

Note 8, page 144, line 22.

And teach the messenger what fate *etc.*

When a pacha is sufficiently strong to resist, the single messenger, who is always the first bearer of the order for his death, is strangled instead, and sometimes five or six, one after the other, on the same errand, by command of the refractory patient; if, on the contrary, he is weak or loyal, he bows, kisses the sultan's respectable signature, and is bowstrung with great complacency. In 1810, several of these presents were exhibited in the niche of the seraglio gate; among others, the head of the Pacha of Bagdat, a brave young man, cut off by treachery, after a desperate resistance.

Note 9, page 145, line 12.

Thrice clapp'd his hands, and call'd his steed, *etc.*

Clapping of the hands calls the servants. The Turks hate a superfluous expenditure of voice, and they have no bells.

Note 10, page 145, line 13.

Resign'd his gem-adorn'd chibouque, *etc.*

Chibouque, the Turkish pipe, of which the amber mouth-piece, and sometimes the ball which contains the leaf, is adorned with precious stones, if in possession of the wealthier orders.

Note 11, page 145, line 15.

With Maugrabee and Mamaluke, *etc.*

Maugrabee, Moorish mercenaries.

Note 12, page 145, line 16.

His way amid his delis took, *etc.*

Deli, bravos who form the forlorn hope of the cavalry, and always begin the action.

Note 13, page 145, line 29.

Careering cleave the folded felt *etc.*

A twisted fold of *felt* is used for scimitar practice by the Turks, and few but mussulman arms can cut through it at a single stroke: sometimes a tough turban is used for the same purpose. The jerreed is a game of blunt javelins, animated and graceful.

Note 14, page 146, line 2.

Nor heard their ollahs wild and loud—*etc.*

«Ollahs,» Alla il Allah, the «Leilies,» as the Spanish poets call them, the sound is ollah; a cry of which the Turks, for a silent people, are somewhat profuse, particularly during the jerreed, or in the chase, but mostly in battle. Their animation in the field, and gravity in the chamber, with their pipes and comboloios, form an amusing contrast.

Note 15, page 146, line 22.

The Persian atar-gul's perfume, *etc.*

«Atar-gul,» ottar of roses. The Persian is the finest.

Note 16, page 146, line 24.

The pictured roof and marble floor: *etc.*

The ceiling and wainscots, or rather walls, of the mussulman apartments are generally painted, in great houses, with one eternal and highly-coloured view of Constantinople, wherein the principal feature is a noble contempt of perspective; below, arms, scimitars, etc. are in general fancifully and not inelegantly disposed.

Note 17, page 147, line 10.

A message from the bulbul bears; *etc.*

It has been much doubted whether the notes of this «lover of the rose» are sad or merry; and Mr Fox's remarks on the subject have provoked some learned controversy as to the opinions of the ancients on the subject. I dare not venture a conjecture on the point, though a little inclined to the «errare mallem,» etc. *if* Mr Fox *was* mistaken.

Note 18, page 148, line 15.

E'en Azrael, from his deadly quiver *etc.*

«Azrael»—the angel of death.

Note 19, page 149, line 19.

Within the caves of Istakar.

The treasures of the Pre-Adamite sultans. See D'Herbelot, article *Istakar.*

Note 20, page 150, line 2.

Holds not a musselim's controul: *etc.*

Musselim, a governor, the next in rank after a pacha; a waywode is the third; and then come the agas.

Note 21, page 150, line 3.

Was he not bred in Egripo?

Egripo—the Negrepont.—According to the proverb, the Turks of Egripo, the Jews of Salonica, and the Greeks of Athens, are the worst of their respective races.

Note 22, page 152, line 17.

Ah! yonder see the tchocadar, *etc.*

«Tchocadar»—one of the attendants who precedes a man of authority.

THE

BRIDE OF ABYDOS.

CANTO II.

I.

The winds are high on Helle's wave,
  As on that night of stormy water
When love, who sent, forgot to save
The young, the beautiful, the brave,
  The lonely hope of Sestos' daughter.
Oh, when alone along the sky
Her turret-torch was blazing high,
Though rising gale, and breaking foam,
And shrieking sea-birds warn'd him home;
And clouds aloft and tides below,
With signs and sounds, forbade to go,
He could not see, he would not hear
Or sound or sign foreboding fear;
His eye but saw that light of love,
The only star it hail'd above;

His ear but rang with Hero's song,
« Ye waves, divide not lovers long! » —
That tale is old, but love anew
May nerve young hearts to prove as true.

II.

The winds are high, and Helle's tide
Rolls darkly heaving to the main;
And night's descending shadows hide
That field with blood bedew'd in vain,
The desert of old Priam's pride;
The tombs, sole relics of his reign,
All—save immortal dreams that could beguile
The blind old man of Scio's rocky isle!

III.

Oh! yet—for there my steps have been;
These feet have press'd the sacred shore,
These limbs that buoyant wave hath borne—
Minstrel! with thee to muse, to mourn,
To trace again those fields of yore,
Believing every hillock green
Contains no fabled hero's ashes,
And that around the undoubted scene
Thine own « broad Hellespont »[1] still dashes,
Be long my lot! and cold were he
Who there could gaze denying thee!

IV.

The night hath closed on Helle's stream,
Nor yet hath risen on Ida's hill

That moon, which shone on his high theme:
No warrior chides her peaceful beam,
But conscious shepherds bless it still.
Their flocks are grazing on the mound
Of him who felt the Dardan's arrow:
That mighty heap of gather'd ground
Which Ammon's[2] son ran proudly round,
By nations raised, by monarchs crown'd,
Is now a lone and nameless barrow!
Within—thy dwelling-place how narrow!
Without—can only strangers breathe
The name of him that *was* beneath:
Dust long outlasts the storied stone;
But thou—thy very dust is gone!

V.

Late, late to-night will Dian cheer
The swain, and chase the boatman's fear;
Till then—no beacon on the cliff
May shape the course of struggling skiff;
The scatter'd lights that skirt the bay,
All, one by one, have died away;
The only lamp of this lone hour
Is glimmering in Zuleika's tower.
Yes! there is light in that lone chamber,
And o'er her silken ottoman
Are thrown the fragrant beads of amber,
O'er which her fairy fingers ran;[3]
Near these, with emerald rays beset,
(How could she thus that gem forgot?)
Her mother's sainted amulet,[4]

Whereon engraved the koorsee text.
Could smooth this life, and win the next;
And by her comboloio[5] lies
A Koran of illumined dyes;
And many a bright emblazon'd rhyme
By Persian scribes redeem'd from time;
And o'er those scrolls, not oft so mute,
Reclines her now neglected lute;
And round her lamp of fretted gold
Bloom flowers in urns of China's mould;
The richest work of Iran's loom,
And Sheeraz' tribute of perfume;
All that can eye or sense delight
   Are gather'd in that gorgeous room:
   But yet it hath an air of gloom.
She, of this peri cell the sprite,
What doth she hence, and on so rude a night?

VI.

Wrapt in the darkest sable vest,
   Which none save noblest moslem wear,
To guard from winds of heaven the breast
   As heaven itself to Selim dear,
With cautious steps the thicket threading,
   And starting oft, as through the glade
   The gust its hollow moanings made,
Till on the smoother pathway treading,
More free her timid bosom beat,
   The maid pursued her silent guide;
And though her terror urged retreat,
   How could she quit her Selim's side?
   How teach her tender lips to chide?

VII.

They reach'd at length a grotto, hewn
By nature, but enlarged by art,
Where oft her lute she wont to tune,
And oft her Koran conn'd apart;
And oft in youthful reverie
She dream'd what Paradise might be:
Where woman's parted soul shall go
Her Prophet had disdain'd to show;
But Selim's mansion was secure,
Nor deem'd she, could he long endure
His bower in other worlds of bliss,
Without *her*, most beloved in this!
Oh! who so dear with him could dwell?
What houri soothe him half so well!

VIII.

Since last she visited the spot
Some change seem'd wrought within the grot:
It might be only that the night
Disguised things seen by better light:
That brazen lamp but dimly threw
A ray of no celestial hue;
But in a nook within the cell
Her eye on stranger objects fell.
There arms were piled, not such as wield
The turban'd delis in the field;
But brands of foreign blade and hilt,
And one was red—perchance with guilt!
Ah! how without can blood be spilt?

A cup too on the board was set
That did not seem to hold sherbet.
What may this mean? she turn'd to see
Her Selim—« Oh! can this be he? »

IX.

His robe of pride was thrown aside,
His brow no high-crown'd turban bore,
But in its stead a shawl of red,
Wreathed lightly round his temples wore:
That dagger, on whose hilt the gem
Were worthy of a diadem,
No longer glitter'd at his waist,
Where pistols unadorn'd were braced;
And from his belt a sabre swung,
And from his shoulder loosely hung
The cloak of white, the thin capote
That decks the wandering Candiote:
Beneath—his golden-plated vest
Clung like a cuirass to his breast;
The greaves below his knee that wound
With silvery scales were sheathed and bound.
But were it not that high command
Spake in his eye, and tone, and hand,
All that a careless eye could see
In him was some young galiongée.[6]

X.

« I said I was not what I seem'd;
And now thou seest my words were true:
I have a tale thou hast not dream'd,
If sooth—its truth must others rue,

My story now 't were vain to hide,
I must not see thee Osman's bride:
But had not thine own lips declared
How much of that young heart I shared,
I could not, must not, yet have shown
The darker secret of my own.
In this I speak not now of love;
That, let time, truth, and peril prove:
But first—Oh! never wed another—
Zuleika! I am not thy brother!»

XI.

«Oh! not my brother!—yet unsay—
  God! am I left alone on earth
To mourn—I dare not curse—the day
  That saw my solitary birth?
Oh! thou wilt love me now no more!
  My sinking heart foreboded ill;
But know *me* all I was before,
  Thy sister—friend—Zuleika still.
Thou ledst me here perchance to kill;
  If thou hast cause for vengeance, see!
My breast is offer'd—take thy fill!
  Far better with the dead to be
  Than live thus nothing now to thee:
Perhaps far worse, for now I know
Why Giaffir always seem'd thy foe;
And I, alas! am Giaffir's child,
For whom thou wert contemn'd, reviled.
If not thy sister—would'st thou save
My life. Oh! bid me be thy slave!»

XII.

« My slave, Zuleika!—nay, I 'm thine:
But, gentle love, this transport calm,
Thy lot shall yet be link'd with mine;
I swear it by our Prophet's shrine,
And be that thought thy sorrow's balm.
So may the Koran[7] verse display'd
Upon its steel direct my blade,
In danger's hour to guard us both,
As I preserve that awful oath!
The name in which thy heart hath prided
Must change; but, my Zuleika, know,
That tie is widen'd, not divided,
Although thy sire's my deadliest foe.
My father was to Giaffir all
That Selim late was deem'd to thee;
That brother wrought a brother's fall,
But spared, at least, my infancy;
And lull'd me with a vain deceit
That yet a like return may meet.
He rear'd me, not with tender help,
But like the nephew of a Cain;[8]
He watch'd me like a lion's whelp,
That gnaws and yet may break his chain.
My father's blood in every vein
Is boiling; but for thy dear sake
No present vengeance will I take;
Though here I must no more remain.
But first, beloved Zuleika! hear
How Giaffir wrought this deed of fear.

XIII.

"How first their strife to rancour grew,
  If love or envy made them foes,
It matters little if I knew;
In fiery spirits, slights, though few
  And thoughtless, will disturb repose.
  In war Abdallah's arm was strong,
Remember'd yet in Bosniac song,
And Paswan's[9] rebel hordes attest
How little love they bore such guest:
His death is all I need relate,
The stern effect of Giaffir's hate;
And how my birth disclosed to me,
Whate'er beside it makes, hath made me free.

XIV.

"When Paswan, after years of strife,
At last for power, but first for life,
In Widin's walls too proudly sate,
Our pachas rallied round the state;
Nor last nor least in high command
Each brother led a separate band;
They gave their horsetails[10] to the wind,
  And mustering in Sophia's plain,
Their tents were pitch'd, their post assign'd;
  To one, alas! assign'd in vain!
What need of words? the deadly bowl,
  By Giaffir's order drugg'd and given,
With venom subtle as his soul,
  Dismiss'd Abdallah's hence to heaven.

Reclined and feverish in the bath,
He, when the hunter's sport was up,
But little deem'd a brother's wrath
To quench his thirst had such a cup:
The bowl a bribed attendant bore;
He drank one draught,[11] nor needed more!
If thou my tale, Zuleika, doubt,
Call Haroun—he can tell it out.

XV.

« The deed once done and Paswan's feud
In part suppress'd, though ne'er subdued,
Abdallah's pachalick was gain'd:—
Thou know'st not what in our divan
Can wealth procure for worse than man—
Abdallah's honours were obtain'd
By him a brother's murder stain'd;
'T is true, the purchase nearly drain'd
His ill-got treasure, soon replaced.
Would'st question whence? Survey the waste,
And ask the squalid peasant how
His gains repay his broiling brow!—
Why me the stern usurper spared,
Why thus with me his palace shared,
I know not. Shame, regret, remorse,
And little fear from infant's force;
Besides, adoption as a son
By him whom Heaven accorded none,
Or some unknown cabal, caprice,
Preserved me thus;—but not in peace:
He cannot curb his haughty mood,
Nor I forgive a father's blood.

XVI.

« Within thy father's house are foes;
Not all who break his bread are true:
To these should I my birth disclose,
His days, his very hours were few:
They only want a heart to lead,
A hand to point them to the deed.
But Haroun only knows, or knew
This tale, whose close is almost nigh:
He in Abdallah's palace grew,
And held that post in his serai
Which holds he here—he saw him die:
But what could single slavery do?
Avenge his lord? alas! too late;
Or save his son from such a fate?
He chose the last, and when elate
With foes subdued, or friends betray'd,
Proud Giaffir in high triumph sate,
He led me helpess to his gate,
And not in vain it seems essay'd
To save the life for which he pray'd.
The knowledge of my birth secured
From all and each, but most from me;
Thus Giaffir's safety was ensured.
Removed he too from Roumelie
To this our Asiatic side,
Far from our seats by Danube's tide,
With none but Haroun, who retains
Such knowledge—and that Nubian feels
A tyrant's secrets are but chains,

From which the captive gladly steals.
And this and more to me reveals:
Such still to guilt just Alla sends—
Slaves, tools, accomplices—no friends!

XVII.

« All this, Zuleika, harshly sounds;
But harsher still my tale must be:
Howe'er my tongue thy softness wounds,
Yet I must prove all truth to thee.
I saw thee start this garb to see,
Yet is it one I oft have worn,
And long must wear: this galiongee,
To whom thy plighted vow is sworn,
Is leader of those pirate hordes,
Whose laws and lives are on their swords;
To hear whose desolating tale
Would make thy waning cheek more pale:
These arms thou seest my band have brought,
The hands that wield are not remote;
This cup too for the rugged knaves
Is fill'd—once quaff'd, they ne'er repine:
Our prophet might forgive the slaves;
They 're only infidels in wine.

XVIII.

« What could I be? Proscribed at home,
And taunted to a wish to roam;
And listless left—for Giaffir's fear
Denied the courser and the spear—
Though oft—oh, Mahomet! how oft!—
In full divan the despot scoff'd,

As if *my* weak unwilling hand
Refused the bridle or the brand:
He ever went to war alone,
And pent me here untried—unknown;
To Haroun's care with women left,
By hope unblest, of fame bereft.
While thou—whose softness long endear'd,
Though it unmann'd me, still had cheer'd—
To Brusa's walls for safety sent,
Awaited'st there the field's event.
Haroun, who saw my spirit pining
  Beneath inaction's sluggish yoke,
His captive, though with dread resigning,
  My thraldom for a season broke,
On promise to return before
The day when Giaffir's charge was o'er.
'T is vain—my tongue can not impart
My almost drunkenness of heart,
When first this liberated eye
Survey'd earth, ocean, sun and sky,
As if my spirit pierced them through,
And all their immost wonders knew!
One word alone can paint to thee
That more than feeling—I was free!
E'en for thy presence ceased to pine,
The world—nay—heaven itself was mine!

XIX.

"The shallop of a trusty Moor
Convey'd me from this idle shore;
I long'd to see the isles that gem
Old ocean's purple diadem:

I sought by turns, and saw them all;[12]
But when and where I join'd the crew,
With whom I 'm pledged to rise or fall,
When all that we design to do
Is done, 't will then be time more meet
To tell thee, when the tale 's complete.

XX.

«'T is true, they are a lawless brood,
But rough in form, nor mild in mood;
And every creed, and every race,
With them hath found—may find a place:
But open speech, and ready hand,
Obedience to their chief's command;
A soul for every enterprise,
That never sees with terror's eyes;
Friendship for each, and faith to all,
And vengeance vow'd for those who fall,
Have made them fitting instruments
For more than e'en my own intents.
And some—and I have studied all
Distinguish'd from the vulgar rank,
But chiefly to my council call
The wisdom of the cautious Frank—
And some to higher thoughts aspire,
The last of Lambro's[13] patriots there
Anticipated freedom share;
And oft around the cavern fire
On visionary schemes debate,
To snatch the rayahs[14] from their fate.
So let them ease their hearts with prate

Of equal rights, which man ne'er knew;
I have a love for freedom too.
Ay! let me like the ocean-patriarch[15] roam,
Or only know on land the Tartar's home![16]
My tent on shore, my galley on the sea,
Are more than cities and serais to me:
Borne by my steed, or wafted by my sail,
Across the desert, or before the gale,
Bound where thou wilt, my barb! or glide, my prow!
But be the star that guides the wanderer, thou!
Thou, my Zuleika, share and bless my bark;
The dove of peace and promise to mine ark!
Or, since that hope denied in worlds of strife,
Be thou the rainbow to the storms of life!
The evening beam that smiles the clouds away,
And tints to-morrow with prophetic ray!
Blest—as the muezzin's strain from Mecca's wall
To pilgrims pure and prostrate at his call;
Soft—as the melody of youthful days,
That steals the trembling tear of speechless praise;
Dear—as his native song to exile's ears,
Shall sound each tone thy long-loved voice endears.
For thee in those bright isles is built a bower,
Blooming as Aden[17] in its earliest hour.
A thousand swords, with Selim's heart and hand,
Wait—wave—defend—destroy—at thy command!
Girt by my band, Zuleika at my side,
The spoil of nations shall bedeck my bride.
The haram's languid years of listless ease
Are well resign'd for cares—for joys like these:
Not blind to fate, I see, where'er I rove,
Unnumber'd perils—but one only love!

Yet well my toils shall that fond breast repay,
Though fortune frown, or falser friends betray.
How dear the dream in darkest hours of ill,
Should all be changed, to find thee faithful still!
Be but thy soul, like Selim's, firmly shown;
To thee be Selim's tender as thine own;
To soothe each sorrow, share in each delight,
Blend every thought, do all—but disunite!
Once free, 't is mine our horde again to guide;
Friends to each other, foes to aught beside:
Yet there we follow but the bent assign'd
By fatal nature to man 's warring kind:
Mark! where his carnage and his conquests cease!
He makes a solitude, and calls it—peace!
I like the rest must use my skill or strength,
But ask no land beyond my sabre's length:
Power sways but by division—her resource
The blest alternative of fraud or force!
Ours be the last; in time deceit may come
When cities cage us in a social home:
There e'en thy soul might err—how oft the heart
Corruption shakes which peril could not part!
And woman, more than man, when death or woe
Or even disgrace would lay her lover low,
Sunk in the lap of luxury will shame—
Away suspicion!—*not* Zuleika's name!
But life is hazard at the best; and here
No more remains to win, and much to fear:
Yes, fear!—the doubt, the dread of losing thee,
By Osman's power, and Giaffir's stern decree.
That dread shall vanish with the favouring gale,
Which love to-night hath promised to my sail:

No danger daunts the pair his smile hath blest,
Their steps still roving, but their hearts at rest.
With thee all toils are sweet, each clime hath charms;
Earth—sea alike—our world within our arms!
Ay—let the loud winds whistle o'er the deck,
So that those arms cling closer round my neck:
The deepest murmur of this lip shall be
No sigh for safety, but a prayer for thee!
The war of elements no fears impart
To love, whose deadliest bane is human art:
There lie the only rocks our course can check;
Here moments menace—*there* are years of wreck!
But hence ye thoughts that rise in horror's shape!
This hour bestows, or ever bars escape.
Few words remain of mine my tale to close;
Of thine but *one* to waft us from our foes;
Yea—foes—to me will Giaffir's hate decline?
And is not Osman, who would part us, thine?

XXI.

"His head and faith from doubt and death
Return'd in time my guard to save;
Few heard, none told, that o'er the wave
From isle to isle I roved the while:
And since, though parted from my band,
Too seldom now I leave the land,
No deed they 've done, nor deed shall do,
Ere I have heard and doom'd it too:
I form the plan, decree the spoil,
'T is fit I oftener share the toil.
But now too long I 've held thine ear;

Time presses, floats my bark, and here
We leave behind but hate and fear.
To-morrow Osman with his train
Arrives--to-night must break thy chain:
And would'st thou save that haughty bey,
  Perchance, *his* life who gave thee thine,
With me this hour away—away!
  But yet, though thou art plighted mine,
Would'st thou recal thy willing vow,
Appall'd by truths imparted now,
Here rest I—not to see thee wed:
But be that peril on *my* head!»

XXII.

Zuleika, mute and motionless,
Stood like that statue of distress,
When, her last hope for ever gone,
The mother harden'd into stone;
All in the maid that eye could see
Was but a younger Niobe.
But ere her lip, or e'en her eye,
Essay'd to speak, or look reply,
Beneath the garden's wicket porch
Far flash'd on high a blazing torch!
Another—and another—and another—
«Oh! fly—no more—yet now my more than brother!»
Far, wide, through every thicket spread,
The fearful lights are gleaming red;
Nor these alone—for each right hand
Is ready with a sheathless brand.
They part, pursue, return, and wheel
With searching flambeau, shining steel;

And last of all, his sabre waving,
Stern Giaffir in his fury raving:
And now almost they touch the cave—
Oh! must that grot be Selim's grave?

XXIII.

Dauntless he stood—« 'T is come—soon past—
One kiss, Zuleika—'t is my last:
  But yet my band not far from shore
May hear this signal, see the flash;
Yet now too few—the attempt were rash:
  No matter—yet one effort more.»
Forth to the cavern mouth he stept;
  His pistol's echo rang on high.
Zuleika started not, nor wept,
  Despair benumb'd her breast and eye!—
«They hear me not, or if they ply
Their oars, 't is but to see me die;
That sound hath drawn my foes more nigh.
Then forth my father's scimitar,
Thou ne'er hast seen less equal war!
Farewell, Zuleika!—Sweet! retire:
  Yet stay within—here linger safe,
  At thee his rage will only chafe.
  Stir not—lest even to thee perchance
  Some erring blade or ball should glance.
Fear'st thou for him?—may I expire
If in this strife I seek thy sire!
No—though by him that poison pour'd;
No—though again he call me coward!
But tamely shall I meet their steel?
No—as each crest save *his* may feel!

XXIV.

One bound he made, and gain'd the sand:
Already at his feet hath sunk
The foremost of the prying band,
A gasping head, a quivering trunk:
Another falls—but round him close
A swarming circle of his foes;
From right to left his path he cleft,
And almost met the meeting wave:
His boat appears—not five oars' length—
His comrades strain with desperate strength—
Oh! are they yet in time to save?
His feet the foremost breakers lave;
His band are plunging in the bay,
Their sabres glitter through the spray;
Wet—wild—unwearied to the strand
They struggle—now they touch the land!
They come—'t is but to add to slaughter—
His heart's best blood is on the water.

XXV.

Escaped from shot, unharm'd by steel,
Or scarcely grazed its force to feel,
Had Selim won, betray'd, beset,
To where the strand and billows met:
There as his last step left the land,
And the last death-blow dealt his hand—
Ah! wherefore did he turn to look
For her his eye but sought in vain?
That pause, that fatal gaze he took,
Hath doom'd his death, or fix'd his chain.

Sad proof, in peril and in pain,
How late will lover's hope remain!
His back was to the dashing spray;
Behind, but close, his comrades lay,
When, at the instant, hiss'd the ball—
« So may the foes of Giaffir fall! »
Whose voice is heard? whose carbine rang?
Whose bnllet through the night-air sang,
Too nearly, deadly aim'd to err?
'T is thine—Abdallah's murderer!
The father slowly rued thy hate,
The son hath found a quicker fate:
Fast from his breast the blood is bubbling,
The whiteness of the sea-foam troubling—
If aught his lips essay'd to groan,
The rushing billows choked the tone!

XXVI.

Morn slowly rolls the clouds away;
 Few trophies of the fight are there:
The shouts that shook the midnight-bay
Are silent; but some signs of fray
 That strand of strife may bear,
And fragments of each shiver'd brand;
Steps stamp'd; and dash'd into the sand
The print of many a struggling hand
 May there be mark'd; nor far remote
 A broken torch, an oarless boat;
And tangled on the weeds that heap
The beach where shelving to the deep
 There lies a white capote!

'T is rent in twain—one dark-red stain
The wave yet ripples o'er in vain:
  But where is he who wore?
Ye! who would o'er his relics weep,
Go, seek them where the surges sweep
Their burthen round Sigæum's steep
  And cast on Lemnos' shore:
The sea-birds shriek above the prey,
O'er which their hungry beaks delay,
As shaken on his restless pillow,
His head heaves with the heaving billow;
That hand, whose motion is not life,
Yet feebly seems to menace strife,
Flung by the tossing tide on high,
  Then levell'd with the wave—
What recks it, though that corse shall lie
  Within a living grave?
The bird that tears that prostrate form
Hath only robb'd the meaner worm;
The only heart, the only eye
Had bled or wept to see him die,
Had seen those scatter'd limbs composed,
  And mourn'd above his turban-stone,[18]
That heart hath burst—that eye was closed—
  Yea—closed before his own!

XXVII.

By Helle's stream there is a voice of wail!
And woman's eye is wet—man's cheek is pale:
Zuleika! last of Giaffir's race,
  Thy destined lord is come too late;
He sees not—ne'er shall see thy face!

Can he not hear
The loud wul-wulleh [19] warn his distant ear?
Thy handmaids weeping at the gate,
The Koran-chanters of the hymn of fate,
The silent slaves with folded arms that wait,
Sighs in the hall, and shrieks upon the gale,
Tell him thy tale!
Thou didst not view thy Selim fall!
That fearful moment when he left the cave
Thy heart grew chill:
He was thy hope—thy joy—thy love—thine all—
And that last thought on him thou could'st not save
Sufficed to kill;
Burst forth in one wild cry—and all was still.

Peace to thy broken heart, and virgin grave!
Ah! happy! but of life to lose the worst!
That grief—though deep—though fatal—was thy first!
Thrice happy! ne'er to feel nor fear the force
Of absence, shame, pride, hate, revenge, remorse!
And, oh! that pang where more than madness lies!
The worm that will not sleep—and never dies;
Thought of the gloomy day and ghastly night,
That dreads the darkness, and yet loathes the light,
That winds around, and tears the quivering heart!
Ah! wherefore not consume it—and depart!
Woe to thee, rash and unrelenting chief!
Vainly thou heap'st the dust upon thy head,
Vainly the sackcloth o'er thy limbs dost spread:
By that same hand Abdallah—Selim bled.
Now let it tear thy beard in idle grief:
Thy pride of heart, thy bride for Osman's bed,

She, whom thy sultan had but seen to wed,
Thy daughter's dead!
Hope of thine age, thy twilight's lonely beam,
The star hath set that shone on Helle's stream.
What quench'd its ray?—the blood that thou hast shed!
Hark! to the hurried question of despair:
«Where is my child?» an echo answers—«Where?»[20]

XXVIII.

Within the place of thousand tombs
That shine beneath, while dark above
The sad but living cypress glooms
And withers not, though branch and leaf
Are stamp'd with an eternal grief,
Like early unrequited love,
One spot exists, which ever blooms,
E'en in that deadly grove—
A single rose is shedding there
Its lonely lustre, meek and pale:
It looks as planted by despair—
So white—so faint—the slightest gale
Might whirl the leaves on high;
And yet, though storms and blight assail,
And hands more rude than wintry sky
May wring it from the stem—in vain—
To-morrow sees it bloom again!
The stalk some spirit gently rears,
And waters with celestial tears;
For well may maids of Helle deem
That this can be no earthly flower,
Which mocks the tempest's withering hour,

And buds unshelter'd by a bower;
Nor droops, though spring refuse her shower,
  Nor woos the summer beam:
To it the livelong night there sings
  A bird unseen—but not remote:
Invisible his airy wings,
But soft as harp that houri strings
  His long entrancing note!
It were the bulbul; but his throat,
  Though mournful, pours not such a strain:
For they who listen cannot leave
The spot, but linger there and grieve
  As if they loved in vain!
And yet so sweet the tears they shed,
'T is sorrow so unmix'd with dread,
They scarce can bear the morn to break
  That melancholy spell,
And longer yet would weep and wake,
  He sings so wild and well!
But when the day-blush bursts from high
Expires that magic melody.
And some have been who could believe,
(So fondly youthful dreams deceive,
  Yet harsh be they that blame)
That note so piercing and profound
Will shape and syllable its sound
  Into Zuleika's name.[21]
'T is from her cypress' summit heard,
That melts in air the liquid word:
'T is from her lowly virgin earth
That white rose takes its tender birth.

There late was laid a marble stone;
Eve saw it placed—the morrow gone!
It was no mortal arm that bore
That deep-fix'd pillar to the shore;
For there, as Helle's legends tell,
Next morn 't was found where Selim fell;
Lash'd by the tumbling tide, whose wave
Denied his bones a holier grave:
And there by night, reclined, 't is said,
Is seen a ghastly turban'd head:
And hence extended by the billow,
'T is named the « Pirate-phantom's pillow! »
Where first it lay that mourning flower
Hath flourish'd; flourisheth this hour,
Alone and dewy, coldly pure and pale;
As weeping Beauty's cheek at Sorrow's tale!

NOTES TO CANTO II.

Note 1, page 162, line 23.

Thine own «broad Hellespont» still dashes, *etc.*

The wrangling about this epithet, «the broad Hellespont» or the «boundless Hellespont,» whether it means one or the other, or what it means at all, has been beyond all possibility of detail. I have even heard it disputed on the spot; and foreseeing no speedy conclusion to the controversy, amused myself with swimming across it in the mean time, and probably may again, before the point is settled. Indeed, the question as to the truth of «the tale of Troy divine» still continues, much of it resting upon the talismanic word «ἀπειρος:» probably Homer had the same notion of distance that a coquette has of time, and when he talks of boundless, means half-a-mile; as the latter, by a like figure, when she says *eternal* attachment, simply specifies three weeks.

Note 2, page 163, line 7.

Which Ammon's son ran proudly round, *etc.*

Before his Persian invasion, and crowned the altar with laurel, etc. He was afterwards imitated by Caracalla in his race. It is believed that the last also poisoned a friend, named Festus, for the sake of new Patroclan games. I have seen the sheep feeding on the tombs of Æsietes and Antilochus; the first is in the centre of the plain.

Note 3, page 163, line 27.

O'er which her fairy fingers ran; *etc.*

When rubbed, the amber is susceptible of a perfume, which is slight but not disagreeable.

Note 4, page 163, line 30.

Her mother's sainted amulet, *etc.*

The belief in amulets engraved on gems, or enclosed in gold boxes, containing scraps from the Koran, worn round the neck, wrist, or arm, is still universal in the east. The koorsee (throne) verse in the second cap. of the Koran describes the attributes of the Most High, and is engraved in this manner, and worn by the pious, as the most esteemed and sublime of all sentences.

Note 5, page 164, line 3.

And by her comboloio lies, *etc.*

«Comboloio»—a Turkish rosary. The MSS. particularly those of the Persians, are richly adorned and illuminated. The Greek females are kept in utter ignorance; but many of the Turkish girls are highly accomplished, though not actually qualified for a christian coterie. Perhaps some of our own *blues* might not be the worse for *bleaching*.

Note 6, page 166, line 25.

In him was some young galiongée.

«Galiongée»—or galiongi, a sailor that is, a *Turkish* sailor; the Greeks navigate, the Turks work the guns. Their dress is picturesque; and I have seen the Capitan Pacha more than once wearing it as a kind of *incog.* Their legs, however, are generally naked. The buskins, described in the text as sheathed behind with silver, are those of an Arnaut robber, who was my host (he had quitted the profession) at his Pyrgo, near Gastouni in the Morea; they were plated in scales one over the other, like the back of an armadillo.

Note 7, page 168, line 7.

So may the Koran verse display'd *etc.*

The characters on all Turkish scimitars contain sometimes the name of the place of their manufacture, but more generally a text from the Koran, in letters of gold. Amongst those in my possession is one with a blade of singular construction; it is very broad, and the edge notched into serpentine curves like the ripple of water, or the wavering of flame. I asked the Armenian who sold it, what possible use such a figure could add: he said, in Italian, that he did not know; but the mussulmans had an idea that those of this form gave a severer wound; and liked it because it was «piu feroce.» I did not much admire the reason, but bought it for its peculiarity.

Note 8, page 168, line 22.

But like the nephew of a Cain; *etc.*

It is to be observed, that every allusion to any thing or personage in the Old Testament, such as the Ark, or Cain, is equally the privilege of mussulman and Jew: indeed the former profess to be much better acquainted with the lives, true and fabulous, of the patriarchs, than is warranted by our own sacred writ; and not content with Adam, they have a biography of Pre-Adamites. Solomon is the monarch of all necromancy, and Moses a prophet inferior only to Christ and Mahomet. Zuleika is the Persian name of Potiphar's wife, and her amour with Joseph constitutes one of the finest poems in their language. It is therefore no violation of costume to put the names of Cain, or Noah, into the mouth of a moslem.

Note 9, page 169, line 9.

And Paswan's rebel hordes attest *etc.*

Paswan Oglou, the rebel of Widin, who for the last years of his life set the whole power of the Porte at defiance.

Note 10, page 169, line 22.

They gave their horsetails to the wind, *etc.*

Horsetail, the standard of a pacha.

Note 11, page 170, line 6.

He drank one draught, nor needed more!

Giaffir, Pacha of Argyro Castro, or Scutari, I am not sure which, was actually taken off by the Albanian Ali, in the manner described in the text. Ali Pacha, while I was in the country, married the daughter of his victim, some years after the event had taken place at a bath in Sophia, or Adrianople. The poison was mixed in the cup of coffee, which is presented before the sherbet by the bath-keeper, after dressing.

Note 12, page 174, line 1.

I sought by turns, and saw them all; *etc.*

The Turkish notions of almost all islands are confined to the Archipelago, the sea alluded to.

Note 13, page 174, line 25.

The last of Lambro's patriots there, *etc.*

Lambro Canzani, a Greek, famous for his efforts in 1789-90 for the independence of his country: abandoned by the Russians, he became a pirate, and the Archipelago was the scene of his enterprises. He is said to be still alive at Petersburg. He and Riga are the two most celebrated of the Greek revolutionists.

Note 14, page 174, line 29.

To snatch the rayahs from their fate.

« Rayahs, » all who pay the capitation-tax, called the « haratch. »

Note 15, page 175, line 3.

Ay! let me like the ocean-patriarch roam, *etc.*

This first of voyages is one of the few with which the mussulmans profess much acquaintance.

Note 16, page 175, line 4.

Or only know on land the Tartar's home.

The wandering life of the Arabs, Tartars, and Turkomans, will be found well detailed in any book of eastern travels. That it possesses a charm peculiar to itself cannot be denied. A young French renegado confessed to Chateaubriand, that he never found himself alone, galloping in the desert, without a sensation approaching to rapture, which was indescribable.

Note 17, page 175, line 24.

Blooming as Aden in its earliest hour.

« Jannat al Aden, » the perpetual abode, the mussulman Paradise.

Note 18, page 182, line 23.

And mourn'd above his turban-stone, *etc.*

A turban is carved in stone above the graves of *men* only.

Note 19, page 183, line 2.

The loud wul-wulleh warn his distant ear?

The death-song of the Turkish women. The «silent slaves» are the men whose notions of decorum forbid complaint in *public*.

Note 20, page 184, line 7.

«Where is my child?—an echo answers—«Where?»

«I came to the place of my birth and cried, 'The friends of my youth, where are they?' and an echo answered, 'Where are they?'»

From an Arabic MS.

The above quotation (from which the idea in the text is taken) must be already familiar to every reader— it is given in the first annotation, p. 67, of «The Pleasures of Memory;» a poem so well known as to render a reference almost superfluous; but to whose pages all will be delighted to recur.

Note 21, page 185, line 27.

Into Zuleika's name.

«And airy tongues that *syllable* men's names.»

MILTON.

For a belief that the souls of the dead inhabit the form of birds, we need not travel to the east. Lord Lyttleton's ghost-story, the belief of the Duchess of Kendal, that George I. flew into her window in the shape of a raven (see Orford's Reminiscences), and many other instances, bring this superstition nearer home. The most singular was the whim of a Worcester lady, who, believing her daughter to exist in the shape of a singing bird, literally furnished her pew in the cathedral with cages-full of the kind, and, as she was rich, and a benefactress in beautifying the church, no objection was made to her harmless folly.—For this anecdote, see Orford's Letters.

THE CORSAIR.

A TALE.

«———I suoi pensieri in lui dormir non ponno.»

TASSO, *Canto X, Gerusalemme Liberata.*

DEDICATION

TO

THOMAS MOORE, ESQ.

MY DEAR MOORE,

I DEDICATE to you the last production with which I shall trespass on public patience, and your indulgence, for some years; and I own that I feel anxious to avail myself of this latest and only opportunity of adorning my pages with a name, consecrated by unshaken public principle, and the most undoubted and various talents. While Ireland ranks you among the firmest of her patriots; while you stand alone the first of her bards in her estimation, and Britain repeats and ratifies the decree, permit one, whose only regret, since our first acquaintance, has been the years he had lost before it commenced, to add the humble, but sincere suffrage of friendship, to the voice of more than one

13.

nation. It will at least prove to you, that I have neither forgotten the gratification derived from your society, nor abandoned the prospect of its renewal, whenever your leisure or inclination allows you to atone to your friends for too long an absence. It is said among those friends, I trust truly, that you are engaged in the composition of a poem whose scene will be laid in the east; none can do those scenes so much justice. The wrongs of your own country, the magnificent and fiery spirit of her sons, the beauty and feeling of her daughters, may there be found; and Collins, when he denominated his Oriental his Irish Eclogues, was not aware how true, at least, was a part of his parallel. Your imagination will create a warmer sun, and less clouded sky; but wildness, tenderness, and originality are part of your national claim of oriental descent, to which you have already thus far proved your title more clearly than the most zealous of your country's antiquarians.

May I add a few words on a subject on which all men are supposed to be fluent, and none agreeable?—Self. I have written much, and published more than enough to demand a longer silence than I now meditate; but for some years to come it is my intention to tempt no further the award of « gods, men, nor columns. » In the present composition I have attempted not the most difficult, but, perhaps, the best adapted measure to our language, the good old and now neglected heroic couplet. The stanza of Spenser is perhaps too slow and dignified for narrative; though, I confess, it is the measure most after my own heart: Scott alone, of the present generation, has hitherto completely triumphed over the fatal facility of the octosyllabic verse; and this is not the least victory of his fertile and mighty genius: in blank verse, Milton, Thomson, and our dramatists, are the beacons that shine along the deep, but warn us from the rough and barren rock on which they are kindled. The heroic couplet is not the most popular measure certainly; but as I did not deviate into the other from a wish to flatter what is called public opinion, I shall quit it without further apology, and take my chance once more with that versification, in which I have hitherto published nothing but compositions whose former circulation is part of my present and will be of my future regret.

With regard to my story, and stories in general, I should have been glad to have rendered my personages perfect and amiable, if possible, inasmuch as I have been sometimes criticised, and considered no less responsible for their deeds and qualities than if all had been personal. Be it so—if I have deviated into the gloomy vanity of « drawing from self, » the pictures are probably like, since they are unfavourable; and if not, those who know me are undeceived, and those who do not, I have little interest in undeceiving. I have no particular desire that any but my acquaintance should think the author better than the beings of his imagining; but I cannot help a little surprise, and perhaps amusement, at some odd critical exceptions in the present instance, when I see several bards (far more deserving, I allow) in very reputable plight, and quite exempted from all participation in the faults of those heroes, who, nevertheless, might be found with little more morality than «The Giaour,» and perhaps—but no—I must admit Childe Harold to be a very repulsive personage; and as to his identity, those who like it must give him whatever «alias» they please.

If, however, it were worth while to remove the impression, it might be of some service to me, that the man who is alike the delight of his readers and his friends, the poet of all circles, and the idol of his own, permits me here and elsewhere to subscribe myself,

most truly,

and affectionately,

his obedient servant,

BYRON.

January 1, 1814.

THE CORSAIR.

CANTO I.

« ——— nessun maggior dolore.
Che ricordarsi del tempo felice
Nella miseria,————————— »

DANTE.

I.

« O'ER the glad waters of the dark blue sea,
Our thoughts as boundless, and our souls as free,
Far as the breeze can bear, the billows foam,
Survey our empire, and behold our home!
These are our realms, no limits to their sway—
Our flag the sceptre all who meet obey.
Ours the wild life in tumult still to range
From toil to rest, and joy in every change.
Oh, who can tell? not thou, luxurious slave!
Whose soul would sicken o'er the heaving wave;

Not thou, vain lord of wantonness and ease!
Whom slumber soothes not—pleasure cannot please—
Oh, who can tell, save he whose heart hath tried,
And danced in triumph o'er the waters wide,
The exulting sense—the pulse's maddening play,
That thrills the wanderer of that trackless way?
That for itself can woo the approaching fight,
And turn what some deem danger to delight;
That seeks what cravens shun with more than zeal,
And where the feebler faint—can only feel—
Feel—to the rising bosom's inmost core,
Its hope awaken and its spirit soar?
No dread of death—if with us die our foes—
Save that it seems e'en duller than repose:
Come when it will—we snatch the life of life—
When lost—what recks it—by disease or strife?
Let him who crawls enamour'd of decay,
Cling to his couch, and sicken years away;
Heave his thick breath, and shake his palsied head;
Ours—the fresh turf, and not the feverish bed.
While gasp by gasp he falters forth his soul,
Ours with one pang—one bound—escapes controul.
His corse may boast its urn and narrow cave,
And they who loath'd his life may gild his grave:
Ours are the tears, though few, sincerely shed,
When ocean shrouds and sepulchres our dead.
For us, even banquets fond regret supply
In the red cup that crowns our memory;
And the brief epitaph in danger's day,
When those who win at length divide the prey,
And cry, remembrance saddening o'er each brow,
How had the brave who fell exulted *now!*»

II.

Such were the notes that from the pirate's isle,
Around the kindling watch-fire rang the while;
Such were the sounds that thrill'd the rocks along,
And unto ears as rugged seem'd a song!
In scatter'd groups upon the golden sand,
They game—carouse—converse—or whet the brand;
Select the arms—to each his blade assign,
And careless eye the blood that dims its shine:
Repair the boat, replace the helm or oar,
While others straggling muse along the shore;
For the wild bird the busy springes set,
Or spread beneath the sun the dripping net;
Gaze where some distant sail a speck supplies,
With all the thirsting eye of enterprise;
Tell o'er the tales of many a night of toil,
And marvel where they next shall seize a spoil:
No matter where—their chief's allotment this;
Theirs, to believe no prey nor plan amiss.
But who that CHIEF? his name on every shore
Is famed and fear'd—they ask and know no more.
With these he mingles not but to command;
Few are his words, but keen his eye and hand.
Ne'er seasons he with mirth their jovial mess,
But they forgive his silence for success.
Ne'er for his lip the purpling cup they fill,
That goblet passes him untasted still—
And for his fare—the rudest of his crew
Would that, in turn, have pass'd untasted too;
Earth's coarsest bread, the garden's homeliest roots,
And scarce the summer luxury of fruits,

His short repast in humbleness supply
With all a hermit's board would scarce deny.
But while he shuns the grosser joys of sense,
His mind seems nourish'd by that abstinence.
« Steer to that shore! »—they sail. « Do this! »—'t is done:
« Now form and follow me! »—the spoil is won.
Thus prompt his accents and his actions still,
And all obey and few inquire his will;
To such, brief answer and contemptuous eye
Convey reproof, nor further deign reply.

III.

« A sail!—a sail! »—a promised prize to hope!
Her nation—flag—how speaks the telescope?
No prize, alas!—but yet a welcome sail:
The blood-red signal glitters in the gale.
Yes—she is ours—a home returning bark—
Blow fair, thou breeze!—she anchors ere the dark.
Already doubled is the cape—our bay
Receives that prow which proudly spurns the spray.
How gloriously her gallant course she goes!
Her white wings flying—never from her foes—
She walks the waters like a thing of life,
And seems to dare the elements to strife.
Who would not brave the battle-fire—the wreck—
To move the monarch of her peopled deck?

IV.

Hoarse o'er her side the rustling cable rings;
The sails are furl'd; and anchoring round she swings:
And gathering loiterers on the land discern
Her boat descending from the latticed stern.

'T is mann'd—the oars keep concert to the strand,
Till grates her keel upon the shallow sand.
Hail to the welcome shout!—the friendly speech!
When hand grasps hand uniting on the beach;
The smile, the question, and the quick reply,
And the heart's promise of festivity!

V.

The tidings spread, and gathering grows the crowd:
The hum of voices, and the laughter loud,
And woman's gentler anxious tone is heard—
Friends'—husbands'—lovers' names in each dear word:
« Oh! are they safe? we ask not of success—
But shall we see them? will their accents bless?
From where the battle roars—the billows chafe—
They doubtless boldly did—but who are safe?
Here let them haste to gladden and surprise,
And kiss the doubt from these delighted eyes! »

VI.

« Where is our chief? for him we bear report—
And doubt that joy—which hails our coming—short;
Yet thus sincere—'t is cheering, though so brief;
But, Juan! instant guide us to our chief:
Our greeting paid, we 'll feast on our return,
And all shall hear what each may wish to learn. »
Ascending slowly by the rock-hewn way,
To where his watch-tower beetles o'er the bay,
By bushy brake, and wild flowers blossoming,
And freshness breathing from each silver spring,
Whose scatter'd streams from granite basins burst,
Leap into life, and sparkling woo your thirst;

From crag to cliff they mount—Near yonder cave,
What lonely straggler looks along the wave?
In pensive posture leaning on the brand,
Not oft a resting-staff to that red hand?
« 'T is he—'t is Conrad—here—as wont—alone;
On—Juan! on—and make our purpose known.
The bark he views—and tell him we would greet
His ear with tidings he must quickly meet:
We dare not yet approach—thou know'st his mood,
When strange or uninvited steps intrude.»

VII.

Him Juan sought, and told of their intent—
He spake not—but a sign express'd assent.
These Juan calls—they come—to their salute
He bends him slightly, but his lips are mute.
« These letters, chief, are from the Greek—the spy,
Who still proclaims our spoil or peril nigh:
Whate'er his tidings, we can well report,
Much that»—« Peace, peace!»—he cuts their prating short.
Wondering they turn, abash'd, while each to each
Conjecture whispers in his muttering speech:
They watch his glance with many a stealing look,
To gather how that eye the tidings took;
But, this as if he guess'd, with head aside,
Perchance from some emotion, doubt, or pride,
He read the scroll—« My tablets, Juan, hark—
Where is Gonsalvo?»

« In the anchor'd bark.»

« There let him stay—to him this order bear.
Back to your duty—for my course prepare:
Myself this enterprise to-night will share.»

«To-night, lord Conrad?»

«Ay! at set of sun:

«The breeze will freshen when the day is done.
My corslet—cloak—one hour—and we are gone.
Sling on thy bugle—see that free from rust,
My carbine-lock springs worthy of my trust;
Be the edge sharpen'd of my boarding-brand,
And give its guard more room to fit my hand.
This let the armourer with speed dispose;
Last time it more fatigued my arm than foes:
Mark that the signal-gun be duly fired,
To tell us when the hour of stay 's expired.»

VIII.

They make obeisance, and retire in haste,
Too soon to seek again the watery waste:
Yet they repine not—so that Conrad guides,
And who dare question aught that he decides?
That man of loneliness and mystery,
Scarce seen to smile, and seldom heard to sigh;
Whose name appals the fiercest of his crew,
And tints each swarthy cheek with sallower hue;
Still sways their souls with that commanding art
That dazzles, leads, yet chills the vulgar heart.
What is that spell, that thus his lawless train
Confess and envy, yet oppose in vain?
What should it be? that thus their faith can bind?
The power of thought—the magic of the mind!
Link'd with success, assumed and kept with skill,
That moulds another's weakness to its will;

Wields with their hands, but, still to these unknown,
Makes e'en their mightiest deeds appear his own.
Such hath it been—shall be—beneath the sun
The many still must labour for the one!
'T is nature's doom—but let the wretch who toils,
Accuse not, hate not *him* who wears the spoils.
Oh! if he knew the weight of splendid chains,
How light the balance of his humbler pains!

IX.

Unlike the heroes of each ancient race,
Demons in act, but gods at least in face,
In Conrad's form seems little to admire,
Though his dark eyebrow shades a glance of fire:
Robust but not Herculean—to the sight
No giant frame sets forth his common height;
Yet, in the whole, who paused to look again,
Saw more than marks the crowd of vulgar men;
They gaze and marvel how—and still confess
That thus it is, but why they cannot guess.
Sun-burnt his cheek, his forehead high and pale
The sable curls in wild profusion veil;
And oft perforce his rising lip reveals
The haughtier thought it curbs, but scarce conceals.
Though smooth his voice, and calm his general mien,
Still seems there something he would not have seen:
His features' deepening lines and varying hue
At times attracted, yet perplex'd the view,
As if within that murkiness of mind
Work'd feelings fearful, and yet undefined;
Such might it be—that none could truly tell—
Too close inquiry his stern glance would quell.

There breathe but few whose aspect might defy
The full encounter of his searching eye:
He had the skill, when cunning's gaze would seek
To probe his heart and watch his changing cheek,
At once the observer's purpose to espy,
And on himself roll back his scrutiny,
Lest he to Conrad rather should betray
Some secret thought, than drag that chief's to day.
There was a laughing devil in his sneer,
That raised emotions both of rage and fear;
And where his frown of hatred darkly fell,
Hope withering fled—and mercy sigh'd farewell!

X.

Slight are the outward signs of evil thought,
Within—within—'t was there the spirit wrought!
Love shows all changes—hate, ambition, guile,
Betray no further than the bitter smile;
The lip's least curl, the lightest paleness thrown
Along the govern'd aspect, speak alone
Of deeper passions; and to judge their mien,
He, who would see, must be himself unseen.
Then—with the hurried tread, the upward eye,
The clenched hand, the pause of agony,
That listens, starting, lest the step too near
Approach intrusive on that mood of fear:
Then—with each feature working from the heart,
With feelings loosed to strengthen—not depart:
That rise—convulse—contend—that freeze, or glow,
Flush in the cheek, or damp upon the brow;
Then—stranger! if thou canst, and tremblest not,
Behold his soul—the rest that soothes his lot!

Mark—how that lone and blighted bosom sears
The scathing thought of execrated years!
Behold—but who hath seen, or e'er shall see,
Man as himself—the secret spirit free?

XI.

Yet was not Conrad thus by nature sent
To lead the guilty—guilt's worst instrument—
His soul was changed, before his deeds had driven
Him forth to war with man and forfeit heaven.
Warp'd by the world in disappointment's school,
In words too wise, in conduct *there* a fool;
Too firm to yield, and far too proud to stoop,
Doom'd by his very virtues for a dupe,
He cursed those virtues as the cause of ill,
And not the traitors who betray'd him still;
Nor deem'd that gifts bestow'd on better men
Had left him joy, and means to give again.
Fear'd—shunn'd—belied—ere youth had lost her force,
He hated man too much to feel remorse,
And thought the voice of wrath a sacred call,
To pay the injuries of some on all.
He knew himself a villain—but he deem'd
The rest no better that the thing he seem'd;
And scorn'd the best as hypocrites who hid
Those deeds the bolder spirit plainly did.
He knew himself detested, but he knew
The hearts that loath'd him, crouch'd and dreaded too.
Lone, wild, and strange, he stood alike exempt
From all affection and from all contempt:
His name could sadden, and his acts surprise;
But they that fear'd him dared not to despise:

Man spurns the worm, but pauses ere he wake
The slumbering venom of the folded snake:
The first may turn—but not avenge the blow;
The last expires—but leaves no living foe;
Fast to the doom'd offender's form it clings,
And he may crush—not conquer—still it stings!

XII.

None are all evil—quickening round his heart,
One softer feeling would not yet depart;
Oft could he sneer at others as beguiled
By passions worthy of a fool or child;
Yet 'gainst that passion vainly still he strove,
And e'en in him it asks the name of love!
Yes, it was love—unchangeable—unchanged,
Felt but for one from whom he never ranged;
Though fairest captives daily met his eye,
He shunn'd, nor sought, but coldly pass'd them by;
Though many a beauty droop'd in prison'd bower,
None ever soothed his most unguarded hour.
Yes—it was love—if thoughts of tenderness,
Tried in temptation, strengthen'd by distress,
Unmoved by absence, firm in every clime,
And yet—oh more than all!—untired by time;
Which nor defeated hope, nor baffled wile,
Could render sullen were she near to smile,
Nor rage could fire, nor sickness fret to vent
On her one murmur of his discontent;
Which still would meet with joy, with calmness part,
Lest that his look of grief should reach her heart;
Which nought removed, nor menaced to remove—
If there be love in mortals—this was love!

He was a villain—ay—reproaches shower
On him—but not the passion, nor its power,
Which only proved, all other virtues gone,
Not guilt itself could quench this loveliest one!

XIII.

He paused a moment—till his hastening men
Pass'd the first winding downward to the glen.
« Strange tidings!—many a peril have I past,
Nor know I why this next appears the last!
Yet so my heart forebodes, but must not fear,
Nor shall my followers find me falter here.
'T is rash to meet, but surer death to wait
Till here they hunt us to undoubted fate;
And, if my plan but hold, and fortune smile,
We 'll furnish mourners for our funeral-pile.
Ay—let them slumber—peaceful be their dreams!
Morn ne'er awoke them with such brilliant beams
As kindle high to-night (but blow, thou breeze!)
To warm these slow avengers of the seas.
Now to Medora—Oh! my sinking heart,
Long may her own be lighter than thou art!
Yet was I brave—mean boast where all are brave!
E'en insects sting for aught they seek to save.
This common courage which with brutes we share,
That owes its deadliest efforts to despair,
Small merit claims—but 't was my nobler hope
To teach my few with numbers still to cope;
Long have I led them—not to vainly bleed:
No medium now—we perish or succeed!
So let it be—it irks not me to die;
But thus to urge them whence they cannot fly.

My lot hath long had little of my care,
But chafes my pride thus baffled in the snare;
Is this my skill? my craft! to set at last
Hope, power, and life upon a single cast?
Oh, fate!—accuse thy folly, not thy fate—
She may redeem thee still—nor yet too late.»

XIV.

Thus with himself communion held he, till
He reach'd the summit of his tower-crown'd hill:
There at the portal paused—for wild and soft
He heard those accents never heard too oft;
Through the high lattice far yet sweet they rung,
And these the notes his bird of beauty sung:

1.

«Deep in my soul that tender secret dwells,
Lonely and lost to light for evermore,
Save when to thine my heart responsive swells,
Then trembles into silence as before.

2.

«There, in its centre, a sepulchral lamp
Burns the slow flame, eternal—but unseen;
Which not the darkness of despair can damp,
Though vain its ray as it had never been.

3.

«Remember me—oh! pass not thou my grave
Without one thought whose relics there recline:
The only pang my bosom dares not brave
Must be to find forgetfulness in thine.

4.

« My fondest—faintest—latest accents hear
  Grief for the dead not virtue can reprove;
Then give me all I ever ask'd—a tear,
  The first—last—sole reward of so much love!»

He pass'd the portal—cross'd the corridore,
And reach'd the chamber as the strain gave o'er:
« My own Medora! sure thy song is sad—»
« In Conrad's absence wouldst thou have it glad?
Without thine ear to listen to my lay,
Still must my song my thoughts, my soul betray:
Still must each accent to my bosom suit,
My heart unhush'd—although my lips were mute!
Oh! many a night on this lone couch reclined,
My dreaming fear with storms hath wing'd the wind,
And deem'd the breath that faintly fann'd thy sail
The murmuring prelude of the ruder gale;
Though soft, it seem'd the low prophetic dirge,
That mourn'd thee floating on the savage surge:
Still would I rise to rouse the beacon-fire,
Lest spies less true should let the blaze expire;
And many a restless hour outwatch'd each star,
And morning came—and still thou wert afar.
Oh! how the chill blast on my bosom blew,
And day broke dreary on my troubled view,
And still I gazed and gazed—and not a prow
Was granted to my tears—my truth—my vow!
At length—'t was noon—I hail'd and blest the mast
That met my sight—it near'd—alas! it past!
Another came—oh God! t' was thine at last!

Would that those days were over! wilt thou ne'er,
My Conrad! learn the joys of peace to share?
Sure thou hast more than wealth, and many a home
As bright as this invites us not to roam:
Thou know'st it is not peril that I fear,
I only tremble when thou art not here;
Then not for mine, but that far dearer life,
Which flies from love and languishes for strife—
How strange that heart, to me so tender still,
Should war with nature and its better will!»

«Yea, strange indeed—that heart hath long been changed:
Worm-like 't was trampled—adder-like avenged,
Without one hope on earth beyond thy love,
And scarce a glimpse of mercy from above.
Yet the same feeling which thou dost condemn,
My very love to thee is hate to them,
So closely mingling here, that disentwined,
I cease to love thee when I love mankind;
Yet dread not this—the proof of all the past
Assures the future that my love will last;
But—oh, Medora! nerve thy gentler heart,
«This hour again—but not for long—we part.»

« This hour we part!—my heart foreboded this:
Thus ever fade my fairy dreams of bliss.
This hour—it cannot be—this hour away!
Yon bark hath hardly anchor'd in the bay:
Her consort still is absent, and her crew
Have need of rest before they toil anew;
My love! thou mock'st my weakness; and wouldst steel
My breast before the time when it must feel;

But trifle now no more with my distress,
Such mirth hath less of play than bitterness.
Be silent, Conrad!—dearest! come and share
The feast these hands delighted to prepare;
Light toil! to cull and dress thy frugal fare!
See, I have pluck'd the fruit that promised best,
And where not sure, perplex'd, but pleased, I guess'd
At such as seem'd the fairest: thrice the hill
My steps have wound to try the coolest rill;
Yes! thy sherbet to-night will sweetly flow,
See how it sparkles in its vase of snow!
The grapes' gay juice thy bosom never cheers;
Thou more than moslem when the cup appears:
Think not I mean to chide—for I rejoice
What others deem a penance is thy choice.
But come, the board is spread; our silver lamp
Is trimm'd, and heeds not the sirocco's damp;
Then shall my handmaids wile the time along,
And join with me the dance, or wake the song;
Or my guitar, which still thou lov'st to hear,
Shall soothe or lull—or, should it vex thine ear,
We'll turn the tale, by Ariosto told,
Of fair Olympia loved and left of old.'
Why—thou wert worse than he who broke his vow
To that lost damsel, shouldst thou leave me now;
Or even that traitor chief—I've seen thee smile,
When the clear sky show'd Ariadne's Isle,
Which I have pointed from these cliffs the while:
And thus half sportive, half in fear, I said,
Lest time should raise that doubt to more than dread,
Thus Conrad, too, will quit me for the main:
And he deceived me—for—he came again!»

« Again—again—and oft again—my love!
If there be life below, and hope above,
He will return—but now, the moments bring
The time of parting with redoubled wing:
The why—the where—what boots it now to tell?
Since all must end in that wild word—farewell!
Yet would I fain—did time allow—disclose—
Fear not—these are no formidable foes;
And here shall watch a more than wonted guard,
For sudden siege and long defence prepared:
Nor be thou lonely—though thy lord 's away,
Our matrons and thy handmaids with thee stay;
And this thy comfort—that, when next we meet,
Security shall make repose more sweet.
List!—'t is the bugle—Juan shrilly blew—
One kiss—one more—another—oh! adieu!»
She rose—she sprung—she clung to his embrace,
Till his heart heaved beneath her hidden face.
She dared not raise to his that deep-blue eye,
Which downcast droop'd in tearless agony.
Her long fair hair lay floating o'er his arms,
In all the wildness of dishevell'd charms;
Scarce beat that bosom where his image dwelt
So full—*that* feeling seem'd almost unfelt!
Hark—peals the thunder of the signal-gun!
It told 't was sunset—and he cursed that sun.
Again—again—that form he madly press'd,
Which mutely clasp'd, imploringly caress'd!
And tottering to the couch his bride he bore,
One moment gazed—as if to gaze no more;
Felt—that for him earth held but her alone,
Kiss'd her cold forehead—turn'd—is Conrad gone?

XV.

« And is he gone?» — On sudden solitude
How oft that fearful question will intrude!
« 'T was but an instant past—and here he stood!
And now» —without the portal's porch she rush'd,
And then at length her tears in freedom gush'd;
Big—bright—and fast, unknown to her they fell;
But still her lips refused to send— « Farewell!»
For in that word—that fatal word—howe'er
We promise—hope—believe—there breathes despair.
O'er every feature of that still, pale face,
Had sorrow fix'd what time can ne'er erase;
The tender blue of that large loving eye
Grew frozen with its gaze on vacancy,
Till—oh, how far!—it caught a glimpse of him,
And then it flow'd—and phrensied seem'd to swim
Through those long, dark, and glistening lashes dew'd
With drops of sadness oft to be renew'd.
« He 's gone!» —against her heart that hand is driven,
Convulsed and quick—then gently raised to heaven;
She look'd and saw the heaving of the main;
The white sail set—she dared not look again;
But turn'd with sickening soul within the gate—
« It is no dream—and I am desolate!»

XVI.

From crag to crag descending—swiftly sped
Stern Conrad down, nor once he turn'd his head;
But shrunk whene'er the windings of his way
Forced on his eye what he would not survey,

His lone, but lovely dwelling on the steep,
That hail'd him first when homeward from the deep:
And she—the dim and melancholy star,
Whose ray of beauty reach'd him from afar,
On her he must not gaze, he must not think,
There he might rest—but on destruction's brink:
Yet once almost he stopp'd—and nearly gave
His fate to chance, his projects to the wave;
But no—it must not be—a worthy chief
May melt, but not betray to woman's grief.
He sees his bark, he notes how fair the wind,
And sternly gathers all his might of mind:
Again he hurries on—and as he hears
The clang of tumult vibrate on his ears,
The busy sounds, the bustle of the shore,
The shout, the signal, and the dashing oar;
As marks his eye the sea-boy on the mast,
The anchors rise, the sails unfurling fast,
The waving kerchiefs of the crowd that urge
That mute adieu to those who stem the surge;
And more than all, his blood-red flag aloft,
He marvell'd how his heart could seem so soft.
Fire in his glance, and wildness in his breast,
He feels of all his former self possest;
He bounds—he flies—until his footsteps reach
The verge where ends the cliff, begins the beach,
There checks his speed; but pauses less to breathe
The breezy freshness of the deep beneath,
Than there his wonted statelier step renew;
Nor rush, disturb'd by haste, to vulgar view:
For well had Conrad learn'd to curb the crowd,
By arts that veil, and oft preserve the proud;

His was the lofty port, the distant mien,
That seems to shun the sight—and awes if seen:
The solemn aspect, and the high-born eye,
That checks low mirth, but lacks not courtesy;
All these he wielded to command assent:
But where he wish'd to win, so well unbent,
That kindness cancell'd fear in those who heard,
And other's gifts show'd mean beside his word,
When echo'd to the heart as from his own
His deep yet tender melody of tone:
But such was foreign to his wonted mood,
He cared not what he soften'd, but subdued;
The evil passions of his youth had made
Him value less who loved—than what obey'd.

XVII.

Around him mustering ranged his ready guard.
Before him Juan stands.—« Are all prepared?»

«They are—nay more—embark'd: the latest boat
Waits but my chief——»

« My sword, and my capote.»
Soon firmly girded on, and lightly slung,
His belt and cloak were o'er his shoulders flung;
«Call Pedro here!» He comes—and Conrad bends,
With all the courtesy he deign'd his friends;
Receive these tablets, and peruse with care,
Words of high trust and truth are graven there;
Double the guard, and when Anselmo's bark
Arrives, let him alike these orders mark:
In three days (serve the breeze) the sun shall shine
On our return—till then all peace be thine!»

This said, his brother pirate's hand he wrung,
Then to his boat with haughty gesture sprung.
Flash'd the dipt oars, and sparkling with the stroke,
Around the waves' phosphoric[2] brightness broke;
They gain the vessel—on the deck he stands,
Shrieks the shrill whistle—ply the busy hands—
He marks how well the ship her helm obeys,
How gallant all her crew—and deigns to praise.
His eyes of pride to young Gonsalvo turn—
Why doth he start, and inly seem to mourn?
Alas! those eyes beheld his rocky tower,
And live a moment o'er the parting hour;
She—his Medora—did she mark the prow?
Ah! never loved he half so much as now!
But much must yet be done ere dawn of day—
Again he mans himself and turns away;
Down to the cabin with Gonsalvo bends,
And there unfolds his plan—his means—and ends;
Before them burns the lamp, and spreads the chart,
And all that speaks and aids the naval art;
They to the midnight-watch protract debate;
To anxious eyes what hour is ever late?
Meantime, the steady breeze serenely blew,
And fast and falcon-like the vessel flew;
Pass'd the high headlands of each clustering isle,
To gain their port—long—long ere morning smile:
And soon the night-glass through the narrow bay
Discovers where the pacha's galleys lay.
Count they each sail—and mark how there supine
The lights in vain o'er heedless moslem shine.
Secure, unnoted, Conrad's prow pass'd by,
And anchor'd where his ambush meant to lie;

Screen'd from espial by the jutting cape,
That rears on high its rude fantastic shape.
Then rose his band to duty—not from sleep—
Equipp'd for deeds alike on land or deep;
While lean'd their leader o'er the fretting flood,
And calmly talk'd—and yet he talk'd of blood!

NOTES TO CANTO I.

The time in this poem may seem too short for the occurrences, but the whole of the Ægean isles are within a few hours' sail of the continent, and the reader must be kind enough to take the *wind* as I have often found it.

Note 1, page 214, line 23.

Of fair Olympia loved and left of old.
Orlando, Canto X.

Note 2, page 219, line 4.

Around the waves' phosphoric brightness broke; *etc.*

By night, particularly in a warm latitude, every stroke of the oar, every motion of the boat or ship, is followed by a slight flash like sheet lightning from the water.

THE CORSAIR.

CANTO II.

« Conosceste i dubiosi desiri? »

DANTE.

I.

IN Coron's bay floats many a galley light,
Through Coron's lattices the lamps are bright,
For Seyd, the pacha, makes a feast to-night:
A feast for promised triumph yet to come,
When he shall drag the fetter'd rovers home;
This hath he sworn by Alla and his sword,
And faithful to his firman and his word,
His summon'd prows collect along the coast,
And great the gathering crews, and loud the boast;
Already shared the captives and the prize,
Though far the distant foe they thus despise;
'T is but to sail—no doubt to-morrow's sun
Will see the pirates bound—their haven won!

Meantime the watch may slumber, if they will,
Nor only wake to war, but dreaming kill.
Though all, who can, disperse on shore and seek
To flesh their glowing valour on the Greek;
How well such deed becomes the turban'd brave—
To bare the sabre's edge before a slave!
Infest his dwelling—but forbear to slay,
Their arms are strong, yet merciful to-day,
And do not deign to smite because they may!
Unless some gay caprice suggests the blow,
To keep in practice for the coming foe.
Revel and rout the evening hours beguile,
And they who wish to wear a head must smile;
For moslem mouths produce their choicest cheer,
And hoard their curses, till the coast is clear.

II.

High in his hall reclines the turban'd Seyd;
Around—the bearded chiefs he came to lead.
Removed the banquet, and the last pilaff—
Forbidden draughts, 't is said, he dared to quaff,
Though to the rest the sober berry's juice,[1]
The slaves bear round for rigid moslem's use;
The long chibouque's[2] dissolving clouds supply,
While dance the almas[3] to wild minstrelsy.
The rising morn will view the chiefs embark;
But waves are somewhat treacherous in the dark:
And revellers may more securely sleep
On silken couch than o'er the rugged deep;
Feast there who can—nor combat till they must,
And less to conquest than to korans trust;

And yet the numbers crowded in his host
Might warrant more than e'en the pacha's boast.

III.

With cautious reverence from the outer gate
Slow stalks the slave, whose office there to wait,
Bows his bent head—his hand salutes the floor,
Ere yet his tongue the trusted tidings bore:
« A captive dervise, from the pirate's nest
Escaped, is here—himself would tell the rest. »[4]
He took the sign from Seyd's assenting eye,
And led the holy man in silence nigh.
His arms were folded on his dark-green vest,
His step was feeble, and his look deprest;
Yet worn he seem'd of hardship more than years,
And pale his cheek with penance, not from fears.
Vow'd to his God—his sable locks he wore,
And these his lofty cap rose proudly o'er:
Around his form his loose long robe was thrown,
And wrapt a breast bestow'd on Heaven alone;
Submissive, yet with self-possession mann'd,
He calmly met the curious eyes that scann'd;
And question of his coming fain would seek,
Before the pacha's will allow'd to speak.

IV.

« Whence com'st thou, dervise? »
« From the outlaw's den,
A fugitive— »
« Thy capture where and when? »
« From Scalanovo's port to Scio's isle,
The saick was bound; but Alla did not smile

Upon our course—the moslem merchant's gains
The rovers won: our limbs have worn their chains.
I had no death to fear, nor wealth to boast,
Beyond the wandering freedom which I lost;
At length a fisher's humble boat by night
Afforded hope, and offer'd chance of flight:
I seized the hour, and find my safety here—
With thee—most mighty pacha! who can fear?»

« How speed the outlaws? stand they well prepared,
Their plunder'd wealth and robber's rock to guard?
Dream they of this our preparation, doom'd
To view with fire their scorpion-nest consumed?»

« Pacha! the fetter'd captive's mourning eye
That weeps for flight, but ill can play the spy;
I only heard the reckless waters roar,
Those waves that would not bear me from the shore;
I only mark'd the glorious sun and sky,
Too bright—too blue—for my captivity;
And felt—that all which freedom's bosom cheers,
Must break my chain before it dried my tears.
This may'st thou judge, at least, from my escape,
They little deem of aught in peril's shape;
Else vainly had I pray'd or sought the chance
That leads me here—if eyed with vigilance:
The careless guard that did not see me fly,
May watch as idly when thy power is nigh:
Pacha!—my limbs are faint—and nature craves
Food for my hunger, rest from tossing waves:
Permit my absence—peace be with thee! Peace
With all around!—now grant repose—release.»

« Stay, dervise! I have more to question—stay,
I do command thee—sit—dost hear?—obey!
More I must ask, and food the slaves shall bring;
Thou shalt not pine where all are banqueting:
The supper done—prepare thee to reply,
Clearly and full—I love not mystery.»

'T were vain to guess what shook the pious man,
Who look'd not lovingly on that divan;
Nor show'd high relish for the banquet prest,
And less respect for every fellow-guest.
'T was but a moment's peevish hectic past
Along his cheek, and tranquillized as fast:
He sate him down in silence, and his look
Resumed the calmness which before forsook:
The feast was usher'd in—but sumptuous fare
He shunn'd as if some poison mingled there.
For one so long condemn'd to toil and fast,
Methinks he strangely spares the rich repast.
« What ails thee, dervise? eat—dost thou suppose
This feast a christian's? or my friends thy foes?
Why dost thou shun the salt? that sacred pledge,
Which, once partaken, blunts the sabre's edge,
Makes even contending tribes in peace unite,
And hated hosts seem brethren to the sight!»

« Salt seasons dainties—and my food is still
The humblest root, my drink the simplest rill;
And my stern vow and order's[5] laws oppose
To break or mingle bread with friends or foes;
It may seem strange—if there be aught to dread,
That peril rests upon my single head;

But for thy sway—nay more—thy sultan's throne,
I taste nor bread nor banquet—save alone;
Infringed our order's rule, the prophet's rage
To Mecca's dome might bar my pilgrimage.»

« Well—as thou wilt—ascetic as thou art—
One question answer; then in peace depart.
How many?—Ha! it cannot sure be day?
What star—what sun is bursting on the bay?
It shines a lake of fire!—away—away!
Ho! treachery! my guards! my scimitar!
The galleys feed the flames—and I afar!
Accursed dervise!—these thy tidings—thou
Some villain spy—seize—cleave him—slay him now!»

Up rose the dervise with that burst of light,
Nor less his change of form appall'd the sight:
Up rose that dervise—not in saintly garb,
But like a warrior bounding on his barb,
Dash'd his high cap, and tore his robe away—
Shone his mail'd breast, and flash'd his sabre's ray!
His close but glittering casque, and sable plume,
More glittering eye, and black brow's sabler gloom,
Glared on the moslems' eyes some afrit sprite,
Whose demon death-blow left no hope for fight.
The wild confusion, and the swarthy glow
Of flames on high, and torches from below;
The shriek of terror, and the mingling yell—
For swords began to clash, and shouts to swell,
Flung o'er that spot of earth the air of hell!
Distracted, to and fro, the flying slaves
Behold but bloody shore and fiery waves;

Nought heeded they the pacha's angry cry,
They seize that dervise!—seize on Zatanai![6]
He saw their terror—check'd the first despair
That urged him but to stand and perish there,
Since far too early and too well obey'd,
The flame was kindled ere the signal made;
He saw their terror—from his baldric drew
His bugle—brief the blast—but shrilly blew,
'T is answer'd—« Well ye speed, my gallant crew!
Why did I doubt their quickness of career?
And deem design had left me single here?»
Sweeps his long arm—that sabre's whirling sway
Sheds fast atonement for its first delay;
Completes his fury, what their fear begun,
And makes the many basely quail to one.
The cloven turbans o'er the chamber spread,
And scarce an arm dare rise to guard its head:
Even Seyd, convulsed, o'erwhelm'd with rage, surprise,
Retreats before him, though he still defies.
No craven he—and yet he dreads the blow,
So much confusion magnifies his foe!
His blazing galleys still distract his sight,
He tore his beard, and foaming fled the fight;[7]
For now the pirates pass'd the haram gate,
And burst within—and it were death to wait;
Where wild amazement shrieking—kneeling—throws
The sword aside—in vain—the blood o'erflows!
The corsairs pouring, haste to where within,
Invited Conrad's bugle, and the din
Of groaning victims, and wild cries for life,
Proclaim'd how well he did the work of strife.

They shout to find him grim and lonely there,
A glutted tiger mangling in his lair!
But short their greeting—shorter his reply—
« 'T is well—but Seyd escapes—and he must die—
Much hath been done—but more remains to do—
Their galleys blaze—why not their city too?»

V.

Quick at the word—they seized him each a torch,
And fire the dome from minaret to porch.
A stern delight was fix'd in Conrad's eye,
But sudden sunk—for on his ear the cry
Of women struck, and like a deadly knell
Knock'd at that heart unmoved by battle's yell.
« Oh! burst the haram—wrong not on your lives
One female form—remember—*we* have wives.
On them such outrage vengeance will repay;
Man is our foe, and such 't is ours to slay:
But still we spared—must spare the weaker prey.
Oh! I forgot—but Heaven will not forgive
If at my word the helpless cease to live;
Follow who will—I go—we yet have time
Our souls to lighten of at least a crime.»
He climbs the crackling stair—he bursts the door,
Nor feels his feet glow scorching with the floor;
His breath choked gasping with the volumed smoke,
But still from room to room his way he broke.
They search—they find—they save: with lusty arms
Each bears a prize of unregarded charms;
Calm their loud fears; sustain their sinking frames
With all the care defenceless beauty claims:

So well could Conrad tame their fiercest mood,
And check the very hands with gore imbrued.
But who is she? whom Conrad's arms convey
From reeking pile and combat's wreck—away—
Who but the love of him he dooms to bleed?
The haram-queen—but still the slave of Seyd!

VI.

Brief time had Conrad now to greet Gulnare,[8]
Few words to reassure the trembling fair;
For in that pause compassion snatch'd from war,
The foe before retiring, fast and far,
With wonder saw their footsteps unpursued,
First slowlier fled—then rallied—then withstood.
This Seyd perceives, then first perceives how few,
Compared with his, the corsair's roving crew,
And blushes o'er his error, as he eyes
The ruin wrought by panic and surprise.
Alla il Alla! Vengeance swells the cry—
Shame mounts to rage that must atone or die!
And flame for flame and blood for blood must tell,
The tide of triumph ebbs that flow'd too well—
When wrath returns to renovated strife,
And those who fought for conquest strike for life.
Conrad beheld the danger—he beheld
His followers faint by freshening foes repell'd:
« One effort—one—to break the circling host! »
They form—unite—charge—waver—all is lost!
Within a narrower ring compress'd, beset,
Hopeless, not heartless, strive and struggle yet—
Ah! now they fight in firmest file no more,
Hemm'd in—cut off—cleft down—and trampled o'er;

But each strikes singly, silently, and home,
And sinks outwearied rather than o'ercome,
His last faint quittance rendering with his breath,
Till the blade glimmers in the grasp of death!

VII.

But first, ere came the rallying host to blows,
And rank to rank, and hand to hand oppose,
Gulnare and all her haram handmaids freed,
Safe in the dome of one who held their creed,
By Conrad's mandate safely were bestow'd,
And dried those tears for life and fame that flow'd:
And when that dark-eyed lady, young Gulnare,
Recall'd those thoughts late wandering in despair,
Much did she marvel o'er the courtesy
That smooth'd his accents; soften'd in his eye:
'T was strange—*that* robber thus with gore bedew'd,
Seem'd gentler then than Seyd in fondest mood.
The pacha woo'd as if he deem'd the slave
Must seem delighted with the heart he gave;
The corsair vow'd protection, soothed affright,
As if his homage were a woman's right.
« The wish is wrong—nay, worse for female—vain:
Yet much I long to view that chief again;
If but to thank for, what my fear forgot,
The life—my loving lord remember'd not! »

VIII.

And him she saw, where thickest carnage spread,
But gather'd breathing from the happier dead;
Far from his band, and battling with a host
That deem right dearly won the field he lost,

Fell'd—bleeding—baffled of the death he sought,
And snatch'd to expiate all the ills he wrought;
Preserved to linger and to live in vain,
While vengeance ponder'd o'er new plans of pain,
And stanch'd the blood she saves to shed again—
But drop by drop, for Seyd's unglutted eye
Would doom him ever dying—ne'er to die!
Can this be he? triumphant late she saw,
When his red hand's wild gesture waved, a law!
'T is he indeed—disarm'd but undeprest,
His sole regret the life he still possest;
His wounds too slight, though taken with that will,
Which would have kiss'd the hand that then could kill.
Oh were there none, of all the many given,
To send his soul—he scarcely ask'd to heaven?
Must he alone of all retain his breath,
Who more than all had striven and struck for death?
He deeply felt—what mortal hearts must feel,
When thus reversed on faithless fortune's wheel,
For crimes committed, and the victor's threat
Of lingering tortures to repay the debt—
He deeply, darkly felt; but evil pride
That led to perpetrate—now serves to hide.
Still in his stern and self-collected mien
A conqueror's more than captive's air is seen,
Though faint with wasting toil and stiffening wound,
But few that saw—so calmly gazed around:
Though the far shouting of the distant crowd,
Their tremors o'er, rose insolently loud,
The better warriors, who beheld him near,
Insulted not the foe who taught them fear;

And the grim guards that to his durance led,
In silence eyed him with a secret dread.

IX.

The leech was sent—but not in mercy—there
To note how much the life yet left could bear;
He found enough to load with heaviest chain,
And promise feeling for the wrench of pain:
To-morrow—yea—to-morrow's evening sun
Will sinking see impalement's pangs begun,
And rising with the wonted blush of morn
Behold how well or ill those pangs are borne.
Of torments this the longest and the worst,
Which adds all other agony to thirst,
That day by day death still forbears to slake,
While famish'd vultures flit around the stake.
« Oh! water—water! »—smiling hate denies
The victim's prayer—for if he drinks—he dies.
This was his doom:—the leech, the guard were gone,
And left proud Conrad fetter'd and alone.

X.

'T were vain to paint to what his feelings grew—
It e'en were doubtful if their victim knew.
There is a war, a chaos of the mind,
When all its elements convulsed—combined—
Lie dark and jarring with perturbed force,
And gnashing with impenitent remorse;
That juggling fiend—who never spake before—
But cries « I warn'd thee! » when the deed is o'er.
Vain voice! the spirit burning but unbent,
May writhe—rebel—the weak alone repent!

E'en in that lonely hour when most it feels,
And, to itself, all—all that self reveals,
No single passion, and no ruling thought
That leaves the rest as once unseen, unsought;
But the wild prospect when the soul reviews—
All rushing through their thousand avenues.
Ambition's dreams expiring, love's regret,
Endanger'd glory, life itself beset;
The joy untasted, the contempt or hate
'Gainst those who fain would triumph in our fate;
The hopeless past, the hasting future driven
Too quickly on to guess if hell or heaven;
Deeds, thoughts, and words, perhaps remember'd not
So keenly till that hour, but ne'er forgot;
Things light or lovely in their acted time,
But now to stern reflection each a crime;
The withering sense of evil unreveal'd,
Not cankering less because the more conceal'd—
All, in a word, from which all eyes must start,
That opening sepulchre—the naked heart
Bares with its buried woes, till pride awake,
To snatch the mirror from the soul—and break.
Ay—pride can veil, and courage brave it all,
All—all—before—beyond—the deadliest fall.
Each hath some fear, and he who least betrays,
The only hypocrite deserving praise:
Not the loud recreant wretch who boasts and flies;
But he who looks on death—and silent dies.
So steel'd by pondering o'er his far career,
He half-way meets him should he menace near!

XI.

In the high chamber of his highest tower
Sate Conrad fetter'd in the pacha's power.
His palace perish'd in the flame—this fort
Contain'd at once his captive and his court.
Not much could Conrad of his sentence blame,
His foe, if vanquish'd, had but shared the same:—
Alone he sate—in solitude had scann'd
His guilty bosom, but that breast he mann'd:
One thought alone he could not—dared not meet—
« Oh, how these tidings will Medora greet? »
Then—only then—his clanking hands he raised,
And strain'd with rage the chain on which he gazed;
But soon he found—or feign'd—or dream'd relief,
And smiled in self-derision of his grief,
« And now come torture when it will—or may,
More need of rest to nerve me for the day! »
This said, with languor to his mat he crept,
And, whatsoe'er his visions, quickly slept.
'T was hardly midnight when that fray begun,
For Conrad's plans matured, at once were done;
And havoc loathes so much the waste of time,
She scarce had left an uncommitted crime.
One hour beheld him since the tide he stemm'd—
Disguised—discover'd—conquering—ta'en—condemn'
A chief on land—an outlaw on the deep—
Destroying—saving—prison'd—and asleep!

XII.

He slept in calmest seeming—for his breath
Was hush'd so deep—ah! happy if in death!

He slept—Who o'er his placid slumber bends?
His foes are gone—and here he hath no friends;
Is it some seraph sent to grant him grace?
No, 't is an earthly form with heavenly face!
Its white arm raised a lamp—yet gently hid,
Lest the ray flash abruptly on the lid
Of that closed eye, which opens but to pain,
And once unclosed—but once may close again.
That form, with eye so dark, and cheek so fair,
And auburn waves of gemm'd and braided hair;
With shape of fairy lightness—naked foot,
That shines like snow, and falls on earth as mute—
Through guards and dunnest night how came it there?
Ah! rather ask, what will not woman dare?
Whom youth and pity lead like thee, Gulnare!
She could not sleep—and while the pacha's rest
In muttering dreams yet saw his pirate-guest,
She left his side—his signet-ring she bore,
Which oft in sport adorn'd her hand before—
And with it, scarcely question'd, won her way
Through drowsy guards that must that sign obey.
Worn out with toil, and tired with changing blows,
Their eyes had envied Conrad his repose;
And chill and nodding at the turret door,
They stretch their listless limbs, and watch no more:
Just raised their heads to hail the signet-ring,
Nor ask or what or who the sign may bring.

XIII.

She gazed in wonder, « Can he calmly sleep,
While other eyes his fall or ravage weep?

And mine in restlessness are wandering here—
What sudden spell hath made this man so dear?
True—'t is to him my life, and more, I owe,
And me and mine he spared from worse than woe:
'T is late to think—but soft—his slumber breaks—
How heavily he sighs!—he starts—awakes!»
He raised his head—and dazzled with the light,
His eye seem'd dubious if it saw aright:
He moved his hand—the grating of his chain
Too harshly told him that he lived again.
«What is that form? if not a shape of air,
Methinks, my jailor's face shows wondrous fair!»

«Pirate! thou know'st me not—but I am one,
Grateful for deeds thou hast too rarely done;
Look on me—and remember her thy hand
Snatch'd from the flames, and thy more fearful band.
I come through darkness—and I scarce know why—
Yet not to hurt—I would not see thee die.»

«If so, kind lady! thine the only eye
That would not here in that gay hope delight:
Theirs is the chance—and let them use their right.
But still I thank their courtesy or thine,
That would confess me at so fair a shrine!»

Strange though it seem—yet with extremest grief
Is link'd a mirth—it doth not bring relief—
That playfulness of sorrow ne'er beguiles,
And smiles in bitterness—but still it smiles;
And sometimes with the wisest and the best,
Till even the scaffold 9 echoes with their jest!

Yet not the joy to which it seems akin—
It may deceive all hearts, save that within.
Whate'er it was that flash'd on Conrad, now
A laughing wildness half unbent his brow:
And these his accents had a sound of mirth,
As if the last he could enjoy on earth;
Yet 'gainst his nature—for through that short life,
Few thoughts had he to spare from gloom and strife.

XIV.

«Corsair! thy doom is named—but I have power
To soothe the pacha in his weaker hour.
Thee would I spare—nay more—would save thee now,
But this—time—hope—nor e'en thy strength allow;
But all I can I will: at least delay
The sentence that remits thee scarce a day.
More now were ruin—even thyself were loth
The vain attempt should bring but doom to both.»

«Yes!—loth indeed:—my soul is nerved to all,
Or fall'n too low to fear a further fall:
Tempt not thyself with peril; me with hope,
Of flight from foes with whom I could not cope:
Unfit to vanquish—shall I meanly fly,
The one of all my band that would not die?
Yet there is one—to whom my memory clings,
Till to these eyes her own wild softness springs.
My sole resources in the path I trod
Were these—my bark—my sword—my love—my God!
The last I left in youth—he leaves me now—
And man but works His will to lay me low.

I have no thought to mock his throne with prayer
Wrung from the coward crouching of despair;
It is enough—I breathe—and I can bear.
My sword is shaken from the worthless hand
That might have better kept so true a brand;
My bark is sunk or captive—but my love—
For her in sooth my voice would mount above:
Oh! she is all that still to earth can bind—
And this will break a heart so more than kind,
And blight a form—till thine appear'd, Gulnare!
Mine eye ne'er ask'd if others were as fair?»

« Thou lov'st another then! but what to me
Is this?—'t is nothing—nothing e'er can be:
But yet—thou lov'st—and—oh! I envy those
Whose hearts on hearts as faithful can repose,
Who never feel the void—the wandering thought
That sighs o'er visions—such as mine hath wrought.»

« Lady—methought thy love was his, for whom
This arm redeem'd thee from a fiery tomb.»

« My love stern Seyd's! Oh—No—No—not my love—
Yet much this heart, that strives no more, once strove
To meet his passion—but it would not be:
I felt—I feel—love dwells with—with the free.
I am a slave, a favour'd slave at best,
To share his splendour, and seem very blest!
Oft must my soul the question undergo,
Of—'Dost thou love?' and burn to answer 'No!'
Oh! hard it is that fondness to sustain,
And struggle not to feel averse in vain;

But harder still the heart's recoil to bear,
And hide from one—perhaps another there.
He takes the hand I give not—nor withhold—
Its pulse nor check'd—nor quicken'd—calmly cold:
And when resign'd, it drops a lifeless weight
From one I never loved enough to hate.
No warmth these lips return by his imprest,
And chill'd remembrance shudders o'er the rest.
Yes—had I ever proved that passion's zeal,
The change to hatred were at least to feel:
But still—he goes unmourn'd—returns unsought—
And oft when present—absent from my thought.
Or when reflection comes, and come it must—
I fear that henceforth 't will but bring disgust;
I am his slave—but, in despite of pride,
'T were worse than bondage to become his bride.
Oh! that this dotage of his breast would cease!
Or seek another and give mine release,
But yesterday—I could have said, to peace!
Yes—if unwonted fondness now I feign,
Remember—captive! 't is to break thy chain;
Repay the life that to thy hand I owe;
To give thee back to all endear'd below,
Who share such love as I can never know.
Farewell—morn breaks—and I must now away:
'Twill cost me dear—but dread no death to-day!»

XV.

She press'd his fetter'd fingers to her heart,
And bow'd her head, and turn'd her to depart.
And noiseless as a lovely dream is gone.
And was she here? and is he now alone?

What gem hath dropp'd and sparkles o'er his chain?
The tear most sacred, shed for other's pain,
That starts at once—bright—pure—from pity's mine,
Already polish'd by the hand divine!
Oh! too convincing—dangerously dear—
In woman's eye the unanswerable tear!
That weapon of her weakness she can wield,
To save, subdue—at once her spear and shield:
Avoid it—virtue ebbs and wisdom errs,
Too fondly gazing on that grief of hers!
What lost a world, and bade a hero fly?
The timid tear in Cleopatra's eye.
Yet be the soft triumvir's fault forgiven,
By this—how many lose not earth—but heaven!
Consign their souls to man's eternal foe,
And seal their own to spare some wanton's woe!

XVI.

'T is morn—and o'er his alter'd features play
The beams—without the hope of yesterday.
What shall he be ere night? perchance a thing
O'er which the raven flaps her funeral wing:
By his closed eye unheeded and unfelt,
While sets that sun, and dews of evening melt,
Chill—wet—and misty round each stiffen'd limb,
Refreshing earth—reviving all but him!—

NOTES TO CANTO II.

Note 1, page 224, line 21.

Though to the rest the sober berry's juice, *etc.*

Coffee.

Note 2, page 224, line 23.

The long chibouque's dissolving clouds supply, *etc.*

Pipe.

Note 3, page 224, line 24.

While dance the almas to wild minstrelsy.

Dancing-girls.

Note 4, page 225, line 9.

« A captive dervise, from the pirate's nest
Escaped, is here—himself would tell the rest. »

It has been objected that Conrad's entering disguised as a spy is out of nature.—Perhaps so. I find something not unlike it in history.

« Anxious to explore with his own eyes the state of the Vandals, Majorian ventured, after disguising the colour of his hair, to visit Carthage in the character of his own ambassador; and Genseric was afterwards mortified by the discovery, that he had entertained and dismissed the Emperor of the Romans. Such an anecdote may be rejected as an improbable fiction; but it is a fiction which would not have been imagined unless in the life of a hero.» GIBBON, *D. and F. Vol. VI, p.* 180.

That Conrad is a character not altogether out of nature I shall attempt to prove by some historical coincidences, which I have met with since writing «The Corsair.»

«Eccelin, prisonnier,» dit Rolandini, «s'enfermoit dans un silence menaçant; il fixoit sur la terre son visage féroce, et ne donnoit point d'essor à sa profonde indignation.—De toutes parts cependant les soldats et les peuples accouroient; ils vouloient voir cet homme, jadis si puissant, et la joie universelle éclatoit de toutes parts.

. . . .

«Eccelin étoit d'une petite taille; mais tout l'aspect de sa personne, tous ses mouvements indiquoient un soldat.—Son langage étoit amer, son déportement superbe—et par son seul regard il faisoit trembler les plus hardis.» SISMONDI, *tome III, pages* 219, 220.

«Gizericus (Genseric, king of the Vandals, the conqueror of both Carthage and Rome), statura mediocris, et equi casu claudicans, animo profundus, sermone rarus, luxuriæ contemptor, irâ turbidus, habendi cupidus, ad solicitandas gentes providentissimus,» etc. etc. *Jornandes de Rebus Getius*, c. 33.

I beg leave to quote these gloomy realities to keep in countenance my Giaour and Corsair.

Note 5, page 227, line 27.

And my stern vow and order's laws oppose *etc.*

The dervises are in colleges, and of different orders, as the monks.

Note 6, page 229, line 2.

They seize that dervise!—seize on Zatanai!

Satan.

Note 7, page 229, line 23.

He tore his beard, and foaming fled the fight; *etc.*

A common and not very novel effect of mussulman anger. See Prince Eugene's Memoirs, page 24. «The seraskier received a wound in the thigh; he plucked up his beard by the roots, because he was obliged to quit the field.»

Note 8, page 231, line 8.

Brief time had Conrad now to greet Gulnare, *etc*.

Gulnare, a female name; it means, literally, the flower of the pomegranate.

Note 9, page 238, line 29.

Till e'en the scaffold echoes with their jest!

—In Sir Thomas More, for instauce, on the scaffold, and Anne Boleyn in the Tower, when, grasping her neck, she remarked that it «was too slender to trouble the headsman much.» During one part of the French Revolution, it became a fashion to leave some *mot* as a legacy; and the quantity of facetious last words spoken during that period would form a melancholy jest-book of a considerable size.

THE CORSAIR.

CANTO III.

«Come vedi—ancor non m'abbandona.»

DANTE.

I.

SLOW sinks, more lovely ere his race be run,
Along Morea's hills the setting sun;
Not, as in northern climes, obscurely bright,
But one unclouded blaze of living light!
O'er the hush'd deep the yellow beam he throws,
Gilds the green wave, that trembles as it glows.
On old Ægina's rock, and Idra's isle,
The god of gladness sheds his parting smile;
O'er his own regions lingering, loves to shine,
Though there his altars are no more divine.
Descending fast the mountain shadows kiss
Thy glorious gulf, unconquer'd Salamis!
Their azure arches through the long expanse
More deeply purpled meet his mellowing glance,

And tenderest tints, along their summits driven,
Mark his gay course and own the hues of heaven;
Till, darkly shaded from the land and deep,
Behind his Delphian cliff he sinks to sleep.

On such an eve, his palest beam he cast,
When—Athens! here thy wisest look'd his last.
How watch'd thy better sons his farewell ray,
That closed their murder'd sage's [1] latest day!
Not yet—not yet—Sol pauses on the hill—
The precious hour of parting lingers still;
But sad his light to agonizing eyes,
And dark the mountain's once delightful dyes:
Gloom o'er the lovely land he seem'd to pour,
The land where Phœbus never frown'd before,
But ere he sank below Cithæron's head,
The cup of woe was quaff'd—the spirit fled;
The soul of him who scorn'd to fear or fly—
Who lived and died, as none can live or die!

But lo! from high Hymettus to the plain,
The queen of night asserts her silent reign.[2]
No murky vapour, herald of the storm,
Hides her fair face, nor girds her glowing form;
With cornice glimmering as the moon-beams play,
There the white column greets her grateful ray,
And, bright around with quivering beams beset,
Her emblem sparkles o'er the minaret:
The groves of olive scatter'd dark and wide
Where meek Cephisus pours his scanty tide,
The cypress saddening by the sacred mosque,
The gleaming turret of the gay kiosk,[3]

And, dun and sombre 'mid the holy calm,
Near Theseus' fane yon solitary palm,
All tinged with varied hues arrest the eye—
And dull were his that pass'd them heedless by.

Again the Ægean, heard no more afar,
Lulls his chafed breast from elemental war;
Again his waves in milder tints unfold
Their long array of sapphire and of gold,
Mixt with the shades of many a distant isle,
That frown—where gentler ocean seems to smile.[4]

II.

Not now my theme—why turn my thoughts to thee?
Oh! who can look along thy native sea,
Nor dwell upon thy name, whate'er the tale,
So much its magic must o'er all prevail?
Who that beheld that sun upon thee set,
Fair Athens! could thine evening face forget?
Not he—whose heart nor time nor distance frees,
Spell-bound within the clustering Cyclades!
Nor seems this homage foreign to his strain,
His corsair's isle was once thine own domain—
Would that with freedom it were thine again!

III.

The sun hath sunk—and, darker than the night,
Sinks with its beam upon the beacon height
Medora's heart—the third day 's come and gone—
With it he comes not—sends not—faithless one!
The wind was fair though light, and storms were none.

Last eve Anselmo's bark return'd, and yet
His only tidings that they had not met!
Though wild, as now, far different were the tale
Had Conrad waited for that single sail.

The night-breeze freshens—she that day had past
In watching all that hope proclaim'd a mast;
Sadly she sate—on high—impatience bore
At last her footsteps to the midnight shore,
And there she wander'd heedless of the spray
That dash'd her garments oft, and warn'd away:
She saw not—felt not this—nor dared depart,
Nor deem'd it cold—her chill was at her heart;
Till grew such certainty from that suspense—
His very sight had shock'd from life or sense!

It came at last—a sad and shatter'd boat,
Whose inmates first beheld whom first they sought;
Some bleeding—all most wretched—these the few—
Scarce knew they how escaped—*this* all they knew.
In silence, darkling, each appear'd to wait
His fellow's mournful guess at Conrad's fate:
Something they would have said; but seem'd to fear
To trust their accents to Medora's ear.
She saw at once, yet sunk not—trembled not—
Beneath that grief, that loneliness of lot,
Within that meek fair form, were feelings high,
That deem'd not till they found their energy.
While yet was hope—they soften'd—flutter'd—wept—
All lost—that softness died not—but it slept;
And o'er its slumber rose that strength which said,
« With nothing left to love—there 's nought to dread. »

'T is more than nature's; like the burning might
Delirium gathers from the fever's height.

« Silent you stand—nor would I hear you tell
What—speak not—breathe not—for I know it well—
Yet would I ask—almost my lip denies
The—quick your answer—tell me where he lies?»

« Lady! we know not—scarce with life we fled;
But here is one denies that he is dead:
He saw him bound; and bleeding—but alive.»

She heard no further—'t was in vain to strive—
So throbb'd each vein—each thought—till then withstood;
Her own dark soul—these words at once subdued:
She totters—falls—and senseless had the wave
Perchance but snatch'd her from another grave;
But that with hands though rude, yet weeping eyes,
They yield such aid as pity's haste supplies:
Dash o'er her deathlike cheek the ocean dew,
Raise—fan—sustain—till life returns anew;
Awake her handmaids, with the matrons leave
That fainting form o'er which they gaze and grieve;
Then seek Anselmo's cavern, to report
The tale too tedious—when the triumph short.

IV.

In that wild council words wax'd warm and strange,
With thoughts of ransom, rescue, and revenge;
All, save repose or flight: still lingering there
Breathed Conrad's spirit, and forbade despair;

Whate'er his fate—the breasts he form'd and led
Will save him living, or appease him dead.
Woe to his foes! there yet survive a few,
Whose deeds are daring, as their hearts are true.

V.

Within the haram's secret chamber sate
Stern Seyd, still pondering o'er his captive's fate:
His thoughts on love and hate alternate dwell,
Now with Gulnare, and now in Conrad's cell;
Here at his feet the lovely slave reclined
Surveys his brow—would soothe his gloom of mind,
While many an anxious glance her large dark eye
Sends in its idle search for sympathy,
His only bends in seeming o'er his beads,[5]
But inly views his victim as he bleeds.

« Pacha! the day is thine; and on thy crest
Sits triumph—Conrad taken—fall'n the rest!
His doom is fix'd—he dies: and well his fate
Was earn'd—yet much too worthless for thy hate:
Methinks a short release, for ransom told
With all his treasure, not unwisely sold;
Report speaks largely of his pirate-hoard—
Would that of this my pacha were the lord!
While baffled, weaken'd by this fatal fray—
Watch'd—follow'd—he were then an easier prey;
But once cut off—the remnant of his band
Embark their wealth, and seek a safer strand. »

« Gulnare!—if for each drop of blood a gem
Were offer'd rich as Stamboul's diadem;

If for each hair of his a massy mine
Of virgin ore should supplicating shine;
If all our Arab tales divulge or dream
Of wealth were here—that gold should not redeem!
It had not now redeem'd a single hour;
But that I know him fetter'd, in my power;
And, thirsting for revenge, I ponder still
On pangs that longest rack, and latest kill.»

«Nay, Seyd!—I seek not to restrain thy rage,
Too justly moved for mercy to assuage;
My thoughts were only to secure for thee
His riches—thus released, he were not free:
Disabled, shorn of half his might and band,
His capture could but wait thy first command.»

«His capture *could!*—and shall I then resign
One day to him—the wretch already mine?
Release my foe!—at whose remonstrance?—thine!
Fair suitor!—to thy *virtuous* gratitude,
That thus repays this Giaour's relenting mood,
Which thee and thine alone of all could spare,
No doubt—regardless if the prize were fair,
My thanks and praise alike are due—now hear!
I have a counsel for thy gentler ear:
I do mistrust thee, woman! and each word
Of thine stamps truth on all suspicion heard.
Borne in his arms through fire from yon serai—
Say, wert thou lingering there with him to fly?
Thou need'st not answer—thy confession speaks,
Already reddening on thy guilty cheeks;

Then, lovely dame, bethink thee! and beware:
'T is not *his* life alone may claim such care!
Another word and—nay—I need no more.
Accursed was the moment when he bore
Thee from the flames, which better far—but—no—
I then had mourn'd thee with a lover's woe—
Now 't is thy lord that warns—deceitful thing!
Know'st thou that I can clip thy wanton wing?
In words alone I am not wont to chafe:
Look to thyself—nor deem thy falsehood safe!»

He rose—and slowly, sternly thence withdrew,
Rage in his eye and threats in his adieu:
Ah! little reck'd that chief of womanhood—
Which frowns ne'er quell'd, nor menaces subdued;
And little deem'd he what thy heart, Gulnare!
When soft could feel, and well incensed could dare.
Hisd oubts appear'd to wrong—nor yet she knew
How deep the root from whence compassion grew—
She was a slave—from such may captives claim
A fellow-feeling, differing but in name;
Still half unconscious—heedless of his wrath,
Again she ventured on the dangerous path,
Again his rage repell'd—until arose
That strife of thought, the source of woman's woes!

VI.

Meanwhile—long anxious—weary—still—the same
Roll'd day and night—his soul could terror tame—
This fearful interval of doubt and dread,
When every hour might doom him worse than dead,

When every step that echo'd by the gate,
Might entering lead where axe and stake await;
When every voice that grated on his ear
Might be the last that he could ever hear;
Could terror tame—that spirit stern and high
Had proved unwilling as unfit to die;
'T was worn—perhaps decay'd—yet silent bore
That conflict deadlier far than all before:
The heat of fight, the hurry of the gale,
Leave scarce one thought inert enough to quail;
But bound and fix'd in fetter'd solitude,
To pine, the prey of every changing mood;
To gaze on thine own heart; and meditate
Irrevocable faults, and coming fate—
Too late the last to shun—the first to mend—
To count the hours that struggle to thine end,
With not a friend to animate, and tell
To other ears that death became thee well;
Around thee foes to forge the ready lie,
And blot life's latest scene with calumny;
Before thee tortures, which the soul can dare,
Yet doubts how well the shrinking flesh may bear;
But deeply feels a single cry would shame,
To valour's praise thy last and dearest claim;
The life thou leav'st below, denied above
By kind monopolists of heavenly love;
And more than doubtful paradise—thy heaven
Of earthly hope—thy loved one from thee riven.
Such were the thoughts that outlaw must sustain,
And govern pangs surpassing mortal pain:
And those sustain'd he—boots it well or ill?
Since not to sink beneath, is something still?

VII.

The first day pass'd—he saw not her—Gulnare—
The second—third—and still she came not there;
But what her words avouch'd, her charms had done,
Or else he had not seen another sun.
The fourth day roll'd along, and with the night
Came storm and darkness in their mingling might:
Oh! how he listen'd to the rushing deep,
That ne'er till now so broke upon his sleep;
And his wild spirit wilder wishes sent,
Roused by the roar of his own element!
Oft had he ridden on that winged wave,
And loved its roughness for the speed it gave;
And now its dashing echo'd on his ear,
A long-known voice—alas! too vainly near!
Loud sung the wind above; and, doubly loud,
Shook o'er his turret-cell the thunder-cloud;
And flash'd the lightning by the latticed bar,
To him more genial than the midnight star:
Close to the glimmering grate he dragg'd his chain,
And hoped *that* peril might not prove in vain.
He raised his iron hand to Heaven, and pray'd
One pitying flash to mar the form it made:
His steel and impious prayer attract alike—
The storm roll'd onward and disdain'd to strike;
Its peal wax'd fainter—ceased—he felt alone,
As if some faithless friend had spurn'd his groan!

VIII.

The midnight pass'd—and to the massy door
A light step came—it paused—it moved once more;

Slow turns the grating bolt and sullen key;
'T is as his heart foreboded—that fair she!
Whate'er her sins, to him a guardian saint,
And beateous still as hermit's hope can paint;
Yet changed since last within that cell she came,
More pale her cheek, more tremulous her frame:
On him she cast her dark and hurried eye,
Which spoke before her accents—« thou must die!
Yes, thou must die—there is but one resource,
The last—the worst—if torture were not worse.»

« Lady! I look to none—my lips proclaim
What last proclaim'd they—Conrad still the same:
Why shouldst thou seek an outlaw's life to spare,
And change the sentence I deserve to bear?
Well have I earn'd—nor here alone—the meed
Of Seyd's revenge, by many a lawless deed.»

«Why should I seek? because—oh! didst thou not
Redeem my life from worse than slavery's lot?
Why should I seek?—hath misery made thee blind
To the fond workings of a woman's mind!
And must I say! albeit my heart rebel
With all that woman feels, but should not tell—
Because—despite thy crimes—that heart is moved:
It fear'd thee—thank'd thee—pitied—madden'd—loved.
Reply not, tell not now thy tale again,
Thou lov'st another—and I love in vain;
Though fond as mine her bosom, form more fair,
I rush through peril which she would not dare.
If that thy heart to hers were truly dear,
Were I thine own—thou wert not lonely here:

An outlaw's spouse—and leave her lord to roam!
What hath such gentle dame to do with home?
But speak not now—o'er thine and o'er my head
Hangs the keen sabre by a single thread;
If thou hast courage still, and wouldst be free,
Receive this poniard—rise—and follow me!»

« Ay—in my chains! my steps will gently tread,
With these adornments, o'er each slumbering head!
Thou hast forgot—is this a garb for flight?
Or is that instrument more fit for fight?»

« Misdoubting corsair! I have gain'd the guard,
Ripe for revolt, and greedy for reward.
A single word of mine removes that chain:
Without some aid how here could I remain?
Well, since we met, hath sped my busy time,
If in aught evil, for thy sake the crime:
The crime—'t is none to punish those of Seyd.
That hated tyrant, Conrad—he must bleed!
I see thee shudder—but my soul is changed—
Wrong'd, spurn'd, reviled—and it shall be avenged—
Accused of what till now my heart disdain'd—
Too faithful, though to bitter bondage chain'd.
Yes, smile!—but he had little cause to sneer,
I was not treacherous then—nor thou too dear:
But he has said it—and the jealous well,
Those tyrants, teasing, tempting to rebel,
Deserve the fate their fretting lips foretell.
I never loved—he bought me—somewhat high—
Since with me came a heart he could not buy.

I was a slave unmurmuring; he hath said,
But for his rescue I with thee had fled.
'T was false thou know'st—but let such augurs rue,
Their words are omens insult renders true.
Nor was thy respite granted to my prayer;
This fleeting grace was only to prepare
New torments for thy life, and my despair.
Mine too he threatens; but his dotage still
Would fain reserve me for his lordly will:
When wearier of these fleeting charms and me,
There yawns the sack—and yonder rolls the sea!
What, am I then a toy for dotard's play,
To wear but till the gilding frets away?
I saw thee—loved thee—owe thee all—would save,
If but to show how grateful is a slave.
But had he not thus menaced fame and life,
(And well he keeps his oaths pronounced in strife)
I still had saved thee—but the pacha spared.
Now I am all thine own—for all prepared:
Thou lov'st me not—nor know'st—or but the worst.
Alas! this love—that hatred are the first—
Oh! couldst thou prove my truth, thou wouldst not start,
Nor fear the fire that lights an eastern heart,
'T is now the beacon of thy safety—now
It points within the port a mainote prow:
But in one chamber, where our path must lead,
There sleeps—he must not wake—the oppressor Seyd!»

« Gulnare—Gulnare—I never felt till now
My abject fortune, wither'd fame so low:
Seyd is mine enemy; had swept my band
From earth with ruthless but with open hand,

And therefore came I, in my bark of war,
To smite the smiter with the scimitar;
Such is my weapon—not the secret knife—
Who spares a woman's seeks not slumber's life.
Thine saved I gladly, lady, not for this—
Let me not deem that mercy shown amiss.
Now fare thee well—more peace be with thy breast!
Night wears apace—my last of earthly rest!»

«Rest! rest! by sunrise must thy sinews shake,
And thy limbs writhe around the ready stake.
I heard the order—saw—I will not see—
If thou wilt perish, I will fall with thee.
My life—my love—my hatred—all below
Are on this cast—corsair! 't is but a blow!
Without it flight were idle—how evade
His sure pursuit? my wrongs too unrepaid,
My youth disgraced—the long, long wasted years,
One blow shall cancel with our future fears;
But since the dagger suits thee less than brand,
I 'll try the firmness of a female hand.
The guards are gain'd—one moment all were o'er—
Corsair! we meet in safety or no more;
If errs my feeble hand, the morning cloud
Will hover o'er thy scaffold, and my shroud.»

IX.

She turn'd, and vanish'd ere he could reply,
But his glance follow'd far with eager eye;
And gathering, as he could, the links that bound
His form, to curl their length, and curb their sound,

Since bar and bolt no more his steps preclude,
He, fast as fetter'd limbs allow, pursued.
'T was dark and winding, and he knew not where
That passage led; nor lamp nor guard were there:
He sees a dusky glimmering—shall he seek
Or shun that ray so indistinct and weak?
Chance guides his steps—a freshness seems to bear
Full on his brow, as if from morning air—
He reach'd an open gallery—on his eye
Gleam'd the last star of night, the clearing sky:
Yet scarcely heeded these—another light
From a lone chamber struck upon his sight.
Towards it he moved, a scarcely closing door
Reveal'd the ray within, but nothing more.
With hasty step a figure outward past,
Then paused—and turn'd—and paused—'t is she at last!
No poniard in that hand—nor sign of ill—
«Thanks to that softening heart—she could not kill!»
Again he look'd, the wildness of her eye
Starts from the day abrupt and fearfully.
She stopp'd—threw back her dark far-floating hair,
That nearly veil'd her face and bosom fair:
As if she late had bent her leaning head
Above some object of her doubt or dread.
They meet—upon her brow—unknown—forgot—
Her hurrying hand had left—'t was but a spot—
Its hue was all he saw, and scarce withstood—
Oh! slight but certain pledge of crime—'t is blood!

X.

He had seen battle—he had brooded lone
O'er promised pangs to sentenced guilt foreshown;

He had been tempted—chasten'd—and the chain
Yet on his arms might ever there remain:
But ne'er from strife—captivity—remorse—
From all his feelings in their inmost force—
So thrill'd—so shudder'd every creeping vein,
As now they froze before that purple stain.
That spot of blood, that light but guilty streak,
Had banish'd all the beauty from her cheek!
Blood he had view'd—could view unmoved—but then
It flow'd in combat, or was shed by men!

XI.

« 'T is done—he nearly waked—but it is done.
Corsair! he perish'd—thou art dearly won.
All words would now be vain—away—away!
Our bark is tossing—'t is already day.
The few gain'd over, now are wholly mine,
And these thy yet surviving band shall join:
Anon my voice shall vindicate my hand,
When once our sail forsakes this hated strand.»

XII.

She clapp'd her hands—and through the gallery pour,
Equipp'd for flight, her vassals—Greek and Moor;
Silent but quick they stoop, his chains unbind,
Once more his limbs are free as mountain wind!
But on his heavy heart such sadness sate,
As if they there transferr'd that iron weight.
No words are utter'd—at her sign, a door
Reveals the secret passage to the shore;
The city lies behind—they speed, they reach
The glad waves dancing on the yellow beach;

And Conrad following, at her beck, obey'd,
Nor cared he now if rescued or betray'd;
Resistance were as useless as if Seyd
Yet lived to view the doom his ire decreed.

XIII.

Embark'd, the sail unfurl'd, the light breeze blew—
How much had Conrad's memory to review!
Sunk he in contemplation, till the cape
Where last he anchor'd rear'd its giant shape.
Ah!—since that fatal night, though brief the time,
Had swept an age of terror, grief, and crime.
As its far shadow frown'd above the mast,
He veil'd his face, and sorrow'd as he past;
He thought of all—Gonsalvo and his band,
His fleeting triumph and his failing hand;
He thought on her afar, his lonely bride:
He turn'd and saw—Gulnare, the homicide!

XIV.

She watch'd his features till she could not bear
Their freezing aspect and averted air,
And that strange fierceness foreign to her eye,
Fell quench'd in tears, too late to shed or dry.
She knelt beside him and his hand she prest,
«Thou may'st forgive though Alla's self detest;
But for that deed of darkness what wert thou?
Reproach me—but not yet—oh! spare me *now!*
I am not what I seem—this fearful night
My brain bewilder'd—do not madden quite!
If I had never loved—though less my guilt,
Thou hadst not lived to—hate me—if thou wilt.»

XV.

She wrongs his thoughts, they more himself upbraid
Than her, though undesign'd the wretch he made;
But speechless all, deep, dark, and unexprest,
They bleed within that silent cell—his breast.
Still onward, fair the breeze, nor rough the surge,
The blue waves sport around the stern they urge;
Far on the horizon's verge appears a speck,
A spot—a mast—a sail—an armed deck!
Their little bark her men of watch descry,
And ampler canvass woos the wind from high;
She bears her down majestically near,
Speed on her prow, and terror in her tier;
A flash is seen—the ball beyond their bow
Booms harmless, hissing to the deep below.
Up rose keen Conrad from his silent trance,
A long, long absent gladness in his glance;
« 'T is mine—my blood-red flag! again—again—
I am not all deserted on the main! »
They own the signal, answer to the hail,
Hoist out the boat at once, and slacken sail.
« 'T is Conrad! Conrad! » shouting from the deck,
Command nor duty could their transport check!
With light alacrity and gaze of pride,
They view him mount once more his vessel's side,
A smile relaxing in each rugged face,
Their arms can scarce forbear a rough embrace.
He, half forgetting danger and defeat,
Returns their greeting as a chief may greet,
Wrings with a cordial grasp Anselmo's hand,
And feels he yet can conquer and command!

XVI.

These greetings o'er, the feelings that o'erflow,
Yet grieve to win him back without a blow;
They sail'd prepared for vengeance—had they known
A woman's hand secured that deed her own,
She were their queen—less scrupulous are they
Than haughty Conrad how they win their way.
With many an asking smile, and wondering stare,
They whisper round, and gaze upon Gulnare;
And her, at once above—beneath her sex,
Whom blood appall'd not, their regards perplex.
To Conrad turns her faint imploring eye,
She drops her veil, and stands in silence by;
Her arms are meekly folded on that breast,
Which—Conrad safe—to fate resign'd the rest.
Though worse than phrensy could that bosom fill,
Extreme in love or hate, in good or ill,
The worst of crimes had left her woman still!

XVII.

This Conrad mark'd, and felt—ah! could he less?
Hate of that deed—but grief for her distress;
What she has done no tears can wash away,
And Heaven must punish on its angry day:
But—it was done: he knew, whate'er her guilt,
For him that poniard smote, that blood was spilt;
And he was free!—and she for him had given
Her all on earth, and more than all in heaven!
And now he turn'd him to that dark-eyed slave
Whose brow was bow'd beneath the glance he gave,

Who now seem'd changed and humbled:—faint and meek,
But varying oft the colour of her cheek
To deeper shades of paleness—all its red
That fearful spot which stain'd it from the dead!
He took that hand—it trembled—now too late—
So soft in love—so wildly nerved in hate;
He clasp'd that hand—it trembled—and his own
Had lost its firmness, and his voice its tone.
« Gulnare! »—but she replied not—« dear Gulnare! »
She raised her eye—her only answer there—
At once she sought and sunk in his embrace:
If he had driven her from that resting-place,
His had been more or less than mortal heart,
But—good or ill—it bade her not depart.
Perchance, but for the bodings of his breast,
His latest virtue then had join'd the rest.
Yet e'en Medora might forgive the kiss
That ask'd from form so fair no more than this,
The first, the last that frailty stole from faith—
To lips where love had lavish'd all his breath,
To lips—whose broken sighs such fragrance fling,
As he had fann'd them freshly with his wing!

XVIII.

They gain by twilight's hour their lonely isle.
To them the very rocks appear to smile;
The haven hums with many a cheering sound,
The beacons blaze their wonted stations round,
The boats are darting o'er the curly bay,
And sportive dolphins bend them through the spray;
E'en the hoarse sea-bird's shrill, discordant shriek,
Greets like the welcome of his tuneless beak!

Beneath each lamp that through its lattice gleams,
Their fancy paints the friends that trim the beams.
Oh! what can sanctify the joys of home,
Like hope's gay glance from ocean's troubled foam?

XIX.

The lights are high on beacon and from bower,
And midst them Conrad seeks Medora's tower:
He looks in vain—'t is strange—and all remark,
Amid so many, hers alone is dark.
'Tis strange—of yore its welcome never fail'd,
Nor now, perchance, extinguish'd, only veil'd.
With the first boat descends he for the shore,
And looks impatient on the lingering oar.
Oh! for a wing beyond the falcon's flight,
To bear him like an arrow to that height!
With the first pause the resting rowers gave,
He waits not—looks not—leaps into the wave,
Strives through the surge, bestrides the beach, and high
Ascends the path familiar to his eye.

He reach'd his turret-door—he paused—no sound
Broke from within; and all was night around.
He knock'd, and loudly—footstep nor reply
Announced that any heard or deem'd him nigh;
He knock'd—but faintly—for his trembling hand
Refused to aid his heavy heart's demand.
The portal opens—'tis a well-known face—
But not the form he panted to embrace.
Its lips are silent—twice his own essay'd,
And fail'd to frame the question they delay'd;

He snatch'd the lamp—its light will answer all—
It quits his grasp, expiring in the fall.
He would not wait for that reviving ray—
As soon could he have linger'd there for day;
But, glimmering through the dusky corridor,
Another chequers o'er the shadow'd floor;
His steps the chamber gain—his eyes behold
All that his heart believed not—yet foretold!

XX.

He turn'd not—spoke not—sunk not—fix'd his look,
And set the anxious frame that lately shook:
He gazed—how long we gaze despite of pain,
And know, but dare not own, we gaze in vain?
In life itself she was so still and fair,
That death with gentler aspect wither'd there;
And the cold flowers[6] her colder hand contain'd,
In that last grasp as tenderly were strain'd
As if she scarcely felt, but feign'd a sleep,
And made it almost mockery yet to weep:
The long dark lashes fringed her lids of snow,
And veil'd—thought shrinks from all that lurk'd below—
Oh! o'er the eye death most exerts his might,
And hurls the spirit from her throne of light!
Sinks those blue orbs in that long, last eclipse,
But spares, as yet, the charm around her lips—
Yet, yet they seem as they forbore to smile,
And wish'd repose—but only for a while;
But the white shroud, and each extended tress,
Long—fair—but spread in utter lifelessness,
Which, late the sport of every summer wind,
Escaped the baffled wreath that strove to bind;

These—and the pale pure cheek, became the bier—
But she is nothing—wherefore is he here?

XXI.

He ask'd no question—all were answer'd now
By the first glance on that still—marble brow.
It was enough—she died—what reck'd it how?
The love of youth, the hope of better years,
The source of softest wishes, tenderest fears,
The only living thing he could not hate,
Was reft at once—and he deserved his fate,
But did not feel it less;—the good explore,
For peace, those realms where guilt can never soar:
The proud—the wayward—who have fix'd below
Their joy—and find this earth enough for woe,
Lose in that one their all—perchance a mite—
But who in patience parts with all delight?
Full many a stoic eye and aspect stern
Mask hearts where grief hath little left to learn;
And many a withering thought lies hid, not lost,
In smiles that least befit who wear them most.

XXII.

By those, that deepest feel, is ill exprest
The indistinctness of the suffering breast;
Where thousand thoughts begin to end in one,
Which seeks from all the refuge found in none;
No words suffice the secret soul to show,
For truth denies all eloquence to woe.
On Conrad's stricken soul exhaustion prest,
And stupor almost lull'd it into rest;

So feeble now—his mother's softness crept
To those wild eyes, which like an infant's wept:
It was the very weakness of his brain,
Which thus confess'd without relieving pain.
None saw his trickling tears—perchance, if seen,
That useless flood of grief had never been:
Nor long they flow'd—he dried them to depart,
In helpless—hopeless—brokenness of heart:
The sun goes forth—but Conrad's day is dim;
And the night cometh—ne'er to pass from him.
There is no darkness like the cloud of mind,
On grief's vain eye—the blindest of the blind!
Which may not—dare not see—but turns aside
To blackest shade—nor will endure a guide!

XXIII.

His heart was form'd for softness—warp'd to wrong;
Betray'd too early, and beguiled too long;
Each feeling pure—as falls the dropping dew
Within the grot; like that had harden'd too;
Less clear, perchance, its earthly trials pass'd,
But sunk, and chill'd, and petrified at last.
Yet tempests wear, and lightning cleaves the rock;
If such his heart, so shatter'd is the shock.
There grew one flower beneath its rugged brow,
Though dark the shade—it shelter'd—saved till now,
The thunder came—that bolt hath blasted both,
The granite's firmness, and the lily's growth:
The gentle plant hath left no leaf to tell
Its tale, but shrunk and wither'd where it fell,
And of its cold protector, blacken round
But shiver'd fragments on the barren ground!

XXIV.

'T is morn—to venture on his lonely hour
Few dare; though now Anselmo sought his tower.
He was not there—nor seen along the shore;
Ere night, alarm'd, their isle is traversed o'er:
Another morn—another bids them seek,
And shout his name till echo waxeth weak;
Mount—grotto—cavern—valley search'd in vain,
They find on shore a sea-boat's broken chain:
Their hope revives—they follow o'er the main.
'Tis idle all—moons roll on moons away,
And Conrad comes not—came not since that day:
Nor trace, nor tidings of his doom declare
Where lives his grief, or perish'd his despair;
Long mourn'd his band whom none could mourn beside;
And fair the monument they gave his bride:
For him they raise not the recording stone—
His death yet dubious, deeds too widely known;
He left a corsair's name to other times,
Link'd with one virtue, and a thousand crimes.[7]

NOTES TO CANTO III.

Note 1, page 248, line 8.

That closed their murder'd sage's latest day!

Socrates drank the hemlock a short time before sunset (the hour of execution), notwithstanding the entreaties of his disciples to wait till the sun went down.

Note 2, page 248, line 20.

The queen of night asserts her silent reign.

The twilight in Greece is much shorter than in our own country; the days in winter are longer, but in summer of shorter duration.

Note 3, page 248, line 30.

The gleaming turret of the gay kiosk, *etc.*

The kiosk is a Turkish summer-house: the palm is without the present walls of Athens, not far from the Temple of Theseus, between which and the tree the wall intervenes.--Cephisus' stream is indeed scanty, and Ilissus has no stream at all.

Note 4, page 249, line 10.

That frown—where gentler ocean seems to smile.

The opening lines as far as section II. have, perhaps, little business here, and were annexed to an unpublished (though printed) poem;

but they were written on the spot in the spring of 1811, and—I scarce know why—the reader must excuse their appearance here if he can.

Note 5, page 252, line 14.

His only bends in seeming o'er his beads, etc.

The comboloio, or Mahometan rosary; the beads are in number ninety-nine.

Note 6, page 268, line 16.

And the cold flowers her colder hand contain'd, *etc.*

In the Levant it is the custom to strew flowers on the bodies of the dead, and in the hands of young persons to place a nosegay.

Note 7, page 271, last line.

Link'd with one virtue, and a thousand crimes.

That the point of honour which is represented in one instance of Conrad's character has not been carried beyond the bounds of probability, may, perhaps, be in some degree confirmed by the following anecdote of a brother buccaneer in the year 1814.

Our readers have all seen the account of the enterprise against the pirates of Barrataria; but few, we believe, were informed of the situation, history, or nature of that establishment. For the information of such as were unacquainted with it, we have procured from a friend the following interesting narrative of the main facts, of which he has personal knowledge, and which cannot fail to interest some of our readers.

Barrataria is a bay, or a narrow arm of the Gulf of Mexico: it runs through a rich but very flat country, until it reaches within a mile of the Mississippi river, fifteen miles below the city of New-Orleans. The bay has branches almost innumerable, in which persons can lie concealed from the severest scrutiny. It communicates with three lakes which lie on the south-west side, and these with the lake of the same name, and which lies contiguous to the sea, where there is an island formed by the two arms of this lake and the sea. The east and west points of this island were fortified in the year 1811, by a band of pirates, under the command of one Monsieur La Fitte. A large majority of these outlaws are of that class of the population of the state of Louisiana who fled from the island of St Domingo during the troubles there, and took refuge in the island of Cuba: and when the last war between France and Spain commenced, they were compelled to leave that island with the short notice of a few days. Without ceremony they entered the United States, the most of them the state of Louisiana, with all the negroes they had possessed in Cuba. They were notified by the governor of that state of the clause in the constitution which forbade the importation of slaves; but, at the same time, received the assurance of the governor that he would obtain, if possible, the approbation of the general government for their retaining this property.

The Island of Barrataria is situated about lat. 29 deg. 15 min. lon. 92 30. and is as remarkable for its health as for the superior scale and shell-fish with which its waters abound. The chief of this horde, like Charles de Moor, had mixed with his many vices some virtues. In the year 1813, this party had, from its turpitude and boldness, claimed the attention of the governor of Louisiana; and to break up the establishment, he thought proper to strike at the head. He therefore offered a reward of 500 dollars for the head of Monsieur La Fitte, who was well known to the inhabitants of the city of New-Orleans, from his immediate connexion, and his once having been a fencing-master in that city, of great reputation, which art he learnt in Buonaparte's army, where he was a captain. The reward which was offered by the governor for the head of La Fitte was answered by the offer of a reward from the latter of 15,000 for the head of the governor. The governor ordered out a company to march from the city to La Fitte's island, and to burn and destroy all the property, and to bring to the city of New-Orleans all his banditti. This company, under the command of a man who had been the intimate associate of this bold captain, approached very near to the fortified island, before he saw a man, or heard a sound, until he heard a whistle, not unlike a boatswain's call. Then it was he found himself surrounded by armed men who had emerged from the secret avenues which led into Bayou. Here it was that the modern Charles de Moor developed his few noble traits; for to this man, who had come to destroy his life and all that was dear to him, he not only spared his life, but offered him that which would have made the honest soldier easy for the remainder of his days, which was indignantly refused. He then, with the approbation of his captor, returned to the city. This circumstance, and some concomitant events, proved that this band of pirates was not to be taken by land. Our naval force having always been small

18.

in that quarter, exertions for the destruction of this illicit establishment could not be expected from them until augmented; for an officer of the navy, with most of the gun-boats on that station, had to retreat from an overwhelming force of La Fitte's. So soon as the augmentation of the navy authorised an attack, one was made; the overthrow of this banditti has been the result, and now this almost invulnerable point and key to New-Orleans is clear of an enemy, it is to be hoped the government will hold it by a strong military force. — *From an American Newspaper.*

In Noble's continuation of Granger's Biographical Dictionary, there is a singular passage in his account of Archbishop Blackbourne, and as in some measure connected with the profession of the hero of the foregoing poem, I cannot resist the temptation of extracting it.

« There is something mysterious in the history and character of Dr Blackbourne. The former is but imperfectly known; and report has even asserted he was a buccaneer; and that one of his brethren in that profession having asked, on his arrival in England, what had become of his old chum, Blackbourne, was answered, he is archbishop of York. We are informed, that Blackbourne was installed sub-dean of Exeter, in 1694, which office he resigned in 1702; but after his successor, Lewis Barnet's death, in 1704, he regained it. In the following year he became dean; and, in 1714, held with it the archdeanery of Cornwall. He was consecrated bishop of Exeter, February 24, 1716; and translated to York, November 28, 1724, as a reward, according to court scandal, for uniting George I. to the Duchess of Munster. This, however, appears to have been an unfounded calumny. As archbishop he behaved with great prudence, and was equally respectable as the guardian of the revenues of the see. Rumour whispered he retained the vices of his youth, and that a passion for the fair sex formed an item in the list of his weaknesses; but so far from being convicted by seventy witnesses, he does not appear to have been directly criminated by one. In short, I look upon these aspersions as the effects of mere malice. How is it possible a buccaneer should have been so good a scholar as Blackbourne certainly was? he who had so perfect a knowledge of the classics (particularly of the Greek tragedians), as to be able to read them with the same ease as he could Shakspeare, must have taken great pains to acquire the learned languages; and have had both leisure and good masters.

But he was undoubtedly educated at Christ-church College, Oxford. He is allowed to have been a pleasant man: this, however, was turned against him, by its being said, 'he gained more hearts than souls.'"

"The only voice that could soothe the passions of the savage (Alphonso III.) was that of an amiable and virtuous wife, the sole object of his love; the voice of Donna Isabella, the daughter of the Duke of Savoy, and the grand-daughter of Philip II. King of Spain. —Her dying words sunk deep into his memory; his fierce spirit melted into tears; and, after the last embrace, Alphonso retired into his chamber to bewail his irreparable loss, and to meditate on the vanity of human life."—*Miscellaneous Works of Gibbon, New Edition*, 8vo. vol. 3, page 473.

LARA.

A TALE.

LARA.

CANTO I.

I.

The serfs are glad through Lara's wide domain,
And slavery half forgets her feudal chain;
He, their unhoped, but unforgotten lord,
The long self-exiled chieftain is restored:
There be bright faces in the busy hall,
Bowls on the board, and banners on the wall;
Far checkering o'er the pictured window, plays
The unwonted faggots' hospitable blaze;
And gay retainers gather round the hearth,
With tongues all loudness, and with eyes all mirth.

II.

The chief of Lara is return'd again:
And why had Lara cross'd the bounding main?
Left by his sire, too young such loss to know,
Lord of himself;—that heritage of woe,
That fearful empire which the human breast
But holds to rob the heart within of rest!—

With none to check, and few to point in time
The thousand paths that slope the way to crime;
Then, when he most required commandment, then
Had Lara's daring boyhood govern'd men.
It skills not, boots not step by step to trace
His youth through all the mazes of its race;
Short was the course his restlessness had run,
But long enough to leave him half undone.

III.

And Lara left in youth his father-land;
But from the hour he waved his parting hand
Each trace wax'd fainter of his course, till all
Had nearly ceased his memory to recall.
His sire was dust, his vassals could declare,
'T was all they knew, that Lara was not there;
Nor sent, nor came he, till conjecture grew
Cold in the many, anxious in the few.
His hall scarce echoes with his wonted name,
His portrait darkens in its fading frame,
Another chief consoled his destined bride,
The young forgot him, and the old had died;
« Yet doth he live! » exclaims the impatient heir,
And sighs for sables which he must not wear.
A hundred scutcheons deck with gloomy grace
The Laras' last and longest dwelling-place;
But one is absent from the mouldering file,
That now were welcome in that gothic pile.

IV.

He comes at last in sudden loneliness,
And whence they know not, why they need not guess;

They more might marvel, when the greeting's o'er,
Not that he came, but came not long before:
No train is his beyond a single page,
Of foreign aspect, and of tender age.
Years had roll'd on, and fast they speed away
To those that wander as to those that stay;
But lack of tidings from another clime
Had lent a flagging wing to weary time.
They see, they recognise, yet almost deem
The present dubious, or the past a dream.

He lives, nor yet is past his manhood's prime,
Though sear'd by toil, and something touch'd by time;
His faults, whate'er they were, if scarce forgot,
Might be untaught him by his varied lot;
Nor good nor ill of late were known, his name
Might yet uphold his patrimonial fame:
His soul in youth was haughty, but his sins
No more than pleasure from the stripling wins;
And such, if not yet harden'd in their course,
Might be redeem'd, nor ask a long remorse.

V.

And they indeed were changed—'t is quickly seen
Whate'er he be, 't was not what he had been:
That brow in furrow'd lines had fix'd at last,
And spake of passions, but of passions past:
The pride, but not the fire, of early days,
Coldness of mien, and carelessness of praise;
A high demeanour, and a glance that took
Their thoughts from others by a single look;

And that sarcastic levity of tongue,
The stinging of a heart the world hath stung,
That darts in seeming playfulness around,
And makes those feel that will not own the wound;
All these seem'd his, and something more beneath,
Than glance could well reveal, or accent breathe.
Ambition, glory, love, the common aim,
That some can conquer, and that all would claim,
Within his breast appear'd no more to strive,
Yet seem'd as lately they had been alive;
And some deep feeling it were vain to trace
At moments lighten'd o'er his livid face.

VI.

Not much he loved long question of the past,
Nor told of wondrous wilds, and deserts vast,
In those far lands where he had wander'd lone,
And—as himself would have it seem—unknown:
Yet these in vain his eye could scarcely scan,
Nor glean experience from his fellow man;
But what he had beheld he shunn'd to show,
As hardly worth a stranger's care to know;
If still more prying such inquiry grew,
His brow fell darker, and his words more few.

VII.

Not unrejoiced to see him once again,
Warm was his welcome to the haunts of men;
Born of high lineage, link'd in high command,
He mingled with the magnates of his land;
Join'd the carousals of the great and gay,
And saw them smile or sigh their hours away;

But still he only saw, and did not share
The common pleasure or the general care;
He did not follow what they all pursued
With hope still baffled still to be renew'd;
Nor shadowy honour, nor substantial gain,
Nor beauty's preference, and the rival's pain:
Around him some mysterious circle thrown
Repell'd approach, and show'd him still alone;
Upon his eye sate something of reproof,
That kept at least frivolity aloof;
And things more timid that beheld him near,
In silence gazed, or whisper'd mutual fear;
And they the wiser, friendlier few confest
They deem'd him better than his air exprest.

VIII.

'T was strange—in youth all action and all life,
Burning for pleasure, not averse from strife;
Woman—the field—the ocean—all that gave
Promise of gladness, peril of a grave,
In turn he tried—he ransack'd all below,
And found his recompense in joy or woe,
No tame, trite medium; for his feelings sought
In that intenseness an escape from thought:
The tempest of his heart in scorn had gazed
On that the feebler elements had raised;
The rapture of his heart had look'd on high,
And ask'd if greater dwelt beyond the sky:
Chain'd to excess, the slave of each extreme,
How woke he from the wildness of that dream?
Alas! he told not—but he did awake
To curse the wither'd heart that would not break.

IX.

Books, for his volume heretofore was man,
With eye more curious he appear'd to scan,
And oft, in sudden mood, for many a day
From all communion he would start away:
And then, his rarely call'd attendants said,
Through night's long hours would sound his hurried tread
O'er the dark gallery, where his fathers frown'd
In rude but antique portraiture around:
They heard, but whisper'd—« *that* must not be known—
The sound of words less earthly than his own.
Yes, they who chose might smile, but some had seen
They scarce knew what, but more than should have been.
Why gazed he so upon the ghastly head
Which hands profane had gather'd from the dead,
That still beside his open'd volume lay,
As if to startle all save him away?
Why slept he not when others were at rest?
Why heard no music, and received no guest?
All was not well they deem'd—but where the wrong?
Some knew perchance—but 't were a tale too long;
And such besides were too discreetly wise,
To more than hint their knowledge in surmise;
But if they would—they could »—around the board,
Thus Lara's vassals prattled of their lord.

X.

It was the night, and Lara's glassy stream
The stars are studding, each with imaged beam:
So calm, the waters scarcely seem to stray,
And yet they glide like happiness away;

Reflecting far and fairy-like from high
The immortal lights that live along the sky:
Its banks are fringed with many a goodly tree,
And flowers the fairest that may feast the bee;
Such in her chaplet infant Dian wove,
And innocence would offer to her love.
These deck the shore; the waves their channel make
In windings bright and mazy like the snake.
All was so still, so soft in earth and air,
You scarce would start to meet a spirit there;
Secure that nought of evil could delight
To walk in such a scene, on such a night!
It was a moment only for the good:
So Lara deem'd, nor longer there he stood,
But turn'd in silence to his castle-gate;
Such scene his soul no more could contemplate:
Such scene reminded him of other days,
Of skies more cloudless, moons of purer blaze,
Of nights more soft and frequent, hearts that now—
No—no—the storm may beat upon his brow,
Unfelt— unsparing—but a night like this,
A night of beauty, mock'd such breast as his.

XI.

He turn'd within his solitary hall,
And his high shadow shot along the wall;
There were the painted forms of other times,
'T was all they left of virtues or of crimes,
Save vague tradition; and the gloomy vaults
That hid their dust, their foibles, and their faults,
And half a column of the pompous page,
That speeds the specious tale from age to age;

Where history's pen its praise or blame supplies,
And lies like truth, and still most truly lies.
He wandering mused, and as the moon-beam shone
Through the dim lattice o'er the floor of stone,
And the high fretted roof, and saints, that there
O'er gothic windows knelt in pictured prayer,
Reflected in fantastic figures grew,
Like life, but not like mortal life, to view;
His bristling locks of sable, brow of gloom,
And the wide waving of his shaken plume,
Glanced like a spectre's attributes, and gave
His aspect all that terror gives the grave.

XII.

'T was midnight—all was slumber; the lone light
Dimm'd in the lamp, as loth to break the night.
Hark! there be murmurs heard in Lara's hall—
A sound—a voice—a shriek—a fearful call!
A long, loud shriek—and silence—did they hear
That frantic echo burst the sleeping ear?
They heard and rose, and, tremulously brave,
Rush where the sound invoked their aid to save;
They come with half-lit tapers in their hands,
And snatch'd in startled haste unbelted brands.

XIII.

Cold as the marble where his length was laid,
Pale as the beam that o'er his features play'd,
Was Lara stretch'd; his half-drawn sabre near,
Dropp'd it should seem in more than nature's fear;
Yet he was firm, or had been firm till now,
And still defiance knit his gather'd brow;

Though mix'd with terror, senseless as he lay,
There lived upon his lip the wish to slay;
Some half-form'd threat in utterance there had died,
Some imprecation of despairing pride;
His eye was almost seal'd, but not forsook,
E'en in its trance, the gladiator's look,
That oft awake his aspect could disclose,
And now was fix'd in horrible repose.
They raise him—bear him;—hush! he breathes, he speaks,
The swarthy blush recolours in his cheeks,
His lip resumes its red, his eye, though dim,
Rolls wide and wild, each slowly quivering limb
Recalls its function, but his words are strung
In terms that seem not of his native tongue;
Distinct but strange, enough they understand
To deem them accents of another land,
And such they were, and meant to meet an ear
That hears him not—alas! that cannot hear!

XIV.

His page approach'd, and he alone appear'd
To know the import of the words they heard;
And, by the changes of his cheek and brow,
They were not such as Lara should avow,
Nor he interpret, yet with less surprise
Than those around their chieftain's state he eyes.
But Lara's prostrate form he bent beside,
And in that tongue which seem'd his own replied,
And Lara heeds those tones that gently seem
To soothe away the horrors of his dream;
If dream it were, that thus could overthrow
A breast that needed not ideal woe.

XV.

Whate'er his phrensy dream'd or eye beheld,
If yet remember'd ne'er to be reveal'd,
Rests at his heart: the custom'd morning came,
And breathed new vigour in his shaken frame;
And solace sought he none from priest nor leech,
And soon the same in movement and in speech
As heretofore he fill'd the passing hours,
Nor less he smiles, nor more his forehead lours
Than these were wont; and if the coming night
Appear'd less welcome now to Lara's sight,
He to his marvelling vassals show'd it not,
Whose shuddering proved *their* fear was less forgot,
In trembling pairs (alone they dared not) crawl
The astonish'd slaves, and shun the fated hall;
The waving banner, and the clapping door,
The rustling tapestry, and the echoing floor;
The long dim shadows of surrounding trees,
The flapping bat, the night-song of the breeze;
Aught they behold or hear their thought appals,
As evening saddens o'er the dark gray walls.

XVI.

Vain thought! that hour of ne'er unravell'd gloom
Came not again, or Lara could assume
A seeming of forgetfulness, that made
His vassals more amazed nor less afraid—
Had memory vanish'd then with sense restored?
Since word, nor look, nor gesture of their lord
Betray'd a feeling that recall'd to these
That fever'd moment of his mind's disease.

Was it a dream? was his the voice that spoke
Those strange wild accents; his the cry that broke
Their slumber? his the oppress'd o'erlabour'd heart
That ceased to beat, the look that made them start?
Could he, who thus had suffer'd, so forget,
When such as saw that suffering shudder yet?
Or did that silence prove his memory fix'd
Too deep for words, indelible, unmix'd
In that corroding secrecy which gnaws
The heart to show the effect, but not the cause?
Not so in him; his breast had buried both,
Nor common gazers could discern the growth
Of thoughts that mortal lips must leave half told;
They choke the feeble words that would unfold.

XVII.

In him, inexplicably mix'd, appear'd
Much to be loved and hated, sought and fear'd;
Opinion varying o'er his hidden lot,
In praise or railing ne'er his name forgot;
His silence form'd a theme for others' prate—
They guess'd—they gazed—they fain would know his fate.
What had he been? what was he, thus unknown,
Who walk'd their world, his lineage only known?
A hater of his kind? yet some would say,
With them he could seem gay amidst the gay;
But own'd, that smile if oft observed and near,
Waned in its mirth, and wither'd to a sneer;
That smile might reach his lip, but pass'd not by,
None e'er could trace its laughter to his eye:
Yet there was softness too in his regard,
At times, a heart as not by nature hard,

But once perceived, his spirit seem'd to chide
Such weakness, as unworthy of its pride,
And steel'd itself, as scorning to redeem
One doubt from others' half withheld esteem;
In self-inflicted penance of a breast
Which tenderness might once have wrung from rest;
In vigilance of grief that would compel
The soul to hate for having loved too well.

XVIII.

There was in him a vital scorn of all:
As if the worst had fall'n which could befall,
He stood a stranger in this breathing world,
An erring spirit from another hurl'd;
A thing of dark imaginings, that shaped
By choice the perils he by chance escaped;
But 'scaped in vain, for in their memory yet
His mind would half exult and half regret:
With more capacity for love than earth
Bestows on most of mortal mould and birth,
His early dreams of good outstripp'd the truth,
And troubled manhood follow'd baffled youth;
With thought of years in phantom chase mispent,
And wasted powers for better purpose lent;
And fiery passions that had pour'd their wrath
In hurried desolation o'er his path,
And left the better feelings all at strife
In wild reflection o'er his stormy life;
But haughty still, and loth himself to blame,
He call'd on nature's self to share the shame,
And charged all faults upon the fleshly form
She gave to clog the soul, and feast the worm;

Till he at last confounded good and ill,
And half mistook for fate the acts of will:
Too high for common selfishness, he could
At times resign his own for others' good,
But not in pity, not because he ought,
But in some strange perversity of thought,
That sway'd him onward with a secret pride
To do what few or none would do beside;
And this same impulse would, in tempting time,
Mislead his spirit equally to crime;
So much he soar'd beyond, or sunk beneath
The men with whom he felt condemn'd to breathe,
And long'd by good or ill to separate
Himself from all who shared his mortal state;
His mind abhorring this had fix'd her throne
Far from the world, in regions of her own:
Thus coldly passing all that pass'd below,
His blood in temperate seeming now would flow:
Ah! happier if it ne'er with guilt had glow'd,
But ever in that icy smoothness flow'd!
'T is true, with other men their path he walk'd,
And like the rest in seeming did and talk'd,
Nor outraged reason's rules by flaw nor start,
His madness was not of the head, but heart;
And rarely wander'd in his speech, or drew
His thoughts so forth as to offend the view.

XIX.

With all that chilling mystery of mien,
And seeming gladness to remain unseen,
He had (if 't were not nature's boon) an art
Of fixing memory on another's heart:

It was not love perchance—nor hate—nor aught
That words can image to express the thought;
But they who saw him did not see in vain,
And once beheld, would ask of him again:
And those to whom he spake remember'd well,
And on the words, however light, would dwell:
None knew, nor how, nor why, but he entwined
Himself perforce around the hearer's mind;
There he was stamp'd, in liking, or in hate,
If greeted once; however brief the date
That friendship, pity, or aversion knew,
Still there within the inmost thought he grew.
You could not penetrate his soul, but found,
Despite your wonder, to your own he wound;
His presence haunted still; and from the breast
He forced an all-unwilling interest:
Vain was the struggle in that mental net,
His spirit seem'd to dare you to forget!

XX.

There is a festival, where knights and dames,
And aught that wealth or lofty lineage claims
Appear—a high-born and a welcome guest
To Otho's hall came Lara with the rest.
The long carousal shakes the illumined hall,
Well speeds alike the banquet and the ball;
And the gay dance of bounding beauty's train
Links grace and harmony in happiest chain:
Blest are the early hearts and gentle hands
That mingle there in well according bands;
It is a sight the careful brow might smooth,
And make age smile, and dream itself to youth,

And youth forget such hour was past on earth,
So springs the exulting bosom to that mirth!

XXI.

And Lara gazed on these, sedately glad,
His brow belied him if his soul was sad;
And his glance follow'd fast each fluttering fair,
Whose steps of lightness woke no echo there:
He lean'd against the lofty pillar nigh,
With folded arms and long attentive eye,
Nor mark'd a glance so sternly fix'd on his—
Ill brook'd high Lara scrutiny like this:
At length he caught it, 't is a face unknown,
But seems as searching his, and his alone;
Prying and dark, a stranger's by his mien,
Who still till now had gazed on him unseen:
At length encountering meets the mutual gaze
Of keen inquiry, and of mute amaze;
On Lara's glance emotion gathering grew,
As if distrusting that the stranger threw;
Along the stranger's aspect fix'd and stern,
Flash'd more than thence the vulgar eye could learn.

XXII.

«'T is he!» the stranger cried, and those that heard
Re-echoed fast and far the whisper'd word.
«'T is he!»—«'T is who?» they question far and near,
Till louders accents rung on Lara's ear;
So widely spread, few bosoms well could brook
The general marvel, or that single look;
But Lara stirr'd not, changed not, the surprise
That sprung at first to his arrested eyes

Seem'd now subsided, neither sunk nor raised
Glanced his eye round, though still the stranger gazed;
And drawing nigh, exclaim'd, with haughty sneer,
«'T is he!—how came he thence?—what doth he here?»

XXIII.

It were too much for Lara to pass by
Such question, so repeated fierce and high;
With look collected, but with accent cold,
More mildly firm than petulantly bold,
He turn'd, and met the inquisitorial tone—
«My name is Lara!—when thine own is known,
Doubt not my fitting answer to requite
The unlook'd for courtesy of such a knight.
'T is Lara!—further wouldst thou mark or ask?
I shun no question, and I wear no mask.»

«Thou shunn'st no question! Ponder—is there none
Thy heart must answer, though thine ear would shun?
And deem'st thou me unknown too! Gaze again!
At least thy memory was not given in vain.
Oh! never canst thou cancel half her debt,
Eternity forbids thee to forget.»
With slow and searching glance upon his face
Grew Lara's eyes, but nothing there could trace
They knew, or chose to know—with dubious look
He deign'd no answer, but his head he shook,
And half contemptuous turn'd to pass away;
But the stern stranger motion'd him to stay.
«A word!—I charge thee stay, and answer here
To one, who, wert thou noble, were thy peer,

But as thou wast and art—nay, frown not, lord,
If false, 't is easy to disprove the word—
But, as thou wast and art, on thee looks down,
Distrusts thy smiles, but shakes not at thy frown.
Art thou not he? whose deeds——»

«Whate'er I be,
Words wild as these, accusers like to thee
I list no further; those with whom they weigh
May hear the rest, nor venture to gainsay
The wondrous tale no doubt thy tongue can tell,
Which thus begins so courteously and well.
Let Otho cherish here his polish'd guest,
To him my thanks and thoughts shall be exprest.»
And here their wondering host hath interposed—
« Whate'er there be between you undisclosed,
This is no time nor fitting place to mar
The mirthful meeting with a wordy war.
If thou, Sir Ezzelin, hast ought to show
Which it befits Count Lara's ear to know,
To-morrow, here, or elsewhere, as may best
Beseem your mutual judgment, speak the rest;
I pledge myself for thee, as not unknown,
Though like Count Lara now return'd alone
From other lands, almost a stranger grown;
And if from Lara's blood and gentle birth
I augur right of courage and of worth,
He will not that untainted line belie,
Nor aught that knighthood may accord, deny.»

«To-morrow be it,» Ezzelin replied,
« And here our several worth and truth be tried;

I gage my life; my falchion to attest
My words, so may I mingle with the blest!»
What answers Lara? to its centre shrunk
His soul, in deep abstraction sudden sunk;
The words of many, and the eyes of all
That there were gather'd, seem'd on him to fall;
But his were silent, his appear'd to stray
In far forgetfulness away—away—
Alas! that heedlessness of all around
Bespoke remembrance only too profound.

XXIV.

«To-morrow!—ay, to-morrow!» further word
Than those repeated none from Lara heard;
Upon his brow no outward passion spoke,
From his large eye no flashing anger broke;
Yet there was something fix'd in that low tone,
Which show'd resolve, determined, though unknown.
He seized his cloak—his head he slightly bow'd,
And, passing Ezzelin, he left the crowd;
And, as he pass'd him, smiling met the frown
With which that chieftain's brow would bear him down:
It was nor smile of mirth, nor struggling pride
That curbs to scorn the wrath it cannot hide;
But that of one in his own heart secure
Of all that he would do, or could endure.
Could this mean peace? the calmness of the good?
Or guilt grown old in desperate hardihood?
Alas! too like in confidence are each,
For man to trust to mortal look or speech;
From deeds, and deeds alone, may he discern
Truths which it wrings the unpractised heart to learn.

XXV.

And Lara call'd his page, and went his way—
Well could that stripling word or sign obey:
His only follower from those climes afar,
Where the soul glows beneath a brighter star;
For Lara left the shore from whence he sprung,
In duty patient, and sedate though young;
Silent as him he served, his faith appears
Above his station, and beyond his years.
Though not unknown the tongue of Lara's land,
In such from him he rarely heard command;
But fleet his step, and clear his tones would come,
When Lara's lip breathed forth the words of home:
Those accents as his native mountains dear,
Awake their absent echoes in his ear,
Friends', kindred's, parents', wonted voice recall,
Now lost, abjured, for one—his friend, his all:
For him earth now disclosed no other guide;
What marvel then he rarely left his side?

XXVI.

Light was his form, and darkly delicate
That brow whereon his native sun had sate,
But had not marr'd, though in his beams he grew,
The cheek where oft the unbidden blush shone through;
Yet not such blush as mounts when health would show
All the heart's hue in that delighted glow;
But 't was a hectic tint of secret care
That for a burning moment fever'd there;
And the wild sparkle of his eye seem'd caught
From high, and lighten'd with electric thought,

Though its black orb those long low lashes fringe,
Had temper'd with a melancholy tinge;
Yet less of sorrow than of pride was there,
Or if 't were grief, a grief that none should share:
And pleased not him the sports that please his age,
The tricks of youth, the frolics of the page;
For hours on Lara he would fix his glance,
As all-forgotten in that watchful trance;
And from his chief withdrawn, he wander'd lone,
Brief were his answers, and his questions none;
His walk the wood, his sport some foreign book;
His resting-place the bank that curbs the brook:
He seem'd, like him he served, to live apart
From all that lures the eye, and fills the heart;
To know no brotherhood, and take from earth
No gift beyond that bitter boon—our birth.

XXVII.

If aught he loved, 'twas Lara; but was shown
His faith in reverence and in deeds alone;
In mute attention; and his care, which guess'd
Each wish, fulfill'd it ere the tongue express'd.
Still there was haughtiness in all he did,
A spirit deep that brook'd not to be chid;
His zeal, though more than that of servile hands,
In act alone obeys, his air commands;
As if 't was Lara's less than *his* desire
That thus he served, but surely not for hire.
Slight were the tasks enjoin'd him by his lord,
To hold the stirrup, or to bear the sword;
To tune his lute, or if he will'd it more,
On tomes of other times and tongues to pore;

But ne'er to mingle with the menial train,
To whom he show'd nor deference nor disdain,
But that well-worn reserve which proved he knew
No sympathy with that familiar crew:
His soul, whate'er his station or his stem,
Could bow to Lara, not descend to them.
Of higher birth he seem'd, and better days,
Nor mark of vulgar toil that hand betrays,
So femininely white it might bespeak
Another sex, when match'd with that smooth cheek,
But for his garb, and something in his gaze,
More wild and high than woman's eye betrays;
A latent fierceness that far more became
His fiery climate than his tender frame:
True, in his words it broke not from his breast,
But from his aspect might be more than guess'd.
Kaled his name, though rumour said he bore
Another ere he left his mountain-shore;
For sometimes he would hear, however nigh,
That name repeated loud without reply,
As unfamiliar, or, if roused again,
Start to the sound, as but remember'd then;
Unless 't was Lara's wonted voice that spake,
For then, ear, eyes, and heart would all awake.

XXVIII.

He had look'd down upon the festive hall,
And mark'd that sudden strife so mark'd of all;
And when the crowd around and near him told
Their wonder at the calmness of the bold,
Their marvel how the high-born Lara bore
Such insult, from a stranger doubly sore,

The colour of young Kaled went and came,
The lip of ashes, and the cheek of flame;
And o'er his brow the dampening heart-drops threw
The sickening iciness of that cold dew,
That rises as the busy bosom sinks
With heavy thoughts from which reflection shrinks.
Yes—there be things that we must dream and dare,
And execute ere thought be half aware;
Whate'er might Kaled's be, it was enow
To seal his lip, but agonise his brow.
He gazed on Ezzelin till Lara cast
That sidelong smile upon the knight he past;
When Kaled saw that smile his visage fell,
As if on something recognised right well;
His memory read in such a meaning more
Than Lara's aspect unto others wore;
Forward he sprung—a moment, both were gone,
And all within that hall seem'd left alone;
Each had so fix'd his eye on Lara's mien,
All had so mix'd their feelings with that scene,
That when his long dark shadow through the porch
No more relieves the glare of yon high torch,
Each pulse beats quicker, and all bosoms seem
To bound as doubting from too black a dream,
Such as we know is false, yet dread in sooth,
Because the worst is ever nearest truth.
And they are gone—but Ezzelin is there,
With thoughtful visage and imperious air;
But long remain'd not; ere an hour expired
He waved his hand to Otho, and retired.

XXIX.

The crowd are gone, the revellers at rest;
The courteous host, and all-approving guest,
Again to that accustom'd couch must creep
Where joy subsides, and sorrow sighs to sleep,
And man, o'erlabour'd with his being's strife,
Shrinks to that sweet forgetfulness of life:
There lie love's feverish hope, and cunning's guile,
Hate's working brain, and lull'd ambition's wile;
O'er each vain eye oblivion's pinions wave,
And quench'd existence crouches in a grave.
What better name may slumber's bed become?
Night's sepulchre, the universal home,
Where weakness, strength, vice, virtue, sunk supine,
Alike in naked helplessness recline;
Glad for awhile to heave unconscious breath,
Yet wake to wrestle with the dread of death,
And shun, though day but dawn on ills increas'd,
That sleep, the loveliest, since it dreams the least.

LARA.

CANTO II.

I.

NIGHT wanes—the vapours round the mountains curl'd
Melt into morn, and light awakes the world.
Man has another day to swell the past,
And lead him near to little, but his last;
But mighty nature bounds as from her birth,
The sun is in the heavens, and life on earth;
Flowers in the valley, splendour in the beam,
Health on the gale, and freshness in the stream.
Immortal man! behold her glories shine,
And cry, exulting inly, « they are thine! »
Gaze on, while yet thy gladden'd eye may see;
A morrow comes when they are not for thee:
And grieve what may above thy senseless bier,
Nor earth nor sky will yield a single tear;

Nor cloud shall gather more, nor leaf shall fall,
Nor gale breathe forth one sigh for thee, for all;
But creeping things shall revel in their spoil,
And fit thy clay to fertilize the soil.

II.

'T is morn—'t is noon—assembled in the hall,
The gather'd chieftains come to Otho's call;
'T is now the promised hour, that must proclaim
The life or death of Lara's future fame;
When Ezzelin his charge may here unfold,
And whatsoe'er the tale, it must be told.
His faith was pledged, and Lara's promise given,
To meet it in the eye of man and Heaven.
Why comes he not? Such truths to be divulged,
Methinks the accuser's rest is long indulged.

III.

The hour is past, and Lara too is there,
With self-confiding, coldly patient air;
Why comes not Ezzelin? The hour is past,
And murmurs rise, and Otho's brow's o'ercast.
« I know my friend! his faith I cannot fear,
If yet he be on earth, expect him here;
The roof that held him in the valley stands
Between my own and noble Lara's lands;
My halls from such a guest had honour gain'd,
Nor had Sir Ezzelin his host disdain'd,
But that some previous proof forbade his stay,
And urged him to prepare against to-day;
The word I pledged for his I pledge again,
Or will myself redeem his knighthood's stain. »

He ceased—and Lara answer'd, « I am here,
To lend at thy demand a listening ear;
To tales of evil from a stranger's tongue,
Whose words already might my heart have wrung,
But that I deem'd him scarcely less than mad,
Or, at the worst, a foe ignobly bad.
I know him not—but me it seems he knew
In lands where—but I must not trifle too:
Produce this babbler—or redeem the pledge;
Here in thy hold, and with thy falchion's edge.»

Proud Otho on the instant, reddening, threw
His glove on earth, and forth his sabre flew.
« The last alternative befits me best,
And thus I answer for mine absent guest.»

With cheek unchanging from its sallow gloom,
However near his own or other's tomb;
With hand, whose almost careless coolness spoke
Its grasp well-used to deal the sabre-stroke;
With eye, though calm, determined not to spare,
Did Lara too his willing weapon bare.
In vain the circling chieftains round them closed,
For Otho's phrensy would not be opposed;
And from his lip those words of insult fell—
« His sword is good who can maintain them well.»

IV.

Short was the conflict; furious, blindly rash,
Vain Otho gave his bosom to the gash:
He bled, and fell; but not with deadly wound,
Stretch'd by a dextrous sleight along the ground.

«Demand thy life!» He answer'd not: and then
From that red floor he ne'er had risen again,
For Lara's brow upon the moment grew
Almost to blackness in its demon hue;
And fiercer shook his angry falchion now
Than when his foe's was levell'd at his brow;
Then all was stern collectedness and art,
Now rose the unleaven'd hatred of his heart;
So little sparing to the foe he fell'd,
That when the approaching crowd his arm withheld,
He almost turn'd the thirsty point on those,
Who thus for mercy dared to interpose;
But to a moment's thought that purpose bent;
Yet look'd he on him still with eye intent,
As if he loathed the ineffectual strife
That left a foe, howe'er o'erthrown, with life;
As if to search how far the wound he gave
Had sent its victim onward to his grave.

V.

They raised the bleeding Otho, and the leech
Forbade all present question, sign, and speech;
The others met within a neighbouring hall,
And he, incensed and heedless of them all,
The cause and conqueror in this sudden fray,
In haughty silence slowly strode away;
He back'd his steed, his homeward path he took,
Nor cast on Otho's towers a single look.

VI.

But where was he? that meteor of a night,
Who menaced but to disappear with light?

Where was this Ezzelin? who came and went
To leave no other trace of his intent.
He left the dome of Otho long ere morn,
In darkness, yet so well the path was worn
He could not miss it: near his dwelling lay;
But there he was not, and with coming day
Came fast inquiry, which unfolded nought
Except the absence of the chief it sought.
A chamber tenantless, a steed at rest,
His host alarm'd, his murmuring squires distrest:
Their search extends along, around the path,
In dread to meet the marks of prowlers' wrath:
But none are there, and not a brake hath borne
Nor gout of blood, nor shred of mantle torn;
Nor fall nor struggle hath defaced the grass,
Which still retains a mark where murder was;
Nor dabbling fingers left to tell the tale,
The bitter print of each convulsive nail,
When agonised hands that cease to guard,
Wound in that pang the smoothness of the sward.
Some such had been, if here a life was reft,
But these were not; and doubting hope is left;
And strange suspicion, whispering Lara's name,
Now daily mutters o'er his blacken'd fame;
Then sudden silent when his form appear'd,
Awaits the absence of the thing it fear'd
Again its wonted wondering to renew,
And dye conjecture with a darker hue.

VII.

Days roll along, and Otho's wounds are heal'd,
But not his pride, and hate no more conceal'd:

He was a man of power, and Lara's foe,
The friend of all who sought to work him woe,
And from his country's justice now demands
Account of Ezzelin at Lara's hands.
Who else than Lara could have cause to fear
His presence? who had made him disappear,
If not the man on whom his menaced charge
Had sate too deeply were he left at large?
The general rumour ignorantly loud,
The mystery dearest to the curious crowd;
The seeming friendlessness of him who strove
To win no confidence, and wake no love;
The sweeping fierceness which his soul betray'd,
The skill with which he wielded his keen blade;
Where had his arm unwarlike caught that art?
Where had that fierceness grown upon his heart?
For it was not the blind capricious rage
A word can kindle and a word assuage;
But the deep working of a soul unmix'd
With aught of pity where its wrath had fix'd;
Such as long power and overgorged success
Concentrates into all that 's merciless:
These, link'd with that desire which ever sways
Mankind, the rather to condemn than praise,
'Gainst Lara gathering raised at length a storm,
Such as himself might fear, and foes would form,
And he must answer for the absent head
Of one that haunts him still, alive or dead.

VIII.

Within that land was many a malcontent,
Who cursed the tyranny to which he bent;

That soil full many a wringing despot saw,
Who worked his wantonness in form of law;
Long war without and frequent broil within
Had made a path for blood and giant sin,
That waited but a signal to begin
New havock, such as civil discord blends,
Which knows no neuter, owns but foes or friends;
Fix'd in his feudal fortress each was lord,
In word and deed obey'd, in soul abhorr'd.
Thus Lara had inherited his lands,
And with them pining hearts and sluggish hands;
But that long absence from his native clime
Had left him stainless of oppression's crime,
And now diverted by his milder sway,
All dread by slow degrees had worn away:
The menials felt their usual awe alone,
But more for him than them that fear was grown;
They deem'd him now unhappy, though at first
Their evil judgment augur'd of the worst,
And each long restless night, and silent mood,
Was traced to sickness, fed by solitude:
And though his lonely habits threw of late
Gloom o'er his chamber, cheerful was his gate;
For thence the wretched ne'er unsoothed withdrew,
For them, at least, his soul compassion knew.
Cold to the great, contemptuous to the high,
The humble pass'd not his unheeding eye;
Much he would speak not, but beneath his roof
They found asylum oft, and ne'er reproof.
And they who watch'd might mark that day by day,
Some new retainers gather'd to his sway;

But most of late, since Ezzelin was lost,
He play'd the courteous lord and bounteous host:
Perchance his strife with Otho made him dread
Some snare prepared for his obnoxious head;
Whate'er his view, his favour more obtains
With these, the people, than his fellow thanes.
If this were policy, so far 't was sound,
The million judged but of him as they found;
From him by sterner chiefs to exile driven
They but required a shelter, and 't was given.
By him no peasant mourn'd his rifled cot,
And scarce the serf could murmur o'er his lot;
With him old avarice found its hoard secure,
With him contempt forbore to mock the poor;
Youth, present cheer, and promised recompense
Detain'd, till all too late to part from thence:
To hate he offer'd, with the coming change,
The deep reversion of delay'd revenge;
To love, long baffled by the unequal match,
The well-won charms success was sure to snatch.
All now was ripe; he waits but to proclaim
That slavery nothing which was still a name.
The moment came, the hour when Otho thought
Secure at last the vengeance which he sought:
His summons found the destined criminal
Begirt by thousands in his swarming hall,
Fresh from their feudal fetters newly riven,
Defying earth, and confident of heaven.
That morning he had freed the soil-bound slaves
Who dig no land for tyrants but their graves!
Such is their cry—some watch-word for the fight
Must vindicate the wrong, and warp the right:

Religion—freedom—vengeance—what you will,
A word 's enough to raise mankind to kill;
Some factious phrase by cunning caught and spread,
That guilt may reign, and wolves and worms be fed!

IX.

Throughout that clime the feudal chiefs had gain'd
Such sway, their infant monarch hardly reign'd;
Now was the hour for faction's rebel growth,
The serfs contemn'd the one, and hated both:
They waited but a leader, and they found
One to their cause inseparably bound;
By circumstance compell'd to plunge again,
In self-defence, amidst the strife of men.
Cut off by some mysterious fate from those
Whom birth and nature meant not for his foes,
Had Lara from that night, to him accurst,
Prepared to meet, but not alone, the worst:
Some reason urged, whate'er it was, to shun
Inquiry into deeds at distance done;
By mingling with his own the cause of all,
E'en if he fail'd, he still delay'd his fall,
The sullen calm that long his bosom kept,
The storm that once had spent itself and slept,
Roused by events that seem'd foredoom'd to urge
His gloomy fortunes to their utmost verge,
Burst forth, and made him all he once had been,
And is again; he only changed the scene.
Light care had he for life, and less for fame,
But not less fitted for the desperate game:
He deem'd himself mark'd out for others' hate,
And mock'd at ruin so they shared his fate.

What cared he for the freedom of the crowd?
He raised the humble but to bend the proud.
He had hoped quiet in his sullen lair,
But man and destiny beset him there:
Inured to hunters, he was found at bay;
And they must kill, they cannot snare the prey.
Stern, unambitious, silent, he had been
Henceforth a calm spectator of life's scene;
But dragg'd again upon the arena, stood
A leader not unequal to the feud;
In voice—mien—gesture—savage nature spoke,
And from his eye the gladiator broke.

X.

What boots the oft-repeated tale of strife,
The feast of vultures, and the waste of life?
The varying fortune of each separate field,
The fierce that vanquish, and the faint that yield?
The smoking ruin, and the crumbled wall?
In this the struggle was the same with all;
Save that distemper'd passions lent their force
In bitterness that banish'd all remorse.
None sued, for mercy knew her cry was vain,
The captive died upon the battle-slain:
In either cause one rage alone possest
The empire of the alternate victor's breast;
And they that smote for freedom or for sway,
Deem'd few were slain, while more remain'd to slay.
It was too late to check the wasting brand,
And desolation reap'd the famish'd land;
The torch was lighted, and the flame was spread,
And carnage smiled upon her daily dead.

XI.

Fresh with the nerve the new-born impulse strung
The first success to Lara's numbers clung:
But that vain victory hath ruin'd all,
They form no longer to their leader's call;
In blind confusion on the foe they press,
And think to snatch is to secure success.
The lust of booty, and the thirst of hate,
Lure on the broken brigands to their fate;
In vain he doth whate'er a chief may do,
To check the headlong fury of that crew;
In vain their stubborn ardour he would tame,
The hand that kindles cannot quench the flame;
The wary foe alone hath turn'd their mood,
And shown their rashness to that erring brood:
The feign'd retreat, the nightly ambuscade,
The daily harass, and the fight delay'd,
The long privation of the hoped supply,
The tentless rest beneath the humid sky,
The stubborn wall that mocks the leaguer's art,
And palls the patience of his baffled heart,
Of these they had not deem'd: the battle-day
They could encounter as a veteran may;
But more preferr'd the fury of the strife,
And present death, to hourly-suffering life:
And famine wrings, and fever sweeps away
His numbers melting fast from their array;
Intemperate triumph fades to discontent,
And Lara's soul alone seems still unbent:
But few remain to aid his voice and hand,
And thousands dwindled to a scanty band:

Desperate, though few, the last and best remain'd
To mourn the discipline they late disdain'd.
One hope survives, the frontier is not far,
And thence they may escape from native war;
And bear within them to the neighbouring state
An exile's sorrows, or an outlaw's hate:
Hard is the task their father-land to quit,
But harder still to perish or submit.

XII.

It is resolved—they march—consenting night
Guides with her star their dim and torchless flight;
Already they perceive its tranquil beam
Sleep on the surface of the barrier stream;
Already they descry—Is you the bank?
Away! 't is lined with many a hostile rank.
Return or fly!—What glitters in the rear?
'T is Otho's banner—the pursuer's spear!
Are those the shepherds' fires upon the height?
Alas! they blaze too widely for the flight:
Cut off from hope, and compass'd in the toil,
Less blood perchance hath bought a richer spoil!

XIII.

A moment's pause, 't is but to breathe their band,
Or shall they onward press, or here withstand?
It matters little—if they charge the foes
Who by the border-stream their march oppose,
Some few, perchance, may break and pass the line,
However link'd to baffle such design.
«The charge be ours! to wait for their assault
Were fate well worthy of a coward's halt.»

Forth flies each sabre, reined is every steed,
And the next word shall scarce outstrip the deed:
In the next tone of Lara's gathering breath
How many shall but hear the voice of death!

XIV.

His blade is bared, in him there is an air
As deep, but far too tranquil for despair;
A something of indifference more than then
Becomes the bravest, if they feel for men—
He turn'd his eye on Kaled, ever near,
And still too faithful to betray one fear;
Perchance 't was but the moon's dim twilight threw
Along his aspect an unwonted hue
Of mournful paleness, whose deep tint exprest
The truth, and not the terror of his breast.
This Lara mark'd, and laid his hand on his:
It trembled not in such an hour as this;
His lip was silent, scarcely beat his heart,
His eye alone proclaim'd, « we will not part!
Thy band may perish, or thy friends may flee,
Farewell to life, but not adieu to thee! »

The word hath pass'd his lips, and onward driven,
Pours the link'd band through rank asunder riven;
Well has each steed obey'd the armed heel,
And flash the scimitars, and rings the steel;
Outnumber'd not outbraved, they still oppose
Despair to daring, and a front to foes;
And blood is mingled with the dashing stream,
Which runs all redly till the morning beam.

XV.

Commanding, aiding, animating all,
Where foe appear'd to press, or friend to fall,
Cheers Lara's voice, and waves or strikes his steel,
Inspiring hope himself had ceased to feel.
None fled, for well they knew that flight were vain;
But those that waver turn to smite again,
While yet they find the firmest of the foe
Recoil before their leader's look and blow:
Now girt with numbers, now almost alone
He foils their ranks, or re-unites his own;
Himself he spared not—once they seem'd to fly—
Now was the time! he waved his hand on high,
And shook—why sudden droops that plumed crest?
The shaft is sped—the arrow's in his breast!
That fatal gesture left the unguarded side,
And death hath stricken down yon arm of pride.
The word of triumph fainted from his tongue;
That hand, so raised, how droopingly it hung!
But yet the sword instinctively retains,
Though from its fellow shrink the falling reins;
These Kaled snatches: dizzy with the blow,
And senseless bending o'er his saddle-bow,
Perceives not Lara that his anxious page
Beguiles his charger from the combat's rage:
Meantime his followers charge, and charge again;
Too mix'd the slayers now to heed the slain!

XVI.

Day glimmers on the dying and the dead,
The cloven cuirass, and the helmless head;

The war-horse masterless is on the earth,
And that last gasp hath burst his bloody girth;
And near, yet quivering with what life remain'd,
The heel that urged him and the hand that rein'd;
And some too near that rolling torrent lie,
Whose waters mock the lip of those that die;
That panting thirst which scorches in the breath
Of those that die the soldier's fiery death,
In vain impels the burning mouth to crave
One drop—the last—to cool it for the grave;
With feeble and convulsive effort swept,
Their limbs along the crimson'd turf have crept;
The faint remains of life such struggles waste,
But yet they reach the stream, and bend to taste:
They feel its freshness, and almost partake—
Why pause? No further thirst have they to slake—
It is unquench'd, and yet they feel it not;
It was an agony—but now forgot!

XVII.

Beneath a lime, remoter from the scene,
Where but for him that strife had never been,
A breathing but devoted warrior lay:
'T was Lara bleeding fast from life away.
His follower once, and now his only guide,
Kneels Kaled watchful o'er his welling side,
And with his scarf would stanch the tides that rush,
With each convulsion, in a blacker gush;
And then, as his faint breathing waxes low,
In feebler, not less fatal tricklings flow:
He scarce can speak, but motions him 't is vain,
And merely adds another throb to pain.

He clasps the hand that pang which would assuage,
And sadly smiles his thanks to that dark page
Who nothing fears, nor feels, nor heeds, nor sees,
Save that damp brow which rests upon his knees;
Save that pale aspect, where the eye, though dim,
Held all the light that shone on earth for him.

XVIII.

The foe arrives, who long had search'd the field,
Their triumph nought till Lara too should yield;
They would remove him, but they see 't were vain,
And he regards them with a calm disdain,
That rose to reconcile him with his fate,
And that escape to death from living hate:
And Otho comes, and leaping from his steed,
Looks on the bleeding foe that made him bleed,
And questions of his state; he answers not,
Scarce glances on him as on one forgot,
And turns to Kaled:—each remaining word,
They understood not, if distinctly heard;
His dying tones are in that other tongue,
To which some strange remembrance wildly clung.
They spake of other scenes, but what—is known
To Kaled, whom their meaning reach'd alone;
And he replied, though faintly, to their sound,
While gazed the rest in dumb amazement round:
They seem'd even then—that twain—unto the last
To half forget the present in the past;
To share between themselves some separate fate,
Whose darkness none beside should penetrate.

XIX.

Their words though faint were many—from the tone
Their import those who heard could judge alone;
From this, you might have deem'd young Kaled's death
More near than Lara's by his voice and breath,
So sad, so deep, and hesitating broke
The accents his scarce-moving pale lips spoke;
But Lara's voice, though low, at first was clear
And calm, till murmuring death gasp'd hoarsely near:
But from his visage little could we guess,
So unrepentant, dark, and passionless,
Save that when struggling nearer to his last,
Upon that page his eye was kindly cast;
And once as Kaled's answering accents ceas'd,
Rose Lara's hand, and pointed to the east:
Whether (as then the breaking sun from high
Roll'd back the clouds) the morrow caught his eye,
Or that 't was chance, or some remember'd scene
That raised his arm to point where such had been,
Scarce Kaled seem'd to know, but turn'd away,
As if his heart abhorr'd that coming day.
And shrunk his glance before that morning light,
To look on Lara's brow—where all grew night.
Yet sense seem'd left, though better were its loss,
For when one near display'd the absolving cross,
And proffer'd to his touch the holy bead,
Of which his parting soul might own the need,
He look'd upon it with an eye profane,
And smiled—Heaven pardon! if 't were with disdain:
And Kaled, though he spoke not, nor withdrew
From Lara's face his fix'd, despairing view,

With brow repulsive, and with gesture swift,
Flung back the hand which held the sacred gift,
As if such but disturb'd the expiring man,
Nor seem'd to know his life but *then* began,
That life of immortality, secure
To none, save them whose faith in Christ is sure.

XX.

But gasping heaved the breath that Lara drew,
And dull the film along his dim eye grew;
His limbs stretch'd fluttering, and his head droop'd o'er
The weak yet still untiring knee that bore;
He press'd the hand he held upon his heart—
It beats no more, but Kaled will not part
With the cold grasp, but feels, and feels in vain,
For that faint throb which answers not again.
« It beats! »—Away, thou dreamer! he is gone—
It once was Lara which thou look'st upon.

XXI.

He gazed, as if not yet had pass'd away
The haughty spirit of that humble clay;
And those around have roused him from his trance,
But cannot tear from thence his fixed glance;
And when in raising him from where he bore
Within his arms the form that felt no more,
He saw the head his breast would still sustain,
Roll down like earth to earth upon the plain;
He did not dash himself thereby, nor tear
The glossy tendrils of his raven hair,
But strove to stand and gaze, but reel'd and fell,
Scarce breathing more than that he loved so well.

Than that *he* loved! Oh! never yet beneath
The breast of man such trusty love may breathe!
That trying moment hath at once reveal'd
The secret long and yet but half-conceal'd;
In baring to revive that lifeless breast,
Its grief seem'd ended, but the sex confest;
And life return'd, and Kaled felt no shame—
What now to her was womanhood or fame?

XXII.

And Lara sleeps not where his fathers sleep,'
But where he died his grave was dug as deep;
Nor is his mortal slumber less profound,
Though priest nor bless'd, nor marble deck'd the mound;
And he was mourn'd by one whose quiet grief,
Less loud, outlasts a people's for their chief.
Vain was all question ask'd her of the past,
And vain e'en menace—silent to the last;
She told nor whence, nor why she left behind
Her all for one who seem'd but little kind.
Why did she love him? Curious fool!—be still—
Is human love the growth of human will?
To her he might be gentleness; the stern
Have deeper thoughts than your dull eyes discern,
And when they love, your smilers guess not how
Beats the strong heart, though less the lips avow.
They were not common links, that form'd the chain
That bound to Lara Kaled's heart and brain;
But that wild tale she brook'd not to unfold,
And seal'd is now each lip that could have told.

XXIII.

They laid him in the earth, and on his breast,
Besides the wound that sent his soul to rest,
They found the scatter'd dints of many a scar,
Which were not planted there in recent war;
Where'er had pass'd his summer years of life,
It seems they vanish'd in a land of strife;
But all unknown his glory or his guilt,
These only told that somewhere blood was spilt,
And Ezzelin, who might have spoke the past,
Return'd no more—that night appear'd his last.

XXIV.

Upon that night (a peasant's is the tale)
A serf that cross'd the intervening vale,
When Cynthia's light almost gave way to morn,
And nearly veil'd in mist her waning horn;
A serf, that rose betimes to thread the wood,
And hew the bough that bought his children's food,
Pass'd by the river that divides the plain
Of Otho's lands and Lara's broad domain:
He heard a tramp—a horse and horseman broke
From out the wood—before him was a cloak
Wrapt round some burthen at his saddle-bow,
Bent was his head, and hidden was his brow.
Roused by the sudden sight at such a time,
And some foreboding that it might be crime,
Himself unheeded watch'd the stranger's course,
Who reach'd the river, bounded from his horse,
And lifting thence the burthen which he bore,
Heaved up the bank, and dash'd it from the shore,

Then paused, and look'd, and turn'd, and seem'd to watch,
And still another hurried glance would snatch,
And follow with his step the stream that flow'd,
As if even yet too much its surface show'd:
At once he started, stoop'd, around him strown
The winter floods had scatter'd heaps of stone;
Of these the heaviest thence he gather'd there,
And slung them with a more than common care.
Meantime the serf had crept to where unseen
Himself might safely mark what this might mean;
He caught a glimpse, as of a floating breast,
And something glitter'd star-like on the vest,
But ere he well could mark the buoyant trunk,
A massy fragment smote it, and it sunk:
It rose again, but indistinct to view,
And left the waters of a purple hue,
Then deeply disappear'd: the horseman gazed
Till ebb'd the latest eddy it had raised;
Then turning, vaulted on his pawing steed,
And instant spurr'd him into panting speed.
His face was mask'd—the features of the dead,
If dead it were, escaped the observer's dread;
But if in sooth a star its bosom bore,
Such is the badge that knighthood ever wore,
And such 't is known Sir Ezzelin had worn
Upon the night that led to such a morn.
If thus he perish'd, Heaven receive his soul!
His undiscover'd limbs to ocean roll;
And charity upon the hope would dwell
It was not Lara's hand by which he fell.

XXV.

And Kaled—Lara—Ezzelin, are gone,
Alike without their monumental stone!
The first, all efforts vainly strove to wean
From lingering where her chieftain's blood had been;
Grief had so tamed a spirit once too proud,
Her tears were few, her wailing never loud;
But furious, would you tear her from the spot
Where yet she scarce believed that he was not,
Her eye shot forth with all the living fire
That haunts the tigress in her whelpless ire;
But left to waste her weary moments there,
She talk'd all idly unto shapes of air,
Such as the busy brain of sorrow paints,
And woos to listen to her fond complaints:
And she would sit beneath the very tree
Where lay his drooping head upon her knee;
And in that posture where she saw him fall,
His words, his looks, his dying grasp recall;
And she had shorn, but saved her raven hair,
And oft would snatch it from her bosom there,
And fold, and press it gently to the ground,
As if she stanch'd anew some phantom's wound.
Herself would question, and for him reply;
Then rising, start, and beckon him to fly
From some imagined spectre in pursuit;
Then seat her down upon some linden's root,
And hide her visage with her meagre hand,
Or trace strange characters along the sand—
This could not last—she lies by him she loved;
Her tale untold—her truth too dearly proved.

NOTE TO LARA.

Note 1, page 323, line 10.

And Lara sleeps not where his fathers sleep, *etc.*

The event was suggested by the description of the death or rather burial of the Duke of Gandia.

The most interesting and particular account of this mysterious event is given by Burchard; and is in substance as follows : «On the eighth day of June, the Cardinal of Valenza, and the Duke of Gandia, sons of the pope, supped with their mother, Vanozza, near the church of *S. Pietro ad vincula;* several other persons being present at the entertainment. A late hour approaching, and the cardinal having reminded his brother that it was time to return to the apostolic palace, they mounted their horses or mules, with only a few attendants, and proceeded together as far as the palace of Cardinal Ascanio Sforza, when the duke informed the cardinal, that before he returned home, he had to pay a visit of pleasure. Dismissing therefore all his attendants, excepting his *staffiero,* or footman, and a person in a mask, who had paid him a visit whilst at supper, and who, during the space of a month, or thereabouts, previous to this time, had called upon him almost daily, at the apostolic palace, he took this person behind him on his mule, and proceeded to the street of the Jews, where he quitted his servant, directing him to remain there until a certain hour; when, if he did not return, he might repair to the palace. The duke then seated the person in the mask behind him, and rode, I know not whither; but in that night he was assassinated, and thrown into the river.

The servant, after having been dismissed, was also assaulted and mortally wounded; and although he was attended with great care, yet such was his situation, that he could give no intelligible account of what had befallen his master. In the morning, the duke not having returned to the palace, his servants began to be alarmed; and one of them informed the pontiff of the evening excursion of his sons, and that the duke had not yet made his appearance. This gave the pope no small anxiety; but he conjectured that the duke had been attracted by some courtesan to pass the night with her, and, not choosing to quit the house in open day, had waited till the following evening to return home. When, however, the evening arrived, and he found himself disappointed in his expectations, he became deeply afflicted, and began to make inquiries from different persons, whom he ordered to attend him for that purpose. Amongst these was a man named Giorgio Schiavoni, who having discharged some timber from a bark in the river, had remained on board the vessel to watch it, and being interrogated whether he had seen any one thrown into the river, on the night preceding, he replied, that he saw two men on foot, who came down the street, and looked diligently about, to observe whether any person was passing. That seeing no one, they returned, and a short time afterwards two others came, and looked around in the same manner as the former; no person still appearing, they gave a sign to their companions, when a man came, mounted on a white horse, having behind him a dead body, the head and arms of which hung on one side, and the feet on the other side of the horse; the two persons on foot supporting the body, to prevent its falling. They thus proceeded towards that part where the filth of the city is usually discharged into the river, and, turning the horse, with his tail towards the water, the two persons took the dead body by the arms and feet, and with all their strength flung it into the river. The person on horseback then asked if they had thrown it in, to which they replied, *signor, si* (yes, sir.) He then looked towards the river, and seeing a mantle floating on the stream, he inquired what it was that appeared black, to which they answered it was a mantle; and one of them threw stones upon it, in consequence of which it sunk. The attendants of the pontiff then inquired from Giorgio, why he had not revealed this to the governor of the city; to which he replied, that he had seen in his time a hundred dead bodies thrown into the river at the same place, without any inquiry being made respecting them, and that he had not, therefore, considered it as a matter of any importance. The fishermen and seamen were then collected, and ordered to search the river, where, on the following evening, they found the body of the duke, with his habit entire, and thirty ducats in his purse. He was pierced with nine wounds, one of which was in his throat, the others in his head, body, and limbs. No sooner was the pontiff informed of the death of his son, and that he had been thrown, like filth, into the river, than, giving way to his grief, he shut himself up in a chamber, and wept bitterly. The Cardinal of Segovia, and other attendants on the pope, went to the door, and after many hours spent in persuasions and exhortations, prevailed upon him to admit them. From the evening of Wednesday, till the following Saturday, the pope took no food; nor did he sleep from Thursday morning till the same hour on the ensuing day. At length, however, giving way to the entreaties of his attendants, he began to restrain his sorrow, and to consider the injury which his own health might sustain, by the further indulgence of his grief.»—ROSCOE'S *Leo Tenth*, vol. i. page 265.

THE

SIEGE OF CORINTH.

TO

JOHN HOBHOUSE, ESQ.

THIS POEM IS INSCRIBED

BY HIS

FRIEND.

January 22, 1816.

ADVERTISEMENT.

'THE grand army of the Turks (in 1715), under the prime vizier, to open to themselves a way into the heart of the Morea, and to form the siege of Napoli di Romania, the most considerable place in all that country,[1] thought it best in the first place to attack Corinth, upon which they made several storms. The garrison being weakened, and the governor seeing it was impossible

[1] Napoli di Romania is not now the most considerable place in the Morea, but Tripolitza, where the pacha resides, and maintains his government. Napoli is near Argos. I visited all three in 1810-11; and in the course of journeying through the country from my first arrival in 1809, I crossed the Isthmus eight times in my way from Attica to the Morea, over the mountains, or in the other direction, when passing from the Gulf of Athens to that of Lepanto. Both the routes are picturesque and beautiful, though very different: that by sea has more sameness, but the voyage being always within sight of land, and often very near it, presents many attractive views of the islands Salamis, Ægina, Poro, etc. and the coast of the continent.

to hold out against so mighty a force, thought it fit to beat a parley: but while they were treating about the articles, one of the magazines in the Turkish camp, wherein they had six hundred barrels of powder, blew up by accident, whereby six or seven hundred men were killed: which so enraged the infidels, that they would not grant any capitulation, but stormed the place with so much fury, that they took it, and put most of the garrison, with Signior Minotti, the governor, to the sword. The rest, with Antonio Bembo, proveditor extraordinary, were made prisoners of war."—*History of the Turks,* vol. iii. p. 151.

THE

SIEGE OF CORINTH.

I.

Many a vanish'd year and age,
And tempest's breath, and battle's rage,
Have swept o'er Corinth; yet she stands
A fortress form'd to freedom's hands.
The whirlwind's wrath, the earthquake's shock,
Have left untouch'd her hoary rock,
The keystone of a land, which still,
Though fall'n, looks proudly on that hill,
The landmark to the double tide
That purpling rolls on either side,
As if their waters chafed to meet,
Yet pause and crouch beneath her feet.
But could the blood before her shed
Since first Timoleon's brother bled,
Or baffled Persia's despot fled,
Arise from out the earth which drank
The stream of slaughter as it sank,

That sanguine ocean would o'erflow
Her isthmus idly spread below:
Or could the bones of all the slain,
Who perish'd there, be piled again,
That rival pyramid would rise
More mountain-like, through those clear skies,
Than yon tower-capt Acropolis,
Which seems the very clouds to kiss.

II.

On dun Cithæron's ridge appears
The gleam of twice ten thousand spears;
And downward to the Isthmian plain
From shore to shore of either main,
The tent is pitch'd, the crescent shines
Along the moslem's leaguering lines;
And the dusk spahi's bands advance
Beneath each bearded pasha's glance;
And far and wide as eye can reach
The turban'd cohorts throng the beach;
And there the Arab's camel kneels,
And there his steed the Tartar wheels;
The Turcoman hath left his herd,'
The sabre round his loins to gird;
And there the volleying thunders pour,
Till waves grow smoother to the roar.
The trench is dug, the cannon's breath
Wings the far-hissing globe of death;
Fast whirl the fragments from the wall,
Which crumbles with the ponderous ball;
And from that wall the foe replies,
O'er dusty plain and smoky skies,

With fires that answer fast and well
The summons of the infidel.

III.

But near and nearest to the wall
Of those who wish and work its fall,
With deeper skill in war's black art
Than Othman's sons, and high of heart
As any chief that ever stood
Triumphant in the fields of blood;
From post to post, and deed to deed,
Fast spurring on his reeking steed,
Where sallying ranks the trench assail,
And make the foremost moslem quail;
Or where the battery, guarded well,
Remains as yet impregnable,
Alighting cheerly to inspire
The soldier slackening in his fire;
The first and freshest of the host
Which Stamboul's sultan there can boast,
To guide the follower o'er the field,
To point the tube, the lance to wield,
Or whirl around the bickering blade;—
Was Alp, the Adrian renegade!

IV.

From Venice—once a race of worth
His gentle sires—he drew his birth;
But late an exile from her shore,
Against his countrymen he bore
The arms they taught to bear; and now
The turban girt his shaven brow.

Through many a change had Corinth pass'd
With Greece to Venice' rule at last;
And here, before her walls, with those,
To Greece and Venice equal foes,
He stood a foe, with all the zeal
Which young and fiery converts feel,
Within whose heated bosom throngs
The memory of a thousand wrongs.
To him had Venice ceased to be
Her ancient civic boast—« the free, »
And in the palace of St Mark
Unnamed accusers in the dark
Within the « Lion's mouth » had placed
A charge against him uneffaced:
He fled in time, and saved his life,
To waste his future years in strife,
That taught his land how great her loss
In him who triumph'd o'er the cross,
'Gainst which he rear'd the crescent high,
And battled to avenge or die.

V.

Coumourgi[2]—he whose closing scene
Adorn'd the triumph of Eugene,
When on Carlowitz' bloody plain,
The last and mightiest of the slain,
He sank, regretting not to die,
But curst the christian's victory—
Coumourgi—can his glory cease,
That latest conqueror of Greece,
Till christian hands to Greece restore
The freedom Venice gave of yore?

A hundred years have roll'd away
Since he refix'd the moslem sway;
And now he led the mussulman,
And gave the guidance of the van
To Alp, who well repaid the trust
By cities levell'd with the dust;
And proved, by many a deed of death,
How firm his heart in novel faith.

VI.

The walls grew weak; and fast and hot
Against them pour'd the ceaseless shot,
With unabating fury sent
From battery to battlement;
And thunder-like the pealing din
Rose from each heated culverin;
And here and there some crackling dome
Was fired before the exploding bomb:
And as the fabric sank beneath
The shattering shell's volcanic breath,
In red and wreathing columns flash'd
The flame, as loud the ruin crash'd,
Or into countless meteors driven,
Its earth-stars melted into heaven;
Whose clouds that day grew doubly dun,
Impervious to the hidden sun,
With volumed smoke that slowly grew
To one wide sky of sulphurous hue.

VII.

But not for vengeance, long delay'd,
Alone, did Alp, the renegade,

The moslem warriors sternly teach
His skill to pierce the promised breach:
Within these walls a maid was pent,
His hope would win without consent
Of that inexorable sire,
Whose heart refused him in its ire,
When Alp, beneath his christian name,
Her virgin hand aspired to claim.
In happier mood, and earlier time,
While unimpeach'd for traitorous crime,
Gayest in gondola or hall,
He glitter'd through the carnival;
And tuned the softest serenade
That e'er on Adria's waters play'd
At midnight to Italian maid.

VIII.

And many deem'd her heart was won;
For sought by numbers, given to none,
Had young Francesca's hand remain'd
Still by the church's bonds unchain'd;
And when the Adriatic bore
Lanciotto to the Paynim shore,
Her wonted smiles were seen to fail,
And pensive wax'd the maid and pale;
More constant at confessional,
More rare at masque and festival;
Or seen at such with downcast eyes,
Which conquer'd hearts they ceased to prize:
With listless look she seems to gaze;
With humbler care her form arrays;

Her voice less lively in the song;
Her step, though light, less fleet among
The pairs, on whom the morning's glance
Breaks, yet unsated with the dance.

IX.

Sent by the state to guard the land,
(Which, wrested from the moslem's hand,
While Sobieski tamed his pride
By Buda's wall and Danube's side,
The chiefs of Venice wrung away
From Patra to Eubœa's bay,)
Minotti held in Corinth's towers
The doge's delegated powers,
While yet the pitying eye of peace
Smiled o'er her long-forgotten Greece:
And ere that faithless truce was broke
Which freed her from the unchristian yoke.
With him his gentle daughter came;
Nor there, since Menelaus' dame
Forsook her lord and land, to prove
What woes await on lawless love,
Had fairer form adorn'd the shore
Than she, the matchless stranger, bore.

X.

The wall is rent, the ruins yawn;
And, with to-morrow's earliest dawn,
O'er the disjointed mass shall vault
The foremost of the fierce assault,
The bands are rank'd; the chosen van
Of Tartar and of Mussulman,

The full of hope, misnamed «forlorn,»
Who hold the thought of death in scorn,
And win their way with falchions' force,
Or pave the path with many a corse,
O'er which the following brave may rise,
Their stepping-stone—the last who dies!

XI.

'T is midnight: on the mountains brown
The cold, round moon shines deeply down;
Blue roll the waters, blue the sky
Spreads like an ocean hung on high,
Bespangled with those isles of light,
So wildly, spiritually bright;
Who ever gazed upon them shining,
And turn'd to earth without repining,
Nor wish'd for wings to flee away,
And mix with their eternal ray?
The waves on either shore lay there
Calm, clear, and azure as the air;
And scarce their foam the pebbles shook,
But murmur'd meekly as the brook.
The winds were pillow'd on the waves;
The banners droop'd along their staves,
And, as they fell around them furling,
Above them shone the crescent curling;
And that deep silence was unbroke,
Save where the watch his signal spoke,
Save where the steed neigh'd oft and shrill,
And echo answer'd from the hill,
And the wide hum of that wild host
Rustled like leaves from coast to coast,

As rose the muezzin's voice in air
In midnight call to wonted prayer;
It rose, that chanted mournful strain,
Like some lone spirit's o'er the plain:
'T was musical, but sadly sweet,
Such as when winds and harp-strings meet,
And take a long unmeasured tone,
To mortal minstrelsy unknown.
It seem'd to those within the wall
A cry prophetic of their fall:
It struck even the besieger's ear
With something ominous and drear,
An undefined and sudden thrill,
Which makes the heart a moment still,
Then beat with quicker pulse, ashamed
Of that strange sense its silence framed;
Such as a sudden passing-bell
Wakes, though but for a stranger's knell.

XII.

The tent of Alp was on the shore;
The sound was hush'd, the prayer was o'er;
The watch was set, the night-round made,
All mandates issued and obey'd:
'T is but another anxious night,
His pains the morrow may requite
With all revenge and love can pay,
In guerdon for their long delay.
Few hours remain, and he hath need
Of rest, to nerve for many a deed
Of slaughter; but within his soul
The thoughts like troubled waters roll.

He stood alone among the host;
Not his the loud fanatic boast
To plant the crescent o'er the cross,
Or risk a life with little loss,
Secure in paradise to be
By houris loved immortally;
Nor his, what burning patriots feel,
The stern exaltedness of zeal,
Profuse of blood, untired in toil,
When battling on the parent soil.
He stood alone—a renegade
Against the country he betray'd;
He stood alone amidst his band,
Without a trusted heart or hand:
They follow'd him, for he was brave,
And great the spoil he got and gave;
They crouch'd to him, for he had skill
To warp and wield the vulgar will:
But still his christian origin
With them was little less than sin.
They envied even the faithless fame
He earn'd beneath a moslem name;
Since he, their mightiest chief, had been
In youth a bitter Nazarene.
They did not know how pride can stoop,
When baffled feelings withering droop;
They did not know how hate can burn
In hearts once changed from soft to stern;
Nor all the false and fatal zeal
The convert of revenge can feel.
He ruled them—man may rule the worst,
By ever daring to be first:

So lions o'er the jackal sway;
The jackal points, he fells the prey,
Then on the vulgar yelling press,
To gorge the relics of success.

XIII.

His head grows fever'd, and his pulse
The quick successive throbs convulse;
In vain from side to side he throws
His form, in courtship of repose;
Or if he dozed, a sound, a start
Awoke him with a sunken heart.
The turban on his hot brow press'd,
The mail weigh'd lead-like on his breast,
Though oft and long beneath its weight
Upon his eyes had slumber sate,
Without or couch or canopy,
Except a rougher field and sky
Than now might yield a warrior's bed,
Than now along the heaven was spread.
He could not rest, he could not stay
Within his tent to wait for day,
But walk'd him forth along the sand,
Where thousand sleepers strew'd the strand.
What pillow'd them? and why should he
More wakeful than the humblest be?
Since more their peril, worse their toil,
And yet they fearless dream of spoil;
While he alone, where thousands pass'd
A night of sleep, perchance their last,
In sickly vigil wander'd on,
And envied all he gazed upon.

XIV.

He felt his soul become more light
Beneath the freshness of the night.
Cool was the silent sky, though calm,
And bathed his brow with airy balm:
Behind, the camp—before him lay,
In many a winding creek and bay,
Lepanto's gulf; and, on the brow
Of Delphi's hill, unshaken snow,
High and eternal, such as shone
Through thousand summers brightly gone,
Along the gulf, the mount, the clime;
It will not melt, like man, to time:
Tyrant and slave are swept away,
Less form'd to wear before the ray;
But that white veil, the lightest, frailest,
Which on the mighty mount thou hailest,
While tower and tree are torn and rent,
Shines o'er its craggy battlement;
In form a peak, in height a cloud,
In texture like a hovering shroud,
Thus high by parting freedom spread,
As from her fond abode she fled,
And linger'd on the spot, where long
Her prophet spirit spake in song.
Oh, still her step at moments falters
O'er wither'd fields, and ruin'd altars,
And fain would wake, in souls too broken,
By pointing to each glorious token.
But vain her voice, till better days
Dawn in those yet remember'd rays

Which shone upon the Persian flying,
And saw the Spartan smile in dying.

XV.

Not mindless of these mighty times
Was Alp, despite his flight and crimes;
And through this night, as on he wander'd,
And o'er the past and present ponder'd,
And thought upon the glorious dead
Who there in better cause had bled,
He felt how faint and feebly dim,
The fame that could accrue to him,
Who cheer'd the band, and waved the sword,
A traitor in a turban'd horde:
And led them to the lawless siege,
Whose best success were sacrilege.
Not so had those his fancy number'd,
The chiefs whose dust around him slumber'd;
Their phalanx marshall'd on the plain,
Whose bulwarks were not then in vain.
They fell devoted, but undying;
The very gale their names seem'd sighing:
The waters murmur'd of their name;
The woods were peopled with their fame;
The silent pillar, lone and gray,
Claim'd kindred with their sacred clay;
Their spirits wrapt the dusky mountain,
Their memory sparkled o'er the fountain;
The meanest rill, the mightiest river
Roll'd mingling with their fame for ever.
Despite of every yoke she bears,
That land is glory's still and theirs!

'Tis still a watch-word to the earth:
When man would do a deed of worth
He points to Greece, and turns to tread,
So sanction'd, on the tyrant's head:
He looks to her, and rushes on
Where life is lost, or freedom won.

XVI.

Still by the shore Alp mutely mused,
And woo'd the freshness night diffused.
There shrinks no ebb in that tideless sea,[3]
Which changeless rolls eternally;
So that wildest of waves, in their angriest mood,
Scarce break on the bounds of the land for a rood;
And the powerless moon beholds them flow,
Heedless if she come or go:
Calm or high, in main or bay,
On their course she hath no sway.
The rock unworn its base doth bare,
And looks o'er the surf, but it comes not there;
And the fringe of the foam may be seen below,
On the line that it left long ages ago:
A smooth short space of yellow sand
Between it and the greener land.

He wander'd on, along the beach,
Till within the range of a carbine's reach
Of the leaguer'd wall; but they saw him not,
Or how could he 'scape from the hostile shot?
Did traitors lurk in the christians' hold?
Were their hands grown stiff, or their hearts wax'd cold?

I know not, in sooth; but from yonder wall
There flash'd no fire, and there hiss'd no ball,
Though he stood beneath the bastion's frown,
That flank'd the sea-ward gate of the town;
Though he heard the sound, and could almost tell
The sullen words of the sentinel,
As his measured step on the stone below
Clank'd, as he paced it to and fro;
And he saw the lean dogs beneath the wall
Hold o'er the dead their carnival,
Gorging and growling o'er carcass and limb;
They were too busy to bark at him!
From a Tartar's skull they had stripp'd the flesh,
As ye peel the fig when its fruit is fresh;
And their white tusks crunch'd o'er the whiter skull,[4]
As it slipp'd though their jaws, when their edge grew dull,
As they lazily mumbled the bones of the dead,
When they scarce could rise from the spot where they fed;
So well had they broken a lingering fast
With those who had fallen for that night's repast.
And Alp knew, by the turbans that roll'd on the sand,
The foremost of these were the best of his band:
Crimson and green were the shawls of their wear,
And each scalp had a single long tuft of hair,[5]
All the rest was the shaven and bare.
The scalps were in the wild dog's maw,
The hair was tangled round his jaw.
But close by the shore, on the edge of the gulf,
There sat a vulture flapping a wolf,
Who had stolen from the hills, but kept away,
Scared by the dogs, from the human prey;

But he seized on his share of a steed that lay,
Pick'd by the birds, on the sands of the bay.

XVII.

Alp turn'd him from the sickening sight:
Never had shaken his nerves in fight;
But he better could brook to behold the dying,
Deep in the tide of their warm blood lying,
Scorch'd with the death-thirst, and writhing in vain,
Than the perishing dead who are past all pain.
There is something of pride in the perilous hour,
Whate'er be the shape in which death may lower;
For fame is there to say who bleeds,
And honour's eye on daring deeds!
But when all is past, it is bumbling to tread
O'er the weltering field of the tombless dead,
And see worms of the earth, and fowls of the air,
Beasts of the forest, all gathering there;
All regarding man as their prey,
All rejoicing in his decay.

XVIII.

There is a temple in ruin stands,
Fashion'd by long-forgotten hands;
Two or three columns, and many a stone,
Marble and granite, with grass o'ergrown!
Out upon time! it will leave no more
Of the things to come than the things before!
Out upon time! who for ever will leave
But enough of the past for the future to grieve
O'er that which hath been, and o'er that which must be:
What we have seen, our sons shall see;

Remnants of things that have pass'd away,
Fragments of stone, rear'd by creatures of clay!

XIX.

He sate him down at a pillar's base,
And pass'd his hand athwart his face;
Like one in dreary musing mood,
Declining was his attitude;
His head was drooping on his breast,
Fever'd, throbbing, and opprest;
And o'er his brow, so downward bent,
Oft his beating fingers went,
Hurriedly, as you may see
Your own run over the ivory key,
Ere the measured tone is taken
By the chords you would awaken.
There he sate all heavily,
As he heard the night-wind sigh.
Was it the wind, through some hollow stone,[6]
Sent that soft and tender moan?
He lifted his head, and he look'd on the sea,
But it was unrippled as glass may be;
He look'd on the long grass—it waved not a blade;
How was that gentle sound convey'd?
He look'd to the banners—each flag lay still,
So did the leaves on Cithæron's hill,
And he felt not a breath come over his cheek;
What did that sudden sound bespeak?
He turn'd to the left—is he sure of sight?
There sate a lady, youthful and bright!

XX.

He started up with more of fear
Than if an armed foe were near.
« God of my fathers! what is here?
Who art thou, and wherefore sent,
So near a hostile armament? »
His trembling hands refused to sign
The cross he deem'd no more divine:
He had resumed it in that hour,
But conscience wrung away the power.
He gazed, he saw: he knew the face
Of beauty, and the form of grace;
It was Francesca by his side,
The maid who might have been his bride!

The rose was yet upon her cheek,
But mellow'd with a tenderer streak:
Where was the play of her soft lips fled?
Gone was the smile that enliven'd their red.
The ocean's calm within their view,
Beside her eye had less of blue;
But like that cold wave it stood still,
And its glance, though clear, was chill.
Around her form a thin rob twining,
Nought conceal'd her bosom shining;
Through the parting of her hair,
Floating darkly downward there,
Her rounded arm show'd white and bare:
And ere yet she made reply,
Once she raised her hand on high;

It was so wan, and transparent of hue,
You might have seen the moon shine through.

XXI.

« I come from my rest to him I love best,
That I may be happy, and he may be blest.
I have pass'd the guards, the gate, the wall;
Sought thee in safety through foes and all.
'T is said the lion will turn and flee
From a maid in the pride of her purity;
And the power on high, that can shield the good,
Thus from the tyrant of the wood,
Hath extended its mercy to guard me as well
From the hands of the leaguering infidel.
I come—and if I come in vain,
Never, oh never, we meet again!
Thou hast done a fearful deed
In falling away from thy father's creed:
But dash that turban to earth, and sign
The sign of the cross, and for ever be mine;
Wring the black drop from thy heart,
And to-morrow unites us no more to part.»

« And where should our bridal couch be spread?
In the midst of the dying and the dead?
For to-morrow we give to the slaughter and flame
The sons and the shrines of the christian name.
None, save thou and thine, I 've sworn,
Shall be left upon the morn:
But thee will I bear to a lovely spot,
Where our hands shall be join'd, and our sorrow forgot.

There thou yet shalt be my bride,
When once again I 've quell'd the pride
Of Venice; and her hated race
Have felt the arm they would debase
Scourge, with a whip of scorpions, those
Whom vice and envy made my foes.»

Upon his hand she laid her own—
Light was the touch, but it thrill'd to the bone,
And shot a chillness to his heart,
Which fix'd him beyond the power to start.
Though slight was that grasp so mortal cold,
He could not loose him from its hold;
But never did clasp of one so dear
Strike on the pulse with such feeling of fear,
As those thin fingers, long and white,
Froze through his blood by their touch that night.
The feverish glow of his brow was gone,
And his heart sank so still that it felt like stone,
As he look'd on the face, and beheld its hue
So deeply changed from what he knew:
Fair but faint—without the ray
Of mind, that made each feature play
Like sparkling waves on a sunny day;
And her motionless lips lay still as death,
And her words came forth without her breath,
And there rose not a heave o'er her bosom's swell,
And there seem'd not a pulse in her veins to dwell.
Though her eye shone out, yet the lids were fix'd,
And the glance that it gave was wild and unmix'd
With aught of change, as the eyes may seem
Of the restless who walk in a troubled dream;

Like the figures on arras, that gloomily glare,
Stirr'd by the breath of the wintry air,
So seen by the dying lamp's fitful light,
Lifeless, but life-like, and awful to sight;
As they seem, through the dimness, about to come down
From the shadowy wall where their images frown;
Fearfully flitting to and fro,
As the gusts on the tapestry come and go.

« If not for love of me be given
Thus much, then, for the love of Heaven,—
Again I say—that turban tear
From off thy faithless brow, and swear
Thine injured country's sons to spare,
Or thou art lost; and never shalt see
Not earth—that 's past—but heaven or me.
If this thou dost accord, albeit
A heavy doom 't is thine to meet,
That doom shall half absolve thy sin,
And mercy's gate may receive thee within:
But pause one moment more, and take
The curse of Him thou didst forsake;
And look once more to heaven, and see
Its love for ever shut from thee.
There is a light cloud by the moon—7
'T is passing, and will pass full soon—
If, by the time its vapoury sail
Hath ceased her shaded orb to veil,
Thy heart within thee is not changed,
Then God and man are both avenged;
Dark will thy doom be, darker still
Thine immortality of ill. »

Alp look'd to heaven, and saw on high
The sign she spake of in the sky;
But his heart was swollen, and turn'd aside,
By deep interminable pride.
This first false passion of his breast
Roll'd like a torrent o'er the rest.
He sue for mercy! *He* dismay'd
By wild words of a timid maid!
He, wrong'd by Venice, vow to save
Her sons, devoted to the grave!
No—though that cloud were thunder's worst,
And charged to crush him—let it burst!

He look'd upon it earnestly,
Without an accent of reply;
He watch'd it passing; it is flown:
Full on his eye the clear moon shone,
And thus he spake—« Whate'er my fate,
I am no changeling—'t is too late:
The reed in storms may bow and quiver,
Then rise again; the tree must shiver.
What Venice made me, I must be,
Her foe in all, save love to thee:
But thou art safe: oh, fly with me! »
He turn'd, but she is gone!
Nothing is there but the column stone.
Hath she sunk in the earth, or melted in air?
He saw not, he knew not; but nothing is there.

XXII.

The night is past, and shines the sun
As if that morn were a jocund one.

Lightly and brightly breaks away
The morning from her mantle gray,
And the noon will look on a sultry day.
Hark to the trump, and the drum,
And the mournful sound of the barbarous horn,
And the flap of the banners, that flit as they 're borne,
And the neigh of the steed, and the multitude's hum,
And the clash, and the shout, « they come, they come! »
The horsetails[8] are pluck'd from the ground, and the sword
From its sheath; and they form, and but wait for the word.
Tartar, and Spahi, and Turcoman,
Strike your tents, and throng to the van;
Mount ye, spur ye, skirr the plain,
That the fugitive may flee in vain,
When he breaks from the town; and none escape,
Aged or young, in the christian shape;
While your fellows on foot, in a fiery mass,
Bloodstain the breach through which they pass.
The steeds are all bridled, and snort to the rein;
Curved is each neck, and flowing each mane;
White is the foam of their champ on the bit:
The spears are uplifted; the matches are lit;
The cannon are pointed, and ready to roar,
And crush the wall they have crumbled before:
Forms in his phalanx each janizar;
Alp at their head; his right arm is bare,
So is the blade of his scimitar;
The khan and the pachas are all at their post;
The vizier himself at the head of the host.
When the culverin's signal is fired, then on;
Leave not in Corinth a living one—

A priest at her altars, a chief in her halls,
A hearth in her mansions, a stone on her walls,
God and the prophet—Alla hu!
Up to the skies with that wild halloo!
« There the breach lies for passage, the ladder to scale;
And your hands on your sabres, and how should ye fail?
He who first downs with the red cross may crave
His heart's dearest wish; let him ask it, and have! »
Thus utter'd Coumourgi, the dauntless vizier;
The reply was the brandish of sabre and spear,
And the shout of fierce thousands in joyous ire:—
Silence—hark to the signal—fire!

XXIII.

As the wolves, that headlong go
On the stately buffalo,
Though with fiery eyes, and angry roar,
And hoofs that stamp, and horns that gore,
He tramples on earth, or tosses on high
The foremost, who rush on his strength but to die:
Thus against the wall they went,
Thus the first were backward bent;
Many a bosom, sheath'd in brass,
Strew'd the earth like broken glass,
Shiver'd by the shot, that tore
The ground whereon they moved no more:
E'en as they fell, in files they lay,
Like the mower's grass at the close of day,
When his work is done on the levell'd plain;
Such was the fall of the foremost slain.

XXIV.

As the spring-tides, with heavy plash,
From the cliffs invading dash
Huge fragments, sapp'd by the ceaseless flow,
Till white and thundering down they go,
Like the avalanche's snow
On the Alpine vales below;
Thus at length, outbreathed and worn,
Corinth's sons were downward borne
By the long and oft renew'd
Charge of the moslem multitude.
In firmness they stood, and in masses they fell,
Heap'd, by the host of the infidel,
Hand to hand, and foot to foot:
Nothing there, save death, was mute;
Stroke, and thrust, and flash, and cry
For quarter, or for victory,
Mingle there with the volleying thunder,
Which makes the distant cities wonder
How the sounding battle goes,
If with them, or for their foes;
If they must mourn, or may rejoice
In that annihilating voice,
Which pierces the deep hills through and through
With an echo dread and new:
You might have heard it, on that day,
O'er Salamis and Megara
(We have heard the hearers say);
Even unto Piræus bay.

XXV.

From the point of encountering blades to the hilt,
Sabres and swords with blood were gilt;
But the rampart is won, and the spoil begun,
And all but the after carnage done.
Shriller shrieks now mingling come
From within the plunder'd dome:
Hark to the haste of flying feet,
That splash in the blood of the slippery street;
But here and there, where 'vantage ground
Against the foe may still be found,
Desperate groups, of twelve or ten,
Make a pause, and turn again—
With banded backs against the wall,
Fiercely stand, or fighting fall.

There stood an old man—his hairs were white,
But his veteran arm was full of might:
So gallantly bore he the brunt of the fray,
The dead before him, on that day,
In a semicircle lay;
Still he combated unwounded,
Though retreating, unsurrounded.
Many a scar of former fight
Lurk'd beneath his corslet bright;
But of every wound his body bore,
Each and all had been ta'en before:
Though aged, he was so iron of limb,
Few of our youth could cope with him;
And the foes, whom he singly kept at bay,
Outnumber'd his thin hairs of silver gray.

From right to left his sabre swept:
Many an Othman mother wept
Sons that were unborn, when dipp'd
His weapon first in moslem gore,
Ere his years could count a score.
Of all he might have been the sire
Who fell that day beneath his ire:
For, sonless left long years ago,
His wrath made many a childless foe;
And since the day, when in the strait
His only boy had met his fate,
His parent's iron hand did doom
More than a human hecatomb.
If shades by carnage be appeased,
Patroclus' spirit less was pleased
Than his, Minotti's son, who died
Where Asia's bounds and ours divide.
Buried he lay, where thousands before
For thousands of years were inhumed on the shore:
What of them is left, to tell
Where they lie, and how they fell?
Not a stone on their turf, nor a bone in their graves;
But they live in the verse that immortally saves.

XXVI.

Hark to the Alla shout! a band
Of the mussulman bravest and best is at hand:
Their leader's nervous arm is bare,
Swifter to smite, and never to spare—
Unclothed to the shoulder it waves them on;
Thus in the fight is he ever known:

Others a gaudier garb may show,
To tempt the spoil of the greedy foe;
Many a hand 's on a richer hilt,
But none on a steel more ruddily gilt;
Many a loftier turban may wear,—
Alp is but known by the white arm bare;
Look though the thick of the fight, 't is there!
There is not a standard on that shore
So well advanced the ranks before;
There is not a banner in moslem war
Will lure the delhis half so far;
It glances like a falling star!
Where'er that mighty arm is seen,
The bravest be, or late have been;
There the craven cries for quarter
Vainly to the vengeful Tartar;
Or the hero, silent lying,
Scorns to yield a groan in dying;
Mustering his last feeble blow
'Gainst the nearest levell'd foe,
Though faint beneath the mutual wound,
Grappling on the gory ground.

XXVII.

Still the old man stood erect,
And Alp's career a moment check'd.
«Yield thee, Minotti; quarter take,
For thine own, thy daughter's sake.»
Never, renegado, never!
Though the life of thy gift would last for ever.»

« Francesca! Oh my promised bride!
Must she too perish by thy pride?»
« She is safe.»—« Where? where?»—« In heaven;
From whence thy traitor soul is driven—
Far from thee, and undefiled.»
Grimly then Minotti smiled,
As he saw Alp staggering bow
Before his words, as with a blow.
« Oh God! when died she?»—« Yesternight—
Nor weep I for her spirit's flight:
None of my pure race shall be
Slaves to Mahomet and thee—
Come on!»—That challenge is in vain—
Alp's already with the slain!
While Minotti's words were wreaking
More revenge in bitter speaking
Than his falchion's point had found,
Had the time allow'd to wound,
From within the neighbouring porch
Of a long defended church,
Where the last and desperate few
Would the failing fight renew,
The sharp shot dash'd Alp to the ground;
Ere an eye could view the wound
That crash'd through the brain of the infidel,
Round he spun, and down he fell;
A flash like fire within his eyes
Blazed, as he bent no more to rise,
And then eternal darkness sunk
Through all the palpitating trunk;
Nought of life left, save a quivering
Where his limbs were slightly shivering:

They turn'd him on his back; his breast
And brow were stain'd with gore and dust,
And through his lips the life-blood oozed,
From its deep veins lately loosed;
But in his pulse there was no throb,
Nor on his lips one dying sob;
Sigh, nor word, nor struggling breath
Heralded his way to death:
Ere his very thought could pray,
Unanel'd he pass'd away,
Without a hope from mercy's aid,—
To the last a renegade.

XXVIII.

Fearfully the yell arose
Of his followers, and his foes;
These in joy, in fury those:
Then again in conflict mixing,
Clashing swords, and spears transfixing,
Interchanged the blow and thrust,
Hurling warriors in the dust.
Street by street, and foot by foot,
Still Minotti dares dispute
The latest portion of the land
Left beneath his high command;
With him, aiding heart and hand,
The remnant of his gallant band.
Still the church is tenable,
  Whence issued late the fated ball
  That half avenged the city's fall,
When Alp, her fierce assailant, fell:
Thither bending sternly back,

They leave before a bloody track;
And, with their faces to the foe,
Dealing wounds with every blow,
The chief, and his retreating train,
Join to those within the fane;
There they yet may breathe awhile,
Shelter'd by the massy pile.

XXIX.

Brief breathing-time! the turban'd host,
With added ranks and raging boast,
Press onward with such strength and heat,
Their numbers balk their own retreat;
For narrow the way that led to the spot
Where still the christians yielded not;
And the foremost, if fearful, may vainly try
Through the massy column to turn and fly;
They perforce must do or die.
They die; but ere their eyes could close,
Avengers o'er their bodies rose;
Fresh and furious, fast they fill
The ranks unthinn'd, though slaughter'd still;
And faint the weary christians wax
Before the still renew'd attacks:
And now the Othmans gain the gate;
Still resists its iron weight,
And still, all deadly aim'd and hot,
From every crevice comes the shot;
From every shatter'd window pour
The volleys of the sulphurous shower:
But the portal wavering grows and weak—
The iron yields, the hinges creak—

It bends—it falls—and all is o'er;
Lost Corinth may resist no more!

XXX.

Darkly, sternly, and all alone,
Minotti stood o'er the altar stone:
Madonna's face upon him shone,
Painted in heavenly hues above,
With eyes of light and looks of love;
And placed upon that holy shrine
To fix our thoughts on things divine,
When pictured there, we kneeling see
Her, and the Boy-God on her knee,
Smiling sweetly on each prayer
To heaven, as if to waft it there.
Still she smiled; even now she smiles,
Though slaughter streams along her aisles:
Minotti lifted his aged eye,
And made the sign of a cross with a sigh,
Then seized a torch which blazed thereby;
And still he stood, while, with steel and flame,
Inward and onward the mussulman came.

XXXI.

The vaults beneath the mosaic stone
Contain'd the dead of ages gone;
Their names were on the graven floor,
But now illegible with gore;
The carved crests, and curious hues
The varied marble's veins diffuse,
Were smear'd, and slippery—stain'd, and strown
With broken swords, and helms o'erthrown:

There were dead above, and the dead below
Lay cold in many a coffin'd row;
You might see them piled in sable state,
By a pale light through a gloomy grate;
But war had enter'd their dark caves,
And stored along the vaulted graves
Her sulphurous treasures, thickly spread
In masses by the fleshless dead:
Here, throughout the siege, had been
The christians' chiefest magazine;
To these a late form'd train now led,
Minotti's last and stern resource
Against the foe's o'erwhelming force.

XXXII.

The foe came on, and few remain
To strive, and those must strive in vain:
For lack of further lives, to slake
The thirst of vengeance now awake,
With barbarous blows they gash the dead,
And lop the already lifeless head,
And fell the statues from their niche,
And spoil the shrines of offerings rich,
And from each other's rude hands wrest
The silver vessels saints had bless'd.
To the high altar on they go;
Oh, but it made a glorious show!
On its table still behold
The cup of consecrated gold;
Massy and deep, a glittering prize,
Brightly it sparkles to plunderers' eyes:

That morn it held the holy wine,
Converted by Christ to his blood so divine,
Which his worshippers drank at the break of day,
To shrive their souls ere they join'd in the fray.
Still a few drops within it lay;
And round the sacred table glow
Twelve lofty lamps, in splendid row,
From the purest metal cast;
A spoil—the richest, and the last.

XXXIII.

So near they came, the nearest stretch'd
To grasp the spoil he almost reach'd,
When old Minotti's hand
Touch'd with the torch the train—
'Tis fired!
Spire, vaults, the shrine, the spoil, the slain,
The turban'd victors, the christian band,
All that of living or dead remain,
Hurl'd on high with the shiver'd fane,
In one wild roar expired!
The shatter'd town—the walls thrown down—
The waves a moment backward bent—
The hills that shake, although unrent,
As if an earthquake pass'd—
The thousand shapeless things all driven
In cloud and flame athwart the heaven,
By that tremendous blast—
Proclaim'd the desperate conflict o'er
On that too long afflicted shore:
Up to the sky like rockets go
All that mingled there below:

Many a tall and goodly man,
Scorch'd and shrivell'd to a span,
When he fell to earth again
Like a cinder strew'd the plain:
Down the ashes shower like rain;
Some fell in the gulf, which received the sprinkles
With a thousand circling wrinkles;
Some fell on the shore, but, far away,
Scatter'd o'er the isthmus lay;
Christian or moslem, which be they?
Let their mothers see and say!
When in cradled rest they lay,
And each nursing mother smiled
On the sweet sleep of her child,
Little deem'd she such a day
Would rend those tender limbs away.
Not the matrons that them bore
Could discern their offspring more;
That one moment left no trace
More of human form or face
Save a scatter'd scalp or bone:
And down came blazing rafters, strown
Around, and many a falling stone,
Deeply dinted in the clay,
All blacken'd there and reeking lay.
All the living things that heard
That deadly earth-shock disappear'd:
The wild birds flew; the wild dogs fled,
And howling left the unburied dead;
The camels from their keepers broke;
The distant steer forsook the yoke—

The nearer steed plunged o'er the plain,
And burst his girth, and tore his rein;
The bull-frog's note, from out the marsh,
Deep-mouth'd arose, and doubly harsh;
The wolves yell'd on the cavern'd hill
Where echo roll'd in thunder still;
The jackal's troop, in gather'd cry,[10]
Bay'd from afar complainingly,
With a mix'd and mournful sound,
Like crying babe, and beaten hound:
With sudden wing, and ruffled breast,
The eagle left his rocky nest,
And mounted nearer to the sun,
The clouds beneath him seem'd so dun;
Their smoke assail'd his startled beak,
And made him higher soar and shriek—
Thus was Corinth lost and won!

NOTES TO THE SIEGE OF CORINTH.

Note 1, page 338, line 22.

The Turcoman hath left his herd, *etc.*

The life of the Turcomans is wandering and patriarchal, they dwell in tents.

Note 2, page 340, line 22.

Coumourgi—he whose closing scene, *etc*

Ali Coumourgi, the favourite of three sultans, and grand vizier to Achmet III., after recovering Peloponnesus from the Venetians in one campaign, was mortally wounded in the next, against the Germans, at the battle of Peterwaradin (in the plain of Carlowitz), in Hungary, endeavouring to rally his guards. He died of his wounds next day. His last order was the decapitation of General Breuner, and some other German prisoners; and his last words, «Oh that I could thus serve all the christian dogs!» a speech and act not unlike one of Caligula. He was a young man of great ambition and unbounded presumption: on being told that Prince Eugene, then opposed to him, «was a great general,» he said, «I shall become a greater, and at his expense.»

Note 3, page 350, line 10.

There shrinks no ebb in that tideless sea, *etc.*

The reader need hardly be reminded that there are no perceptible tides in the Mediterranean.

Note 4, page 351, line 15.

And their white tusks crunch'd o'er the whiter skull, *etc.*

This spectacle I have seen, such as described, beneath the walls of the seraglio at Constantinople, in the little cavities worn by the Bosphorus in the rock, a narrow terrace of which projects between the wall and the water. I think the fact is also mentioned in Hobhouse's Travels. The bodies were probably those of some refractory janizaries.

Note 5, page 351, line 24.

And each scalp had a single long tuft of hair, *etc.*

This tuft, or long lock, is left from a superstition that Mahomet will draw them into Paradise by it.

Note 6, page 353, line 18.

Was it the wind, through some hollow stone, *etc.*

I must here acknowledge a close, though unintentional, resemblance in these twelve lines to a passage in an unpublished poem of Mr Coleridge, called «Christabel.» It was not till after these lines were written that I heard that wild and singularly original and beautiful poem recited; and the MS. of that production I never saw till very recently, by the kindness of Mr Coleridge himself, who, I hope, is convinced that I have not been a wilful plagiarist. The original idea undoubtedly pertains to Mr Coleridge, whose poem has been composed above fourteen years. Let me conclude by a hope that he will not longer delay the publication of a production, of which I can only add my mite of approbation to the applause of far more competent judges.

Note 7, page 357, line 24.

There is a light cloud by the moon, *etc.*

I have been told that the idea expressed from lines 24 to 31, of the page above noted, has been admired by those whose approbation is valuable. I am glad of it: but it is not original—at least not mine; it may be found much better expressed in pages 182-3-4 of the English version of «Vathek» (I forget the precise page of the French), a work to which I have before referred; and never recur to, or read, without a renewal of gratification.

Note 8, page 359, line 9.

The horsetails are pluck'd from the ground, and the sword, *etc.*

The horsetail, fixed upon a lance, a pacha's standard.

Note 9, page 363, line 10.

And since the day, when in the strait, *etc.*

In the naval battle at the mouth of the Dardanelles, between the Venetians and the Turks.

Note 10, page 372, line 7.

The jackal's troop, in gather'd cry, *etc.*

I believe I have taken a poetical licence to transplant the jackal from Asia. In Greece I never saw nor heard these animals; but among the ruins of Ephesus I have heard them by hundreds. They haunt ruins, and follow armies.

THE

PRISONER OF CHILLON.

A FABLE.

SONNET ON CHILLON.

ETERNAL spirit of the chainless mind!
  Brightest in dungeons, Liberty! thou art,
  For there thy habitation is the heart—
The heart which love of thee alone can bind;
And when thy sons to fetters are consign'd—
  To fetters, and the damp vault's dayless gloom,
  Their country conquers with their martyrdom,
And freedom's fame finds wings on every wind.
Chillon! thy prison is a holy place,
  And thy sad floor an altar—for 't was trod,
Until his very steps have left a trace
  Worn, as if thy cold pavement were a sod,
By Bonnivard![1]—May none those marks efface!
  For they appeal from tyranny to God.

THE

PRISONER OF CHILLON.

I.

My hair is gray, but not with years,
Nor grew it white
In a single night,[2]
As men's have grown from sudden fears;
My limbs are bow'd, though not with toil,
But rusted with a vile repose,
For they have been a dungeon's spoil,
And mine has been the fate of those
To whom the goodly earth and air
Are bann'd, and barr'd—forbidden fare;
But this was for my father's faith
I suffer'd chains and courted death;
That father perish'd at the stake
For tenets he would not forsake;
And for the same his lineal race
In darkness found a dwelling-place;

We were seven—who now are one,
  Six in youth, and one in age,
Finish'd as they had begun,
  Proud of persecution's rage;
One in fire, and two in field,
Their belief with blood have seal'd;
Dying as their father died,
For the God their foes denied;
Three were in a dungeon cast,
Of whom this wreck is left the last.

II.

There are seven pillars of gothic mould,
In Chillon's dungeons deep and old,
There are seven columns, massy and gray,
Dim with a dull imprison'd ray,
A sunbeam which hath lost its way,
And through the crevice and the cleft
Of the thick wall is fallen and left;
Creeping o'er the floor so damp,
Like a marsh's meteor lamp:
And in each pillar there is a ring,
  And in each ring there is a chain;
That iron is a cankering thing,
  For in these limbs its teeth remain,
With marks that will not wear away,
Till I have done with this new day,
Which now is painful to these eyes,
Which have not seen the sun so rise
For years—I cannot count them o'er,
I lost their long and heavy score

When my last brother droop'd and died,
And I lay living by his side.

III.

They chain'd us each to a column-stone,
And we were three—yet, each alone:
We could not move a single pace,
We could not see each other's face,
But with that pale and livid light
That made us strangers in our sight;
And thus together—yet apart,
Fetter'd in hand, but pined in heart;
'T was still some solace in the dearth
Of the pure elements of earth,
To hearken to each other's speech,
And each turn comforter to each
With some new hope, or legend old,
Or song heroically bold;
But even these at length grew cold.
Our voices took a dreary tone,
An echo of the dungeon-stone,
  A grating sound—not full and free
  As they of yore were wont to be:
  It might be fancy—but to me
They never sounded like our own.

IV.

I was the eldest of the three,
  And to uphold and cheer the rest
  I ought to do—and did my best—
And each did well in his degree.

The youngest, whom my father loved,
Because our mother's brow was given
To him—with eyes as blue as heaven,
For him my soul was sorely moved;
And truly might it be distrest
To see such bird in such a nest;
For he was beautiful as day—
(When day was beautiful to me
As to young eagles, being free)—
A polar day, which will not see
A sunset till its summer's gone,
Its sleepless summer of long light,
The snow-clad offspring of the sun:
And thus he was as pure and bright,
And in his natural spirit gay,
With tears for nought but others' ills,
And then they flow'd like mountain rills,
Unless he could assuage the woe
Which he abhorr'd to view below.

V.

The other was as pure of mind,
But form'd to combat with his kind;
Strong in his frame, and of a mood
Which 'gainst the world in war had stood,
And perish'd in the foremost rank
With joy:—but not in chains to pine:
His spirit wither'd with their clank,
I saw it silently decline—
And so perchance in sooth did mine;
But yet I forced it on to cheer
Those relics of a home so dear.

He was a hunter of the hills,
Had follow'd there the deer and wolf;
To him this dungeon was a gulf,
And fetter'd feet the worst of ills.

VI.

Lake Leman lies by Chillon's walls:
A thousand feet in depth below
Its massy waters meet and flow;
Thus much the fathom-line was sent
From Chillon's snow-white battlement,[3]
Which round about the wave enthrals:
A double dungeon wall and wave
Have made—and like a living grave.
Below the surface of the lake
The dark vault lies wherein we lay,
We heard it ripple night and day;
Sounding o'er our heads it knock'd;
And I have felt the winter's spray
Wash through the bars when winds were high
And wanton in the happy sky;
And then the very rock hath rock'd,
And I have felt it shake, unshock'd,
Because I could have smiled to see
The death that would have set me free.

VII.

I said my nearer brother pined,
I said his mighty heart declined,
He loath'd and put away his food;
It was not that 't was coarse and rude,

For we were used to hunter's fare,
And for the like had little care:
The milk drawn from the mountain goat
Was changed for water from the moat,
Our bread was such as captives' tears
Have moisten'd many a thousand years,
Since man first pent his fellow men
Likes brutes within an iron den:
But what were these to us or him?
These wasted not his heart or limb;
My brother's soul was of that mould
Which in a palace had grown cold,
Had his free breathing been denied
The range of the steep mountain's side;
But why delay the truth?—he died.
I saw, and could not hold his head,
Nor reach his dying hand—nor dead,
Though hard I strove, but strove in vain,
To rend and gnash my bonds in twain.
He died—and they unlock'd his chain,
And scoop'd for him a shallow grave
E'en from the cold earth of our cave.
I begg'd them, as a boon, to lay
His corse in dust whereon the day
Might shine—it was a foolish thought,
But then within my brain it wrought,
That e'en in death his freeborn breast
In such a dungeon could not rest.
I might have spared my idle prayer—
They coldly laugh'd—and laid him there:
The flat and turfless earth above
The being we so much did love;

His empty chain above it leant,
Such murder's fitting monument!

VIII.

But he, the favorite and the flower,
Most cherish'd since his natal hour,
His mother's image in fair face,
The infant love of all his race,
His martyr'd father's dearest thought,
My latest care, for whom I sought
To hoard my life, that his might be
Less wretched now, and one day free;
He, too, who yet had held untired
A spirit natural or inspired—
He, too, was struck, and day by day
Was wither'd on the stalk away.
Oh God! it is a fearful thing
To see the human soul take wing
In any shape, in any mood:—
I 've seen it rushing forth in blood,
I 've seen it on the breaking ocean
Strive with a swoln convulsion motion,
I 've seen the sick and ghastly bed
Of sin delirious with its dread:
But these were horrors—this was woe
Unmix'd with such—but sure and slow:
He faded, and so calm and meek,
So softly worn, so sweetly weak,
So tearless, yet so tender—kind,
And grieved for those he left behind;
With all the while a cheek whose bloom
Was as a mockery of the tomb,

Whose tints as gently sunk away
As a departing rainbow's ray—
An eye of most transparent light,
That almost made the dungeon bright,
And not a word of murmur—not
A groan o'er his untimely lot,—
A little talk of better days,
A little hope my own to raise,
For I was sunk in silence—lost
In this last loss, of all the most;
And then the sighs he would suppress
Of fainting nature's feebleness,
More slowly drawn, grew less and less:
I listen'd, but I could not hear—
I call'd, for I was wild with fear;
I knew 't was hopeless, but my dread
Would not be thus admonished;
I call'd, and thought I heard a sound—
I burst my chain with one stroung bound,
And rush'd to him:—I found him not,
I only stirr'd in this black spot,
I only lived—*I* only drew
The accursed breath of dungeon-dew;
The last—the sole—the dearest link
Between me and the eternal brink,
Which bound me to my failing race,
Was broken in this fatal place.
One on the earth, and one beneath—
My brothers—both had ceased to breathe:
I took that hand which lay so still,
Alas! my own was full as chill;

I had not strength to stir, or strive,
But felt that I was still alive—
A frantic feeling, when we know
That what we love shall ne'er be so.
  I know not why
  I could not die,
I had no earthly hope—but faith,
And that forbade a selfish death.

IX.

What next befel me then and there
 I know not well—I never knew—
First came the loss of light, and air,
 And then of darkness too:
I had no thought, no feeling—none—
Among the stones I stood a stone,
And was, scarce conscious what I wist,
As shrubless crags within the mist;
For all was blank, and bleak, and gray,
It was not night—it was not day,
It was not even the dungeon-light,
So hateful to my heavy sight,
But vacancy absorbing space,
And fixedness—without a place;
There were no stars—no earth—no time—
No check—no change—no good—no crime—
But silence, and a stirless breath
Which neither was of life nor death;
A sea of stagnant idleness,
Blind, boundless, mute, and motionless!

X.

A light broke in upon my brain,—
It was the carol of a bird;
It ceased, and then it came again,
The sweetest song ear ever heard,
And mine was thankful till my eyes
Ran over with the glad surprise,
And they that moment could not see
I was the mate of misery;
But then by dull degrees came back
My senses to their wonted track,
I saw the dungeon walls and floor
Close slowly round me as before,
I saw the glimmer of the sun
Creeping as it before had done,
But through the crevice where it came
That bird was perch'd, as fond and tame,
And tamer than upon the tree;
A lovely bird, with azure wings,
And song that said a thousand things,
And seem'd to say them all for me!
I never saw its like before,
I ne'er shall see its likeness more:
It seem'd like me to want a mate,
But was not half so desolate,
And it was come to love me when
None lived to love me so again,
And cheering from my dungeon's brink,
Had brought me back to feel and think.
I know not if it late were free,
Or broke its cage to perch on mine,

But knowing well captivity,
Sweet bird! I could not wish for thine!
Or if it were, in winged guise,
A visitant from Paradise;
For—Heaven forgive that thought! the while
Which made me both to weep and smile;
I sometimes deem'd that it might be
My brother's soul come down to me;
But then at last away it flew,
And then 't was mortal—well I knew,
For he would never thus have flown,
And left me twice so doubly lone,—
Lone—as the corse within its shroud,
Lone—as a solitary cloud,
A single cloud on a sunny day,
While all the rest of heaven is clear,
A frown upon the atmosphere,
That hath no business to appear
When skies are blue, and earth is gay.

XI.

A kind of change came in my fate,
My keepers grew compassionate,
I know not what had made them so,
They were inured to sights of woe,
But so it was:—my broken chain
With links unfasten'd did remain,
And it was liberty to stride
Along my cell from side to side,
And up and down, and then athwart,
And tread it over every part;

And round the pillars one by one,
Returning where my walk begun,
Avoiding only, as I trod,
My brothers' graves without a sod;
For if I thought with heedless tread
My step profaned their lowly bed,
My breath came gaspingly and thick,
And my crush'd heart fell blind and sick.

XII.

I made a footing in the wall,
It was not therefrom to escape,
For I had buried one and all,
Who loved me in a human shape;
And the whole earth would henceforth be
A wider prison unto me:
No child—no sire—no kin had I,
No partner in my misery;
I thought of this, and I was glad,
For thought of them had made me mad;
But I was curious to ascend
To my barr'd windows, and to bend
Once more, upon the mountains high,
The quiet of a loving eye.

XIII.

I saw them—and they were the same,
They were not changed like me in frame;
I saw their thousand years of snow
On high—their wide long lake below,
And the blue Rhone in fullest flow;

I beard the torrents leap and gush
O'er channell'd rock and broken bush;
I saw the white-wall'd distant town,
And whiter sails go skimming down;
And then there was a little isle,[4]
Which in my very face did smile,
The only one in view;
A small green isle, it seem'd no more,
Scarce broader than my dungeon floor,
But in it there were three tall trees,
And o'er it blew the mountain breeze,
And by it there were waters flowing,
And on it there were young flowers growing,
Of gentle breath and hue.
The fish swam by the castle wall,
And they seem'd joyous each and all;
The eagle rode the rising blast,
Methought he never flew so fast
As then to me he seem'd to fly,
And then new tears came in my eye,
And I felt troubled—and would fain
I had not left my recent chain;
And when I did descend again,
The darkness of my dim abode
Fell on me as a heavy load;
It was as is a new-dug grave,
Closing o'er one we sought to save,
And yet my glance, too much opprest,
Had almost need of such a rest.

XIV.

It might be months, or years, or days,
  I kept no count—I took no note,
I had no hope my eyes to raise,
  And clear them of their dreary mote;
At last men came to set me free,
  I ask'd not why, and reck'd not where,
It was at length the same to me,
Fetter'd or fetterless to be,
  I learn'd to love despair.
And thus when they appear'd at last,
And all my bonds aside were cast,
These heavy walls to me had grown
A hermitage—and all my own!
And half I felt as they were come
To tear me from a second home:
With spiders I had friendship made,
And watch'd them in their sullen trade,
Had seen the mice by moonlight play,
And why should I feel less than they?
We were all inmates of one place,
And I, the monarch of each race,
Had power to kill—yet, strange to tell!
In quiet we had learn'd to dwell—
My very chains and I grew friends,
So much a long communion tends
To make us what we are:—even I
Regain'd my freedom with a sigh.

NOTES TO THE PRISONER OF CHILLON.

Note 1, page 379, line 13.

By Bonnivard!—may none those marks efface, *etc.*

François de Bonnivard, fils de Louis de Bonnivard, originaire de Seyssel, et seigneur de Lunes, naquit en 1496; il fit ses études à Turin. En 1510, Jean-Aimé de Bonnivard, son oncle, lui résigna le prieuré de Saint-Victor, qui aboutissait aux murs de Genève, et qui formait un bénéfice considérable.

Ce grand homme (Bonnivard mérite ce titre par la force de son ame, la droiture de son cœur, la noblesse de ses intentions, la sagesse de ses conseils, le courage de ses démarches, l'étendue de ses connaissances, et la vivacité de son esprit), ce grand homme, qui excitera l'admiration de tous ceux qu'une vertu héroïque peut encore émouvoir, inspirera encore la plus vive reconnaissance dans les cœurs des Génevois qui aiment Genève. Bonnivard en fut toujours un des plus fermes appuis : pour assurer la liberté de notre république, il ne craignit pas de perdre souvent la sienne. Il oublia son repos; il méprisa ses richesses; il ne négligea rien pour affermir le bonheur d'une patrie qu'il honora de son choix : dès ce moment, il la chérit comme le plus zélé de ses concitoyens; il la servit avec l'intrépidité d'un héros, et il écrivit son histoire avec la naïveté d'un philosophe, et la chaleur d'un patriote.

Il dit, dans le commencement de son Histoire de Genève, que « dès qu'il eut commencé de lire l'histoire des nations, il se sentit entraîné par son goût pour les républiques, dont il épousa toujours les intérêts. » C'est ce goût pour la liberté qui lui fit sans doute adopter Genève pour sa patrie.

Bonnivard, encore jeune, s'annonça hautement comme le défenseur de Genève contre le duc de Savoie et l'évêque.

En 1519, Bonnivard devint le martyr de sa patrie. Le duc de Savoie étant entré dans Genève avec cinq cents hommes, Bonnivard craignit le ressentiment du duc; il voulut se retirer à Fribourg pour en éviter les suites; mais il fut trahi par deux hommes qui l'accompagnaient, et conduit par ordre du prince à Grolée, où il resta prisonnier pendant deux ans. Bonnivard était malheureux dans ses voyages: comme ses malheurs n'avaient point ralenti son zèle pour Genève, il était toujours un ennemi redoutable pour ceux qui la menaçaient, et par conséquent il devait être exposé à leurs coups. Il fut rencontré, en 1530, sur le Jura, par des voleurs qui le dépouillèrent, et qui le mirent encore entre les mains du duc de Savoie. Ce prince le fit enfermer dans le château de Chillon, où il resta sans être interrogé jusqu'en 1536; il fut alors délivré par les Bernois, qui s'emparèrent du pays de Vaud.

Bonnivard, en sortant de sa captivité, eut le plaisir de trouver Genève libre et réformée; la république s'empressa de lui témoigner sa reconnaissance, et de le dédommager des maux qu'il avait soufferts; elle le reçut bourgeois de la ville au mois de juin 1536; elle lui donna la maison habitée autrefois par le vicaire-général, et elle lui assigna une pension de 200 écus d'or tant qu'il séjournerait à Genève. Il fut admis dans le Conseil des Deux-Cents en 1537.

Bonnivard n'a pas fini d'être utile: après avoir travaillé à rendre Genève libre, il réussit à la rendre tolérante. Bonnivard engagea le Conseil à accorder aux ecclésiastiques et aux paysans un temps suffisant pour examiner les propositions qu'on leur faisait; il réussit par sa douceur: on prêche toujours le christianisme avec succès quand on le prêche avec charité,

Bonnivard fut savant; ses manuscrits, qui sont dans la bibliothèque publique, prouvent qu'il avait bien lu les auteurs classiques latins, et qu'il avait approfondi la théologie et l'histoire. Ce grand homme aimait les sciences, et il croyait qu'elles pouvaient faire la gloire de Genève; aussi il ne négligea rien pour les fixer dans cette ville naissante. En 1551, il donna sa bibliothèque au public; elle fut le commencement de notre bibliothèque publique; et ces livres sont en partie les rares et belles éditions du quinzième siècle qu'on voit dans notre collection. Enfin, pendant la même année, ce bon patriote institua la république son héritière, à condition qu'elle emploierait ses biens à entretenir le collége dont on projettait la fondation.

Il paroit que Bonnivard mourut en 1570; mais on ne peut l'assurer, parcequ'il y a une lacune dans le Nécrologe depuis le mois de juillet 1570 jusqu'en 1571.

Note 2, page 381, line 4.

In a single night, *etc*.

Ludovico Sforza, and others.—The same is asserted of Marie Antoinette's, the wife of Louis XVI., though not in quite so short a period. Grief is said to have the same effect: to such, and not to fear, this change in *hers* was to be attributed.

Note 3, page 385, line 10.

From Chillon's snow-white battlement, *etc*.

The Château de Chillon is situated between Clarens and Villeneuve, which last is at one extremity of the Lake of Geneva. On its left are the entrances of the Rhone, and opposite are the heights of Meillerie and the range of Alps above Boveret and St Gingo.

Near it, on a hill behind, is a torrent; below it, washing its walls, the lake has been fathomed to the depth of 800 feet (French measure); within it are a range of dungeons, in which the early reformers, and subsequently prisoners of state, were confined. Across one of the vaults is a beam black with age, on which we were informed that the condemned were formerly executed. In the cells are seven pillars, or, rather, eight, one being half merged in the wall; in some of these are rings for the fetters and the fettered: in the pavement the steps of Bonnivard have left their traces—he was confined here several years.

It is by this castle that Rousseau has fixed the catastrophe of his Heloise, in the rescue of one of her children by Julie from the water; the shock of which, and the illness produced by the immersion, is the cause of her death.

The chateau is large, and seen along the lake for a great distance. The walls are white.

Note 4, page 393, line 5.

And then there was a little isle, *etc*.

Between the entrances of the Rhone and Villeneuve, not far from Chillon, is a very small island; the only one I could perceive, in my voyage round and over the lake, within its circumference. It contains a few trees (I think not above three), and from its singleness and diminutive size has a peculiar effect upon the view.

When the foregoing poem was composed, I was not sufficiently aware of the history of Bonnivard, or I should have endeavoured to dignify the subject by an attempt to celebrate his courage and his virtues. Some account of his life will be found in a note appended to the «Sonnet on Chillon,» with which I have been furnished by the kindness of a citizen of that Republic which is still proud of the memory of a man worthy of the best age of ancient freedom.

MAZEPPA.

A POEM.

ADVERTISEMENT.

« Celui qui remplissait alors cette place, était un gentilhomme polonais, nommé Mazeppa, né dans le palatinat de Podolie; il avait été élevé page de Jean-Casimir, et avait pris à sa cour quelque teinture des belles-lettres. Une intrigue qu'il eut dans sa jeunesse avec la femme d'un gentilhomme polonais ayant été découverte, le mari le fit lier tout nu sur un cheval farouche, et le laissa aller en cet état. Le cheval, qui était du pays de l'Ukraine, y retourna, et y porta Mazeppa, demi-mort de fatigue et de faim. Quelques paysans le secoururent : il resta long-temps parmi eux, et se signala dans plusieurs courses contre les Tartares. La supériorité de ses lumières lui donna une grande considération parmi les Cosaques : sa réputation, s'augmentant de jour en jour, obligea le czar à le faire prince de l'Ukraine. »—Voltaire, *Hist. de Charles. XII.* p. 196.

« Le roi, fuyant et poursuivi, eut son cheval tué sous

lui; le colonel Gieta, blessé, et perdant tout son sang, lui donna le sien. Ainsi on remit deux fois à cheval, dans la fuite, ce conquérant, qui n'avait pu y monter pendant la bataille. »—VOLTAIRE, *Hist. de Charles XII.* page 216.

« Le roi alla par un autre chemin avec quelques cavaliers. Le carrosse où il était rompit dans la marche; on le remit à cheval. Pour comble de disgrace, il s'égara pendant la nuit dans un bois; là, son courage ne pouvant plus suppléer à ses forces épuisées, les douleurs de sa blessure devenues plus insupportables par la fatigue, son cheval étant tombé de lassitude, il se coucha quelques heures au pied d'un arbre, en danger d'être surpris à tout moment par les vainqueurs, qui le cherchaient de tous côtés. »—VOLTAIRE, *Histoire de Charles XII.* p. 218.

MAZEPPA.

I.

'T WAS after dread Pultowa's day,
When fortune left the royal Swede,
Around a slaughter'd army lay,
No more to combat and to bleed.
The power and glory of the war,
Faithless as their vain votaries, men,
Had pass'd to the triumphant Czar,
And Moscow's walls were safe again,
Until a day more dark and drear,
And a more memorable year,
Should give to slaughter and to shame
A mightier host and haughtier name;
A greater wreck, a deeper fall,
A shock to one—a thunderbolt to all.

II.

Such was the hazard of the die;
The wounded Charles was taught to fly

By day and night, through field and flood,
Stain'd with his own and subjects' blood;
For thousands fell that flight to aid:
And not a voice was heard t' upbraid
Ambition in his humbled hour,
When truth had nought to dread from power.
His horse was slain, and Gieta gave
His own—and died the Russians' slave.
This too sinks after many a league
Of well-sustain'd, but vain fatigue;
And in the depth of forests, darkling
The watch-fires in the distance sparkling—
The beacons of surrounding foes—
A king must lay his limbs at length.
Are these the laurels and repose
For which the nations strain their strength?
They laid him by a savage tree,
In outworn nature's agony;
His wounds were stiff—his limbs were stark—
The heavy hour was chill and dark;
The fever in his blood forbade
A transient slumber's fitful aid:
And thus it was; but yet through all,
King-like the monarch bore his fall,
And made, in this extreme of ill,
His pangs the vassals of his will;
All silent and subdued were they,
As once the nations round him lay.

III.

A band of chiefs!—alas! how few,
Since but the fleeting of a day

Had thinn'd it; but this wreck was true
  And chivalrous: upon the clay
Each sate him down, all sad and mute,
  Beside his monarch and his steed,
For danger levels man and brute,
  And all are fellows in their need.
Among the rest, Mazeppa made
His pillow in an old oak's shade—
Himself as rough, and scarce less old,
The Ukraine's hetman, calm and bold;
But first, outspent with this long course,
The Cossack prince rubb'd down his horse,
And made for him a leafy bed,
  And smooth'd his fetlocks and his mane,
  And slack'd his girth, and stripp'd his rein,
And joy'd to see how well he fed;
For until now he had the dread
His wearied courser might refuse
To browse beneath the midnight dews:
But he was hardy as his lord,
And little cared for bed and board;
But spirited and docile too,
Whate'er was to be done, would do.
Shaggy and swift, and strong of limb,
All Tartar-like he carried him;
Obey'd his voice, and came to call,
And knew him in the midst of all:
Though thousands were around,—and night,
Without a star, pursued her flight,—
That steed from sunset until dawn
His chief would follow like a fawn.

IV.

This done, Mazeppa spread his cloak,
And laid his lance beneath the oak,
Felt if his arms in order good
The long day's march had well withstood—
If still the powder fill'd the pan,
   And flints unloosen'd kept their lock—
His sabre's hilt and scabbard felt,
And whether they had chafed his belt—
And next the venerable man,
From out his haversack and can,
   Prepared and spread his slender stock;
And to the monarch and his men
The whole or portion offer'd then,
With far less of inquietude
Than courtiers at a banquet would.
And Charles of this his slender share
With smiles partook a moment there,
To force of cheer a greater show,
And seem above both wounds and woe;—
And then he said—« Of all our band,
Though firm of heart and strong of hand,
In skirmish, march, or forage, none
Can less have said or more have done
Than thee, Mazeppa! On the earth
So fit a pair had never birth,
Since Alexander's days till now,
As thy Bucephalus and thou:
All Scythia's fame to thine should yield
For pricking on o'er flood and field. »

Mazeppa answer'd—« Ill betide
The school wherein I learn'd to ride! »
Quoth Charles—« Old hetman, wherefore so,
Since thou hast learn'd the art so well? »
Mazeppa said—« 'T were long to tell;
And we have many a league to go,
With every now and then a blow,
And ten to one at least the foe,
Before our steeds may graze at ease
Beyond the swift Borysthenes:
And, sire, your limbs have need of rest,
And I will be the sentinel
Of this your troop. »—« But I request, »
Said Sweden's monarch, « thou wilt tell
This tale of thine, and I may reap,
Perchance, from this the boon of sleep,
For at this moment from my eyes
The hope of present slumber flies. »

« Well, sire, with such a hope, I 'll track
My seventy years of memory back:
I think 't was in my twentieth spring,—
Ay, 't was,—when Casimir was king—
John Casimir,—I was his page
Six summers in my earlier age;
A learned monarch, faith! was he,
And most unlike your majesty:
He made no wars, and did not gain
New realms to lose them back again;
And (save debates in Warsaw's diet)
He reign'd in most unseemly quiet;

Not that he had no cares to vex,
He loved the muses and the sex;
And sometimes these so froward are,
They made him wish himself at war;
But soon his wrath being o'er, he took
Another mistress, or new book:
And then he gave prodigious *fêtes*—
All Warsaw gather'd round his gates
To gaze upon his splendid court,
And dames, and chiefs of princely port:
He was the Polish Solomon,
So sung his poets, all but one,
Who, being unpension'd, made a satire,
And boasted that he could not flatter.
It was a court of jousts and mimes,
Where every courtier tried at rhymes;
Even I for once produced some verses,
And sign'd my odes Despairing Thirsis.
There was a certain palatine,
A count of far and high descent,
Rich as a salt or silver mine;[1]
And he was proud, ye may divine,
As if from heaven he had been sent:
He had such wealth in blood and ore
As few could match beneath the throne;
And he would gaze upon his store,
And o'er his pedigree would pore,
Until by some confusion led,
Which almost look'd like want of head,
He thought their merits were his own.
His wife was not of his opinion—

His junior she by thirty years—
Grew daily tired of his dominion;
And, after wishes, hopes, and fears,
To virtue a few farewell tears,
A restless dream or two, some glances
At Warsaw's youth, some songs, and dances,
Awaited but the usual chances,
Those happy accidents which render
The coldest dames so very tender,
To deck her count with titles given,
'T is said, as passports into heaven;
But, strange to say, they rarely boast
Of these who have deserved them most.

V.

"I was a goodly stripling then;
At seventy years I so may say,
That there were few, or boys or men,
Who, in my dawning time of day,
Of vassal or of knight's degree,
Could vie in vanities with me;
For I had strength, youth, gaiety,
A port, not like to this ye see,
But smooth, as all is rugged now;
For time, and care, and war, have plough'd
My very soul from out my brow;
And thus I should be disavow'd
By all my kind and kin, could they
Compare my day and yesterday;
This change was wrought, too, long ere age
Had ta'en my features for his page:

With years, ye know, have not declined
My strength, my courage, or my mind,
Or at this hour I should not be
Telling old tales beneath a tree,
With starless skies my canopy.
But let me on: Theresa's form—
Methinks it glides before me now,
Between me and yon chestnut's bough,
The memory is so quick and warm;
And yet I find no words to tell
The shape of her I loved so well:
She had the Asiatic eye,
  Such as our Turkish neighbourhood
  Hath mingled with our Polish blood,
Dark as above us is the sky;
But through it stole a tender light,
Like the first moon-rise at midnight;
Large, dark, and swimming in the stream,
Which seem'd to melt to its own beam;
All love, half languor, and half fire,
Like saints that at the stake expire,
And lift their raptured looks on high,
As though it were a joy to die.
A brow like a midsummer lake,
  Transparent with the sun therein,
When waves no murmur dare to make,
  And heaven beholds her face within.
A cheek and lip—but why proceed?
  I loved her then—I love her still;
And such as I am, love indeed
  In fierce extremes—in good and ill.

But still we love e'en in our rage,
And haunted to our very age
With the vain shadow of the past,
As is Mazeppa to the last.

VI.

« We met—we gazed—I saw, and sigh'd,
She did not speak, and yet replied;
There are ten thousand tones and signs
We hear and see, but none defines—
Involuntary sparks of thought,
Which strike from out the heart o'erwrought,
And form a strange intelligence,
Alike mysterious and intense,
Which link the burning chain that binds,
Without their will, young hearts and minds;
Conveying, as the electric wire,
We know not how, the absorbing fire.—
I saw, and sigh'd—in silence wept,
And still reluctant distance kept,
Until I was made known to her,
And we might then and there confer
Without suspicion—then, even then,
  I long'd, and was resolved to speak;
But on my lips they died again,
  The accents tremulous and weak,
Until one hour.—There is a game,
  A frivolous and foolish play,
  Wherewith we wile away the day;
It is—I have forgot the name—
And we to this, it seems, were set,
By some strange chance, which I forget:

I reck'd not if I won or lost,
  It was enough for me to be
  So near to hear, and oh! to see
The being whom I loved the most.—
I watch'd her as a sentinel,
(May ours this dark night watch as well!)
Until I saw, and thus it was,
That she was pensive, nor perceived
Her occupation, nor was grieved
Nor glad to lose or gain; but still
Play'd on for hours, as if her will
Yet bound her to the place, though not
That hers might be the winning lot.
Then through my brain the thought did pass
  Even as a flash of lightning there,
  That there was something in her air
  Which would not doom me to despair;
And on the thought my words broke forth,
  All incoherent as they were—
Their eloquence was little worth,
But yet she listen'd—'t is enough—
  Who listens once will listen twice;
  Her heart, be sure, is not of ice,
And one refusal no rebuff.

VII.

« I loved, and was beloved again—
  They tell me, sire, you never knew
  Those gentle frailties; if 't is true,
I shorten all my joy or pain;
To you 't would seem absurd as vain;
But all men are not born to reign,

Or o'er their passions, or as you
Thus o'er themselves and nations too.
I am—or rather *was*—a prince,
  A chief of thousands, and could lead
  Them on where each would foremost bleed;
But could not o'er myself evince
The like controul—but to resume:
  I loved, and was beloved again;
In sooth, it is a happy doom,
  But yet where happiest ends in pain.—
We met in secret, and the hour
Which led me to that lady's bower
Was fiery expectation's dower.
My days and nights were nothing—all
Except that hour, which doth recall
In the long lapse from youth to age
  No other like itself—I 'd give
  The Ukraine back again to live
It o'er once more—and be a page,
The happy page, who was the lord
Of one soft heart, and his own sword,
And had no other gem nor wealth
Save nature's gift of youth and health.—
We met in secret—doubly sweet,
Some say, they find it so to meet;
I know not that—I would have given
  My life but to have call'd her mine
In the full view of earth and heaven;
  For I did oft and long repine
That we could only meet by stealth.

VIII.

« For lovers there are many eyes,
And such there were on us;—the devil
On such occasions should be civil—
The devil!—I 'm loth to do him wrong,
It might be some untoward saint,
Who would not be at rest too long,
But to his pious bile gave vent—
But one fair night, some lurking spies
Surprised and seized us both.
The count was something more than wroth—
I was unarm'd; but if in steel,
All cap-a-pee from head to heel,
What 'gainst their numbers could I do?—
'T was near his castle, far away
From city or from succour near,
And almost on the break of day;
I did not think to see another,
My moments seem'd reduced to few;
And with one prayer to Mary Mother,
And, it may be, a saint or two,
As I resign'd me to my fate,
They led me to the castle gate:
Theresa's doom I never knew,
Our lot was henceforth separate—
An angry man, ye may opine,
Was he, the proud count palatine;
And he had reason good to be,
But he was most enraged lest such
An accident should chance to touch

Upon his future pedigree;
Nor less amazed, that such a blot
His noble 'scutcheon should have got,
While he was highest of his line;
Because unto himself he seem'd
The first of men, nor less he deem'd
In others' eyes, and most in mine.
'S death! with a *page*—perchance a king
Had reconciled him to the thing;
But with a stripling of a page—
I felt—but cannot paint his rage.

IX.

"'Bring forth the horse!'—the horse was brought;
In truth, he was a noble steed,
A Tartar of the Ukraine breed,
Who look'd as though the speed of thought
Were in his limbs; but he was wild,
Wild as the wild deer, and untaught,
With spur and bridle undefiled—
'T was but a day he had been caught;
And snorting, with erected mane,
And struggling fiercely, but in vain,
In the full foam of wrath and dread
To me the desert-born was led:
They bound me on, that menial throng,
Upon his back with many a thong;
Then loosed him with a sudden lash—
Away!—away!—and on we dash—
Torrents less rapid and less rash.

X.

« Away!—away!—my breath was gone—
I saw not where he hurried on:
'T was scarcely yet the break of day,
And on he foam'd—away!—away!—
The last of human sounds which rose,
As I was darted from my foes,
Was the wild shout of savage laughter,
Which on the wind came roaring after
A moment from that rabble rout:
With sudden wrath I wrench'd my head,
   And snapp'd the cord, which to the mane
   Had bound my neck in lieu of rein,
And, writhing half my form about,
Howl'd back my curse; but 'midst the tread,
The thunder of my courser's speed,
Perchance they did not hear nor heed:
It vexes me—for I would fain
Have paid their insult back again.
I paid it well in after days:
There is not of that castle gate,
Its drawbridge and portcullis' weight,
Stone, bar, moat, bridge, or barrier left;
Nor of its fields a blade of grass,
   Save what grows on a ridge of wall,
   Where stood the hearth-stone of the hall;
And many a time ye there might pass,
Nor dream that e'er that fortress was:
I saw its turrets in a blaze,
Their crackling battlements all cleft,

And the hot lead pour down like rain
From off the scorch'd and blackening roof,
Whose thickness was not vengeance-proof.
They little thought that day of pain,
When lanch'd, as on the lightning's flash,
They bade me to destruction dash,
That one day I should come again,
With twice five thousand horse, to thank
The count for his uncourteous ride.
They play'd me then a bitter prank,
When, with the wild horse for my guide,
They bound me to his foaming flank:
At length I play'd them one as frank—
For time at last sets all things even—
And if we do but watch the hour,
There never yet was human power
Which could evade, if unforgiven,
The patient search and vigil long
Of him who treasures up a wrong.

XI.

« Away, away, my steed and I,
Upon the pinions of the wind,
All human dwellings left behind;
We sped like meteors through the sky,
When with its crackling sound the night
Is chequer'd with the northern light:
Town—village—none were on our track,
But a wild plain of far extent,
And bounded by a forest black;
And, save the scarce-seen battlement

On distant heights of some strong hold,
Against the Tartars built of old,
No trace of man. The year before
A Turkish army had march'd o'er;
And where the spahi's hoof hath trod,
The verdure flies the bloody sod:—
The sky was dull, and dim, and gray,
  And a low breeze crept moaning by—
  I could have answer'd with a sigh—
But fast we fled, away, away—
And I could neither sigh nor pray;
And my cold sweat-drops fell like rain
Upon the courser's bristling mane;
But, snorting still with rage and fear,
He flew upon his far career:
At times I almost thought, indeed,
He must have slacken'd in his speed;
But no—my bound and slender frame
  Was nothing to his angry might,
And merely like a spur became:
Each motion which I made to free
My swoln limbs from their agony
  Increased his fury and affright:
I tried my voice,—'t was faint and low,
But yet he swerved as from a blow;
And, starting to each accent, sprang
As from a sudden trumpet's clang:
Meantime my cords were wet with gore,
Which, oozing through my limbs, ran o'er;
And in my tongue the thirst became
A something fierier far than flame.

XII.

« We near'd the wild wood—'t was so wide,
I saw no bounds on either side;
'T was studded with old sturdy trees,
That bent not to the roughest breeze
Which howls down from Siberia's waste,
And strips the forest in its haste,—
But these were few, and far between
Set thick with shrubs more young and green,
Luxuriant with their annual leaves,
Ere strown by those autumnal eves
That nip the forest's foliage dead,
Discolour'd with a lifeless red,
Which stands thereon like stiffen'd gore
Upon the slain when battle 's o'er,
And some long winter's night hath shed
Its frost o'er every tombless head
So cold and stark, the raven's beak
May peck unpierced each frozen cheek:
'T was a wild waste of underwood,
And here and there a chestnut stood,
The strong oak, and the hardy pine;
 But far apart—and well it were,
Or else a different lot were mine—
 The boughs gave way, and did not tear
My limbs; and I found strength to bear
My wounds, already scarr'd with cold—
My bonds forbade to loose my hold.
We rustled through the leaves like wind,
Left shrubs, and trees, and wolves behind;

27.

By night I heard them on the track,
Their troop came hard upon our back,
With their long gallop, which can tire
The hound's deep hate, and hunter's fire:
Where'er we flew they follow'd on,
Nor left us with the morning sun;
Behind I saw them, scarce a rood,
At day-break winding through the wood,
And through the night had heard their feet
Their stealing, rustling step repeat.
Oh! how I wish'd for spear or sword,
At least to die amidst the horde,
And perish—if it must be so—
At bay, destroying many a foe.
When first my courser's race begun,
I wish'd the goal already won;
But now I doubted strength and speed.
Vain doubt! his swift and savage breed
Had nerved him like the mountain-roe;
Nor faster falls the blinding snow,
Which whelms the peasant near the door
Whose threshold he shall cross no more,
Bewilder'd with the dazzling blast,
Than through the forest-paths he past—
Untired, untamed, and worse than wild;
All furious as a favour'd child
Baulk'd of its wish; or fiercer still—
A woman piqued—who has her will.

XIII.

«The wood was past; 't was more than noon,
But chill the air, although in June;

Or it might be my veins ran cold—
Prolong'd endurance tames the bold;
And I was then not what I seem,
But headlong as a wintry stream,
And wore my feelings out before
I well could count their causes o'er:
And what with fury, fear, and wrath,
The tortures which beset my path,
Cold, hunger, sorrow, shame, distress,
Thus bound in nature's nakedness;
Sprung from a race whose rising blood
When stirr'd beyond its calmer mood,
And trodden hard upon, is like
The rattlesnake's, in act to strike,
What marvel if this worn-out trunk
Beneath its woes a moment sunk?
The earth gave way, the skies roll'd round,
I seem'd to sink upon the ground;
But err'd, for I was fastly bound.
My heart turn'd sick, my brain grew sore,
And throbb'd awhile, then beat no more:
The skies spun like a mighty wheel;
I saw the trees like drunkards reel,
And a slight flash sprang o'er my eyes,
Which saw no farther: he who dies
Can die no more than then I died.
O'ertortured by that ghastly ride,
I felt the blackness come and go,
And strove to wake; but could not make
My senses climb up from below:
I felt as on a plank at sea,
When all the waves that dash o'er thee,

At the same time upheave and whelm,
And hurl thee towards a desert realm.
My undulating life was as
The fancied lights that flitting pass
Our shut eyes in deep midnight, when
Fever begins upon the brain;
But soon it pass'd, with little pain,
  But a confusion worse than such:
  I own that I should deem it much,
Dying, to feel the same again;
And yet I do suppose we must
Feel far more ere we turn to dust:
No matter; I have bared my brow
Full in death's face—before—and now.

XIV.

"My thoughts came back; where was I? Cold,
  And numb, and giddy: pulse by pulse
Life reassumed its lingering hold,
And throb by throb; till grown a pang
  Which for a moment would convulse,
  My blood reflow'd, though thick and chill;
My ear with uncouth noises rang,
  My heart began once more to thrill;
My sight return'd, though dim; alas!
And thicken'd, as it were, with glass.
Methought the dash of waves was nigh;
There was a gleam too of the sky,
Studded with stars;—it is no dream;
The wild horse swims the wilder stream!
The bright broad river's gushing tide
Sweeps, winding onward, far and wide,

And we are half-way, struggling o'er
To yon unknown and silent shore.
The waters broke my hollow trance,
And with a temporary strength
  My stiffen'd limbs were rebaptized.
My courser's broad breast proudly braves,
And dashes off the ascending waves,
And onward we advance!
We reach the slippery shore at length,
  A haven I but little prized,
For all behind was dark and drear,
And all before was night and fear.
How many hours of night or day
In those suspended pangs I lay,
I could not tell; I scarcely knew
If this were human breath I drew.

XV.

« With glossy skin, and dripping mane,
  And reeling limbs, and reeking flank,
The wild steed's sinewy nerves still strain
  Up the repelling bank.
We gain the top: a boundless plain
Spreads through the shadow of the night,
  And onward, onward, onward, seems
  Like precipices in our dreams,
To stretch beyond the sight;
And here and there a speck of white,
  Or scatter'd spot of dusky green,
In masses broke into the light,
As rose the moon upon my right.
  But nought distinctly seen

In the dim waste, would indicate
The omen of a cottage-gate;
No twinkling taper from afar
Stood like a hospitable star;
Not even an ignis-fatuus rose
To make him merry with my woes:
That very cheat had cheer'd me then!
Although detected, welcome still,
Reminding me, through every ill,
Of the abodes of men.

XVI.

"Onward we went—but slack and slow;
His savage force at length o'erspent,
The drooping courser, faint and low,
All feebly foaming went.
A sickly infant had had power
To guide him forward in that hour;
But useless all to me.
His new-born tameness nought avail'd,
My limbs were bound; my force had fail'd,
Perchance, had they been free.
With feeble effort still I tried
To rend the bonds so starkly tied—
But still it was in vain;
My limbs were only wrung the more,
And soon the idle strife gave o'er,
Which but prolong'd their pain:
The dizzy race seem'd almost done,
Although no goal was nearly won:
Some streaks announced the coming sun—

How slow, alas! he came.
Methought that mist of dawning gray
Would never dapple into day;
How heavily it roll'd away—
Before the eastern flame
Rose crimson, and deposed the stars,
And call'd the radiance from their cars,
And fill'd the earth, from his deep throne,
With lonely lustre, all his own.

XVII.

« Up rose the sun; the mists were curl'd
Back from the solitary world
Which lay around—behind—before:
What booted it to traverse o'er
Plain, forest, river? Man nor brute,
Nor dint of hoof, nor print of foot,
Lay in the wild luxuriant soil;
No sign of travel—none of toil;
The very air was mute;
And not an insect's shrill, small horn,
Nor matin bird's new voice was borne
From herb nor thicket. Many a werst,
Panting as if his heart would burst,
The weary brute still stagger'd on;
And still we were—or seem'd—alone;
At length, while reeling on our way,
Methought I heard a courser neigh,
From out yon tuft of blackening firs.
Is it the wind those branches stirs?
No, no! from out the forest prance
A trampling troop; I see them come!

In one vast squadron they advance!
  I strove to cry—my lips were dumb.
The steeds rush on in plunging pride;
But where are they the reins to guide?
A thousand horse—and none to ride!
With flowing tail, and flying mane,
Wide nostrils—never stretch'd by pain,
Mouths bloodless to the bit or rein,
And feet that iron never shod,
And flanks unscarr'd by spur or rod,
A thousand horse, the wild, the free,
Like waves that follow o'er the sea,
  Came thickly thundering on,
As if our faint approach to meet;
The sight re-nerved my courser's feet,
A moment staggering, feebly fleet,
A moment, with a faint low neigh,
  He answer'd, and then fell;
With gasps and glazing eyes he lay,
  And reeking limbs immovable,
  His first and last career is done!
On came the troop—they saw him stoop,
  They saw me strangely bound along
  His back with many a bloody thong:
They stop—they start—they snuff the air,
Gallop a moment here and there,
Approach, retire, wheel round and round,
Then plunging back with sudden bound,
Headed by one black mighty steed,
Who seem'd the patriarch of his breed,
  Without a single speck or hair

Of white upon his shaggy hide;
They snort—they foam—neigh—swerve aside,
And backward to the forest fly,
By instinct, from a human eye.—
  They left me there, to my despair,
Link'd to the dead and stiffening wretch,
Whose lifeless limbs beneath me stretch,
Relieved from that unwonted weight,
From whence I could not extricate
Nor him nor me—and there we lay
  The dying on the dead!
I little deem'd another day
  Would see my houseless, helpless head.

« And there from morn till twilight bound,
I felt the heavy hours toil round,
With just enough of life to see
My last of suns go down on me,
In hopeless certainty of mind,
That makes us feel at length resign'd
To that which our foreboding years
Presents the worst and last of fears
Inevitable—even a boon,
Nor more unkind for coming soon;
Yet shunn'd and dreaded with such care,
As if it only were a snare
  That prudence might escape:
At times both wish'd for and implored,
At times sought with self-pointed sword,
Yet still a dark and hideous close
To even intolerable woes,
  And welcome in no shape.

And, strange to say, the sons of pleasure,
They who have revell'd beyond measure
In beauty, wassail, wine, and treasure,
Die calm, or calmer, oft than he
Whose heritage was misery:
For he who hath in turn run through
All that was beautiful and new,
 Hath nought to hope, and nought to leave;
And, save the future (which is view'd
Not quite as men are base or good,
But as their nerves may be endued),
 With nought perhaps to grieve:—
The wretch still hopes his woes must end,
And death, whom he should deem his friend,
Appears, to his distemper'd eyes,
Arrived to rob him of his prize,
The tree of his new paradise.
To-morrow would have given him all,
Repaid his pangs, repair'd his fall;
To-morrow would have been the first
Of days no more deplored or curst,
But bright, and long, and beckoning years,
Seen dazzling through the mist of tears,
Guerdon of many a painful hour;
To-morrow would have given him power
To rule, to shine, to smite, to save—
And must it dawn upon his grave?

XVIII.

"The sun was sinking—still I lay
 Chain'd to the chill and stiffening steed,
I thought to mingle there our clay;
 And my dim eyes of death had need,

No hope arose of being freed:
I cast my last looks up the sky,
And there, between me and the sun
I saw the expecting raven fly,
Who scarce would wait till both should die,
Ere his repast begun;
He flew, and perch'd, then flew once more,
And each time nearer than before;
I saw his wing through twilight flit,
And once so near me he alit
I could have smote, but lack'd the strength;
But the slight motion of my hand,
And feeble scratching of the sand,
The exerted throat's faint struggling noise,
Which scarcely could be call'd a voice,
Together scared him off at length.—
I know no more—my latest dream
Is something of a lovely star
Which fix'd my dull eyes from afar,
And went and came with wandering beam,
And of the cold, dull, swimming, dense
Sensation of recurring sense,
And then subsiding back to death,
And then again a little breath,
A little thrill, a short suspense,
An icy sickness curdling o'er
My heart, and sparks that cross'd my brain—
A gasp, a throb, a start of pain,
A sigh—and nothing more.

XIX.

« I woke—where was I?—do I see
A human face look down on me?

And doth a roof above me close?
Do these limbs on a couch repose?
Is this a chamber where I lie?
And is it mortal yon bright eye,
That watches me with gentle glance?
  I closed my own again once more,
As doubtful that the former trance
  Could not as yet be o'er.
A slender girl, long-hair'd and tall,
Sate watching by the cottage-wall;
The sparkle of her eye I caught,
E'en with my first return of thought;
For ever and anon she threw
  A prying, pitying glance on me
  With her black eyes so wild and free:
I gazed, and gazed, until I knew
  No vision it could be,—
But that I lived, and was released
From adding to the vulture's feast:
And when the Cossack maid beheld
My heavy eyes at length unseal'd,
She smiled—and I essay'd to speak,
  But fail'd—and she approach'd, and made
  With lip and finger signs that said,
I must not strive as yet to break
The silence, till my strength should be
Enough to leave my accents free;
And then her hand on mine she laid,
And smooth'd the pillow for my head,
And stole along on tiptoe tread,
  And gently oped the door, and spake
In whispers—ne'er was voice so sweet!

Even music follow'd her light feet;—
   But those she call'd were not awake,
And she went forth; but, ere she pass'd,
Another look on me she cast,
   Another sign she made, to say,
That I had nought to fear, that all
Were near, at my command or call,
   And she would not delay
Her due return:—while she was gone,
Methought I felt too much alone.

XX.

« She came with mother and with sire—
What need of more?—I will not tire
With long recital of the rest,
Since I became the Cossacks' guest:
They found me senseless on the plain—
   They bore me to the nearest hut—
They brought me into life again—
Me—one day o'er their realm to reign!
   Thus the vain fool who strove to glut
His rage, refining on my pain,
   Sent me forth to the wilderness,
Bound, naked, bleeding, and alone,
To pass the desert to a throne,—
   What mortal his own doom may guess?—
   Let none despond, let none despair!
To-morrow the Borysthenes
May see our coursers graze at ease
Upon his Turkish bank,—and never
Had I such welcome for a river
   As I shall yield when safely there.

Comrades, good night!»—The hetman threw
His length beneath the oak-tree shade,
With leafy couch already made,
A bed nor comfortless nor new
To him, who took his rest whene'er
The hour arrived, no matter where:—
His eyes the hastening slumbers steep.
And if ye marvel Charles forgot
To thank his tale, *he* wonder'd not,—
The king had been an hour asleep.

NOTE TO MAZEPPA.

Note 1, page 408, line 21.

Rich as a salt or silver mine, *etc.*

This comparison of a «*salt* mine» may perhaps be permitted to a Pole, as the wealth of the country consists greatly in the salt mines.

THE ISLAND;

OR,

CHRISTIAN AND HIS COMRADES.

28.

ADVERTISEMENT.

The foundation of the following story will be found partly in the account of the mutiny of the Bounty in the South Seas (in 1789), and partly in «Mariner's Account of the Tonga Islands.»

THE ISLAND.

CANTO I.

I.

THE morning-watch was come; the vessel lay
Her course, and gently made her liquid way;
The cloven billow flash'd from off her prow
In furrows form'd by that majestic plough;
The waters with their world were all before;
Behind, the South Sea's many an islet shore.
The quiet night, now dappling, 'gan to wane,
Dividing darkness from the dawning main;
The dolphins, not unconscious of the day,
Swam high, as eager of the coming ray;
The stars from broader beams began to creep,
And lift their shining eyelids from the deep;
The sail resumed its lately shadow'd white,
And the wind flutter'd with a freshening flight;
The purpling ocean owns the coming sun,
But ere he break—a deed is to be done.

II.

The gallant chief within his cabin slept,
Secure in those by whom the watch was kept:
His dreams were of Old England's welcome shore,
Of toils rewarded, and of dangers o'er;
His name was added to the glorious roll
Of those who search the storm-surrounded Pole.
The worst was over, and the rest seemed sure,
And why should not his slumber be secure?
Alas! his deck was trod by unwilling feet,
And wilder hands would hold the vessel's sheet;
Young hearts, which languished for some sunny isle,
Where summer years and summer women smile;
Men without country, who, too long estranged,
Had found no native home, or found it changed,
And, half uncivilized, preferr'd the cave
Of some soft savage to the uncertain wave—
The gushing fruits that nature gave untilled;
The wood without a path but where they willed;
The field o'er which promiscuous plenty pour'd
Her horn; the equal land without a lord;
The wish,—which ages have not yet subdued
In man—to have no master save his mood;
The earth, whose mine was on its face, unsold,
The glowing sun and produce all its gold;
The freedom which can call each grot a home;
The general garden, where all steps may roam;
Where nature owns a nation as her child,
Exulting in the enjoyment of the wild;
Their shells, their fruits, the only wealth they know;
Their unexploring navy, the canoe;

Their sport, the dashing breakers and the chase;
Their strangest sight, an European face:—
Such was the country which these strangers yearn'd
To see again, a sight they dearly earn'd.

III.

Awake, bold Bligh! the foe is at the gate!
Awake! awake!——Alas! it is too late!
Fiercely beside thy cot the mutineer
Stands, and proclaims the reign of rage and fear.
Thy limbs are bound, the bayonet at thy breast,
The hands, which trembled at thy voice, arrest;
Dragg'd o'er the deck, no more at thy command
The obedient helm shall veer, the sail expand;
That savage spirit, which would lull by wrath
Its desperate escape from duty's path,
Glares round thee, in the scarce-believing eyes
Of those who fear the chief they sacrifice;
For ne'er can man his conscience all assuage,
Unless he drain the wine of passion, rage.

IV.

In vain, not silenced by the eye of death,
Thou call'st the loyal with thy menaced breath:—
They come not; they are few, and, overawed,
Must acquiesce while sterner hearts applaud.
In vain thou dost demand the cause; a curse
Is all the answer, with the threat of worse.
Full in thine eyes is waved the glittering blade,
Close to thy throat the pointed bayonet laid,
The levell'd muskets circle round thy breast
In hands as steel'd to do the deadly rest.

Thou dar'st them to their worst, exclaiming, « fire! »
But they who pitied not could yet admire;
Some lurking remnant of their former awe
Restrain'd them longer than their broken law;
They would not dip their souls at once in blood,
But left thee to the mercies of the flood.

V.

« Hoist out the boat! » was now the leader's cry;
And who dare answer « no » to mutiny,
In the first dawning of the drunken hour,
The Saturnalia of unhoped-for power?
The boat is lower'd with all the haste of hate,
With its slight plank between thee and thy fate;
Her only cargo such a scant supply
As promises the death their hands deny;
And just enough of water and of bread
To keep, some days, the dying from the dead:
Some cordage, canvass, sails, and lines, and twine,
But treasures all to hermits of the brine,
Were added after, to the earnest prayer
Of those who saw no hope save sea and air;
And last, that trembling vassal of the Pole,
The feeling compass, navigation's soul.

VI.

And now the self-elected chief finds time
To stun the first sensation of his crime,
And raise it in his followers—« ho! the bowl! »
Lest passion should return to reason's shoal.
« Brandy for heroes! » Burke could once exclaim—
No doubt a liquid path to epic fame;

And such the new-born heroes found it here,
And drain'd the draught with an applauding cheer.
« Huzza! for Otaheite! » was the cry;
How strange such shouts from sons of mutiny!
The gentle island, and the genial soil,
The friendly hearts, the feasts without a toil,
The courteous manners but from nature caught,
The wealth unhoarded, and the love unbought;
Could these have charms for rudest sea-boys, driven
Before the mast by every wind of heaven?
And now, e'en now prepared with other's woes
To earn mild virtue's vain desire, repose?
Alas! such is our nature! all but aim
At the same end by pathways not the same;
Our means, our birth, our nation, and our name,
Our fortune, temper, e'en our outward frame,
Are far more potent o'er our yielding clay
Than aught we know beyond our little day.
Yet still there whispers the small voice within,
Heard through gain's silence, and o'er glory's din:
Whatever creed be taught or land be trod,
Man's conscience is the oracle of God!

VII.

The launch is crowded with the faithful few
Who wait their chief, a melancholy crew:
But some remain'd reluctant on the deck
Of that proud vessel—now a moral wreck—
And view'd their captain's fate with piteous eyes;
While others scoff'd his augur'd miseries,
Sneer'd at the prospect of his pigmy sail,
And the slight bark so laden and so frail.

The tender nautilus who steers his prow,
The sea-born sailor of his shell canoe,
The ocean Mab, the fairy of the sea,
Seems far less fragile, and alas! more free.
He, when the lightning-wing'd tornados sweep
The surge, is safe—his port is in the deep—
And triumphs o'er the armadas of mankind,
Which shake the world, yet crumble in the wind.

VIII.

When all was now prepared, the vessel clear
Which hail'd her master in the mutineer—
A seaman, less obdurate than his mates,
Shew'd the vain pity which but irritates;
Watch'd his late chieftain with exploring eye,
And told, in signs, repentant sympathy;
Held the moist shaddock to his parched mouth,
Which felt exhaustion's deep and bitter drouth:
But, soon observed, this guardian was withdrawn,
Nor further mercy clouds rebellion's dawn.
Then forward stepp'd the bold and froward boy
His chief had cherish'd only to destroy,
And, pointing to the helpless prow beneath,
Exclaimed, « depart at once! delay is death! »
Yet then, e'en then, his feelings ceased not all:
In that last moment could a word recall
Remorse for the black deed as yet half done,
And what he hid from many shew'd to one:
When Bligh in stern reproach demanded where
Was now his grateful sense of former care?
Where all his hopes to see his name aspire
And blazon Britain's thousand glories higher?

His feverish lips thus broke their gloomy spell,
« 'T is that! 't is that! I am in hell! in hell! »
No more he said; but urging to the bark
His chief, commits him to his fragile ark:
These the sole accents from his tongue that fell,
But volumes lurk'd below his fierce farewell.

IX.

The arctic sun rose broad above the wave;
The breeze now sunk, now whisper'd from his cave;
As on the Æolian harp, his fitful wings
Now swell'd, now flutter'd o'er his ocean strings.
With slow, despairing oar the abandon'd skiff
Ploughs its drear progress to the scarce-seen cliff,
Which lifts its peak a cloud above the main:
That boat and ship shall never meet again!
But 't is not mine to tell their tale of grief,
Their constant peril and their scant relief;
Their days of danger, and their nights of pain;
Their manly courage e'en when deem'd in vain;
The sapping famine, rendering scarce a son
Known to his mother in the skeleton;
The ills that lessen'd still their little store,
And starved e'en hunger till he wrung no more;
The varying frowns and favours of the deep,
That now almost ingulphs, then leaves to creep
With crazy oar and shatter'd strength along
The tide that yields reluctant to the strong;
The incessant fever of that arid thirst
Which welcomes, as a well, the clouds that burst
Above their naked bones, and feels delight
In the cold drenching of the stormy night,

And from the outspread canvass gladly wrings
A drop to moisten life's all-gasping springs;
The savage foe escaped, to seek again
More hospitable shelter from the main;
The ghastly spectres which were doom'd at last
To tell as true a tale of dangers past,
As ever the dark annals of the deep
Disclosed for man to dread or woman weep.

X.

We leave them to their fate, but not unknown
Nor unredress'd! Revenge may have her own:
Roused discipline aloud proclaims their cause,
And injured navies urge their broken laws.
Pursue we on his track the mutineer,
Whom distant vengeance had not taught to fear.
Wide o'er the wave—away! away! away!
Once more his eyes shall hail the welcome bay;
Once more the happy shores without a law
Receive the outlaws whom they lately saw;
Nature, and nature's goddess—woman—woos
To lands where, save their conscience, none accuse;
Where all partake the earth without dispute,
And bread itself is gather'd as a fruit;[1]
Where none contest the fields, the woods, the streams:—
The goldless age, where gold disturbs no dreams,
Inhabits or inhabited the shore,
Till Europe taught them better than before,
Bestow'd her customs, and amended theirs,
But left her vices also to their heirs.
Away with this! behold them as they were,
Do good with nature, or with nature err.

« Huzza! for Otaheite! » was the cry,
As stately swept the gallant vessel by.
The breeze springs up; the lately flapping sail
Extends its arch before the growing gale;
In swifter ripples stream aside the seas,
Which her bold bow flings off with dashing ease.
Thus Argo plough'd the Euxine's virgin foam;
But those she wafted still look'd back to home—
These spurn their country with their rebel bark,
And fly her as the raven fled the ark;
And yet they seek to nestle with the dove,
And tame their fiery spirits down to love.

NOTE TO CANTO I.

Note 1, page 446, line 23.

And bread itself is gather'd as a fruit; *etc.*

The now celebrated bread-fruit, to transplant which Captain Bligh's expedition was undertaken.

THE ISLAND.

CANTO II.

I.

How pleasant were the songs of Toobonai,[1]
When summer's sun went down the coral bay!
Come, let us to the islet's softest shade,
And hear the warbling birds! the damsels said:
The wood-dove from the forest depth shall coo,
Like voices of the gods from Bolotoo;
We 'll cull the flowers that grow above the dead,
For these most bloom where rests the warrior's head;
And we will sit in twilight's face, and see
The sweet moon glancing through the tooa tree,
The lofty accents of whose sighing bough
Shall sadly please us as we lean below;
Or climb the steep, and view the surf in vain
Wrestle with rocky giants o'er the main,
Which spurn in columns back the baffled spray.
How beautiful are these! how happy they,

Who, from the toil and tumult of their lives,
Steal to look down where nought but ocean strives!
Even he too loves at times the blue lagoon,
And smooths his ruffled mane beneath the moon.

II.

Yes—from the sepulchre we 'll gather flowers,
Then feast like spirits in their promised bowers,
Then plunge and revel in the rolling surf,
Then lay our limbs along the tender turf,
And, wet and shining from the sportive toil,
Anoint our bodies with the fragrant oil,
And plait our garlands gather'd from the grave,
And wear the wreaths that sprung from out the brave.
But lo! night comes, the Mooa woos us back,
The sound of mats are heard along our track;
Anon the torchlight dance shall fling its sheen
In flashing mazes o'er the Marly's green;
And we too will be there; we too recall
The memory bright with many a festival,
Ere Fiji blew the shell of war, when foes
For the first time were wafted in canoes.
Alas! for them the flower of mankind bleeds;
Alas! for them our fields are rank with weeds:
Forgotten is the rapture, or unknown,
Of wandering with the moon and love alone.
But be it so:—*they* taught us how to wield
The club, and rain our arrows o'er the field;
Now let them reap the harvest of their art!
But feast to-night! to-morrow we depart.
Strike up the dance, the cava bowl fill high,
Drain every drop!—to-morrow we may die.

In summer garments be our limbs array'd;
Around our waists the Tappa's white display'd;
Thick wreaths shall form our coronal, like spring's,
And round our necks shall glance the Hooni strings;
So shall their brighter hues contrast the glow
Of the dusk bosoms that beat high below.

III.

But now the dance is o'er—yet stay awhile;
Ah, pause! nor yet put out the social smile.
To-morrow for the Mooa we depart,
But not to-night—to-night is for the heart.
Again bestow the wreaths we gently woo,
Ye young enchantresses of gay Licoo!
How lovely are your forms! how every sense
Bows to your beauties, soften'd, but intense,
Like to the flowers on Mataloco's steep,
Which fling their fragrance far athwart the deep:
We too will see Licoo; but—oh! my heart—
What do I say? to-morrow we depart.

IV.

Thus rose a song—the harmony of times
Before the winds blew Europe o'er these climes.
True, they had vices—such are nature's growth—
But only the barbarian's—we have both:
The sordor of civilization, mix'd
With all the savage which man's fall hath fix'd.
Who hath not seen dissimulation's reign,
The prayers of Abel link'd to deeds of Cain?
Who such would see, may from his lattice view
The old world more degraded than the new,—

Now *new* no more, save where Columbia rears
Twin giants, born by freedom to her spheres,
Where Chimborazo, over air, earth, wave,
Glares with his Titan eye, and sees no slave.

V.

Such was this ditty of tradition's days,
Which to the dead a lingering fame conveys
In song, where fame as yet hath left no sign
Beyond the sound, whose charm is half divine;
Which leaves no record to the sceptic eye,
But yields young history all to harmony;
A boy Achilles, with the centaur's lyre
In hand, to teach him to surpass his sire.
For one long-cherish'd ballad's simple stave,
Rung from the rock, or mingled with the wave,
Or from the bubbling streamlet's grassy side,
Or gathering mountain echoes as they glide,
Hath greater power o'er each true heart and ear,
Than all the columns conquest's minions rear;
Invites, when hieroglyphics are a theme
For sage's labours or the student's dream;
Attracts, when history's volumes are a toil,—
The first, the freshest bud of feeling's soil.
Such was this rude rhyme—rhyme is of the rude—
But such inspired the Norseman's solitude,
Who came and conquer'd; such, wherever rise
Lands which no foes destroy or civilize,
Exist: and what can our accomplish'd art
Of verse do more than reach the awaken'd heart?

VI.

And sweetly now those untaught melodies
Broke the luxurious silence of the skies,
The sweet siesta of a summer day,
The tropic afternoon of Toobonai,
When every flower was bloom, and air was balm,
And the first breath began to stir the palm,
The first yet voiceless wind to urge the wave
All gently to refresh the thirsty cave,
Where sat the songstress with the stranger boy,
Who taught her passion's desolating joy,
Too powerful over every heart, but most
O'er those who know not how it may be lost;
O'er those who, burning in the new-born fire,
Like martyrs revel in their funeral pyre,
With such devotion to their ecstacy,
That life knows no such rapture as to die:
And die they do; for earthly life has nought
Match'd with that burst of nature, even in thought;
And all our dreams of better life above
But close in one eternal gush of love.

VII.

There sate the gentle savage of the wild,
In growth a woman, though in years a child,
As childhood dates within our colder clime,
Where nought is ripen'd rapidly save crime;
The infant of an infant world, as pure
From nature—lovely, warm, and premature;
Dusky like night, but night with all her stars,
Or cavern sparkling with its native spars;

With eyes that were a language and a spell,
A form like Aphrodite's in her shell;
With all her loves around her on the deep,
Voluptuous as the first approach of sleep;
Yet full of life—for through her tropic cheek
The blush would make its way, and all but speak;
The sun-born blood suffused her neck, and threw
O'er her clear nut-brown skin a lucid hue,
Like coral reddening through the darken'd wave,
Which draws the diver to the crimson cave.
Such was this daughter of the southern seas,
Herself a billow in her energies,
To bear the bark of others' happiness,
Nor feel a sorrow till their joy grew less:
Her wild and warm yet faithful bosom knew
No joy like what it gave; her hopes ne'er drew
Aught from experience, that chill touchstone, whose
Sad proof reduces all things from their hues:
She fear'd no ill, because she knew it not,
Or what she knew was soon—too soon—forgot:
Her smiles and tears had pass'd, as light winds pass
O'er lakes, to ruffle, not destroy, their glass,
Whose depths unsearch'd, and fountains from the hill,
Restore their surface, in itself so still,
Until the earthquake tear the naiad's cave,
Root up the spring, and trample on the wave,
And crush the living waters to a mass,
The amphibious desert of the dank morass!
And must their fate be hers? The eternal change
But grasps humanity with quicker range;
And they who fall, but fall as worlds will fall,
To rise, if just, a spirit o'er them all.

VIII.

And who is he? the blue-eyed northern child
Of isles more known to man, but scarce less wild;
The fair-hair'd offspring of the Hebrides,
Where roars the Pentland with its whirling seas;
Rock'd in his cradle by the roaring wind,
The tempest-born in body and in mind,
His young eyes opening on the ocean-foam,
Had from that moment deem'd the deep his home,
The giant comrade of his pensive moods,
The sharer of his craggy solitudes,
The only Mentor of his youth, where'er
His bark was borne; the sport of wave and air;
A careless thing, who placed his choice in chance,
Nurst by the legends of his land's romance;
Eager to hope, but not less firm to bear,
Acquainted with all feelings save despair.
Placed in the Arab's clime, he would have been
As bold a rover as the sands have seen,
And braved their thirst with as enduring lip
As Ishmael, wafted on his desert-ship;[2]
Fix'd upon Chili's shore, a proud Cacique;
On Hellas' mountains, a rebellious Greek;
Born in a tent, perhaps a Tamerlane;
Bred to a throne, perhaps unfit to reign.
For the same soul that rends its path to sway,
If rear'd to such, can find no further prey
Beyond itself, and must retrace its way,[3]
Plunging for pleasure into pain; the same
Spirit which made a Nero, Rome's worst shame,

A humbler state and discipline of heart
Had form'd his glorious namesake's counterpart:[4]
But grant his vices, grant them all his own,
How small their theatre without a throne!

IX.

Thou smilest,—these comparisons seem high
To those who scan all things with dazzled eye;
Link'd with the unknown name of one whose doom
Has nought to do with glory or with Rome,
With Chili, Hellas, or with Araby,
Thou smilest?—Smile, 't is better thus than sigh:
Yet such he might have been; he was a man,
A soaring spirit ever in the van,
A patriot hero or despotic chief,
To form a nation's glory or its grief,
Born under auspices which makes us more
Or less than we delight to ponder o'er.
But these are visions; say, what was he here?
A blooming boy, a truant mutineer,
The fair-hair'd Torquil, free as ocean's spray,
The husband of the bride of Toobonai.

X.

By Neuha's side he sate, and watch'd the waters,—
Neuha, the sun-flower of the island daughters,
Highborn (a birth at which the herald smiles,
Without a scutcheon for these secret isles)
Of a long race, the valiant and the free,
The naked knights of savage chivalry,
Whose grassy cairns ascend along the shore,
And thine,—I 've seen,—Achilles! do no more.

She, when the thunder-bearing strangers came
In vast canoes begirt with bolts of flame,
Topp'd with tall trees, which, loftier than the palm,
Seem'd rooted in the deep amidst its calm;
But when the winds awaken'd, shot forth wings
Broad as the cloud along the horizon flings,
And sway'd the waves, like cities of the sea,
Making the very billows look less free;—
She, with her paddling oar and dancing prow,
Shot through the surf, like rein-deer through the snow,
Swift-gliding o'er the breaker's whitening edge,
Light as a nereid in her ocean sledge,
And gazed and wonder'd at the giant hulk,
Which heaved from wave to wave its trampling bulk:
The anchor dropp'd, it lay along the deep,
Like a huge lion in the sun asleep,
While round it swarm'd the proas' flitting chain,
Like summer bees that hum around his mane.

XI.

The white man landed; need the rest be told?
The new world stretch'd its dusk hand to the old;
Each was to each a marvel, and the tie
Of wonder warm'd to better sympathy.
Kind was the welcome of the sun-born sires,
And kinder still their daughters' gentler fires.
Their union grew: the children of the storm
Found beauty link'd with many a dusky form;
While these in turn admired the paler glow,
Which seem'd so white in climes that knew no snow.
The chace, the race, the liberty to roam,
The soil where every cottage shew'd a home;

The sea-spread net, the lightly-launch'd canoe,
Which stemm'd the studded Archipelago,
O'er whose blue bosom rose the starry isles;
The healthy slumber, earn'd by sportive toils;
The palm, the loftiest dryad of the woods,
Within whose bosom infant Bacchus broods,
While eagles scarce build higher than the crest
Which shadows o'er the vineyard in her breast;
The cava feast, the yam, the cocoa's root,
Which bears at once the cup, and milk, and fruit;
The bread-tree, which, without the ploughshare, yields
The unreap'd harvest of unfurrow'd fields,
And bakes its unadulterated loaves
Without a furnace in unpurchased groves,
And flings off famine from its fertile breast,
A priceless market for the gathering guest;—
These, with the luxuries of seas and woods,
The airy joys of social solitudes,
Tamed each rude wanderer to the sympathies
Of those who were more happy if less wise,
Did more than Europe's discipline had done,
And civilized civilization's son!

XII.

Of these, and there was many a willing pair,
Neuha and Torquil were not the least fair:
Both children of the isles, though distant far;
Both born beneath a sea-presiding star;
Both nourish'd amidst nature's native scenes,
Loved to the last whatever intervenes
Between us and our childhood's sympathy,
Which still reverts to what first caught the eye.

He who first met the highlands' swelling blue,
Will love each peak that shews a kindred hue,
Hail in each crag a friend's familiar face,
And clasp the mountain in his mind's embrace.
Long have I roam'd through lands which are not mine,
Adored the Alp, and loved the Appenine,
Revered Parnassus, and beheld the steep
Jove's Ida and Olympus crown the deep:
But 't was not all long ages' lore, nor all
Their nature held me in their thrilling thrall;
The infant rapture still survived the boy,
And Loch-na-gar with Ida look'd o'er Troy,[5]
Mix'd Celtic memories with the Phrygian mount,
And highland linns with Castalie's clear fount.
Forgive me, Homer's universal shade!
Forgive me, Phœbus! that my fancy stray'd;
The north and nature taught me to adore
Your scenes sublime, from those beloved before.

XIII.

The love which maketh all things fond and fair,
The youth which makes one rainbow of the air,
The dangers past, that make even man enjoy
The pause in which he ceases to destroy,
The mutual beauty, which the sternest feel
Strike to their hearts like lightning to the steel,
United the half savage and the whole,
The maid and boy, in one absorbing soul.
No more the thundering memory of the fight
Wrapp'd his wean'd bosom in its dark delight;
No more the irksome restlessness of rest,
Disturb'd him like the eagle in her nest,

Whose whetted beak and far-pervading eye
Darts for a victim over all the sky;
His heart was tamed to that voluptuous state,
At once Elysian and effeminate,
Which leaves no laurels o'er the hero's urn;—
These wither when for aught save blood they burn;
Yet when their ashes in their nook are laid,
Doth not the myrtle leave as sweet a shade?
Had Cæsar known but Cleopatra's kiss,
Rome had been free, the world had not been his.
And what have Cæsar's deeds and Cæsar's fame
Done for the earth? We feel them in our shame:
The gory sanction of his glory stains
The rust which tyrants cherish on our chains.
Though glory, nature, reason, freedom, bid
Roused millions do what single Brutus did,—
Sweep these mere mock-birds of the despot's song
From the tall bough where they have perch'd so long,
Still are we hawk'd at by such mousing owls,
And take for falcons those ignoble fowls,
When but a word of freedom would dispel
These bugbears, as their terrors show too well.

XIV.

Rapt in the fond forgetfulness of life,
Neuha, the South Sea girl, was all a wife,
With no distracting world to call her off
From love; with no society to scoff
At the new transient flame; no babbling crowd
Of coxcombry in admiration loud,
Or with adulterous whisper to alloy
Her duty, and her glory, and her joy;

With faith and feelings naked as her form,
She stood as stands a rainbow in a storm,
Changing its hues with bright variety,
But still expanding lovelier o'er the sky,
Howe'er its arch may swell, its colours move,
The cloud-compelling harbinger of love.

XV.

Here, in this grotto of the wave-worn shore,
They pass'd the tropic's red meridian o'er;
Nor long the hours—they never paused o'er time,
Unbroken by the clock's funereal chime,
Which deals the daily pittance of our span,
And points and mocks with iron laugh at man.
What deem'd they of the future or the past?
The present, like a tyrant, held them fast:
Their hour-glass was the sea-sand, and the tide,
Like her smooth billow, saw their moments glide;
Their clock the sun, in his unbounded tower;
They reckon'd not, whose day was but an hour;
The nightingale, their only vesper bell,
Sung sweetly to the rose the day's farewell; [6]
The broad sun set, but not with lingering sweep,
As in the north he mellows o'er the deep,
But fiery, full, and fierce, as if he left
The world for ever, earth of light bereft,
Plunged with red forehead down along the wave,
As dives a hero headlong to his grave.
Then rose they, looking first along the skies,
And then for light into each other's eyes,
Wondering that summer show'd so brief a sun,
And asking if indeed the day were done?

XVI.

And let not this seem strange; the devotee
Lives not in earth, but in his ecstasy;
Around him days and worlds are heedless driven,
His soul is gone before his dust to heaven.
Is love less potent? No—his path is trod,
Alike uplifted gloriously to God;
Or link'd to all we know of heaven below,
The other better self, whose joy or woe
Is more than ours; the all-absorbing flame
Which, kindled by another, grows the same,
Wrapt in one blaze; the pure, yet funeral pile,
Where gentle hearts, like Bramins, sit and smile.
How often we forget all time, when lone,
Admiring nature's universal throne,
Her woods, her wilds, her waters, the intense
Reply of *hers* to our intelligence!
Live not the stars and mountains? Are the waves
Without a spirit? Are the dropping caves
Without a feeling in their silent tears?
No, no;—they woo and clasp us to their spheres,
Dissolve this clog and clod of clay before
Its hour, and merge our soul in the great shore.
Strip off this fond and false identity!—
Who thinks of self, when gazing on the sky?
And who, though gazing lower, ever thought,
In the young moments ere the heart is taught
Time's lesson, of man's baseness or his own?
All nature is his realm, and love his throne.

XVII.

Neuha arose, and Torquil: twilight's hour
Came sad and softly to their rocky bower,
Which, kindling by degrees its dewy spars,
Echo'd their dim light to the mustering stars.
Slowly the pair, partaking nature's calm,
Sought out their cottage, built beneath the palm;
Now smiling and now silent, as the scene;
Lovely as love—the spirit! when serene.
The ocean scarce spoke louder with his swell,
Than breathes his mimic murmurer in the shell,[7]
As, far divided from his parent deep,
The sea-born infant cries, and will not sleep,
Raising his little plaint in vain, to rave
For the broad bosom of his nursing wave:
The woods droop'd darkly, as inclined to rest,
The tropic bird wheel'd rock-ward to his nest,
And the blue sky spread round them like a lake
Of peace, where piety her thirst might slake.

XVIII.

But through the palm and plantain, hark, a voice!
Not such as would have been a lover's choice,
In such an hour, to break the air so still;
No dying night-breeze, harping o'er the hill,
Striking the strings of nature, rock and tree,
Those best and earliest lyres of harmony,
With echo for their chorus; nor the alarm
Of the loud war-whoop to dispel the charm;
Nor the soliloquy of the hermit owl,
Exhaling all his solitary soul,

The dim though large-eyed winged anchorite,
Who peals his dreary pæan o'er the night;—
But a loud, long, and naval whistle, shrill
As ever startled through a sea-bird's bill;
And then a pause, and then a hoarse « Hillo!
Torquil! my boy! what cheer? Ho, brother, ho!»
« Who hails?» cried Torquil, following with his eye
The sound. « Here 's one,» was all the brief reply.

XIX.

But here the herald of the self-same mouth
Came breathing o'er the aromatic south,
Not like a « bed of violets» on the gale,
But such as wafts its cloud o'er grog or ale,
Borne from a short frail pipe, which yet had blown
Its gentle odours over either zone,
And puff'd where'er winds rise or waters roll,
Had wafted smoke from Portsmouth to the Pole,
Opposed its vapour as the lightning flash'd,
And reek'd, midst mountain-billows unabash'd,
To Æolus a constant sacrifice,
Through every change of all the varying skies.
And what was he who bore it?—I may err,
But deem him sailor or philosopher.[8]
Sublime tobacco! which from east to west
Cheers the tar's labour or the turkman's rest,
Which on the moslem's ottoman divides
His hours, and rivals opium and his brides;
Magnificent in Stamboul, but less grand,
Though not less loved, in Wapping or the Strand;
Divine in hookas, glorious in a pipe,
When tipp'd with amber, mellow, rich, and ripe;

Like other charmers, wooing the caress
More dazzlingly when daring in full dress;
Yet thy true lovers more admire by far
Thy naked beauties—Give me a cigar!

XX.

Through the approaching darkness of the wood
A human figure broke the solitude,
Fantastically, it may be, array'd,
A seaman in a savage masquerade;
Such as appears to rise out from the deep,
When o'er the line the merry vessels sweep,
And the rough Saturnalia of the tar
Flock o'er the deck, in Neptune's borrow'd car;[9]
And pleased the god of ocean sees his name
Revive once more, though but in mimic game
Of his true sons, who riot in a breeze
Undreamt of in his native Cyclades.
Still the old god delights, from out the main,
To snatch some glimpses of his ancient reign.
Our sailor's jacket, though in ragged trim,
His constant pipe, which never yet burn'd dim,
His foremast air, and somewhat rolling gait,
Like his dear vessel, spoke his former state;
But then a sort of kerchief round his head,
Not over tightly bound, nor nicely spread;
And stead of trowsers (ah! too early torn!
For even the mildest woods will have their thorn)
A curious sort of somewhat scanty mat
Now served for inexpressibles and hat;
His naked feet and neck, and sunburnt face,
Perchance might suit alike with either race.

His arms were all his own, our Europe's growth,
Which two worlds bless for civilizing both;
The musket swung behind his shoulders broad,
And somewhat stoop'd by his marine abode,
But brawny as the boar's; and hung beneath,
His cutlass droop'd, unconscious of a sheath,
Or lost or worn away; his pistols were
Link'd to his belt, a matrimonial pair—
(Let not this metaphor appear a scoff,
Though one miss'd fire, the other would go off);
These, with a bayonet, not so free from rust
As when the arm-chest held its brighter trust,
Completed his accoutrements, as night
Survey'd him in his garb heteroclite.

XXI.

« What cheer, Ben Bunting? » cried (when in full view
Our new acquaintance) Torquil, « Aught of new? »
« Ey, ey, » quoth Ben, « not new, but news enow;
A strange sail in the offing. » — « Sail! and how?
What! could you make her out? It cannot be;
I 've seen no rag of canvass on the sea. »
« Belike, » said Ben, « you might not from the bay,
But from the bluff-head, where I watch'd to-day,
I saw her in the doldrums; for the wind
Was light and baffling. » — « When the sun declined
Where lay she? had she anchor'd? » — « No, but still
She bore down on us, till the wind grew still. »
« Her flag? » — « I had no glass; but fore and aft,
Egad, she seem'd a wicked-looking craft. »
« Armed? » — « I expect so; — sent on the look-out, —
'T is time, belike, to put our helm about. »

« About?—Whate'er may have us now in chace,
We 'll make no running-fight, for that were base;
We will die at our quarters, like true men.»
« Ey, ey; for that, 't is all the same to Ben.»
« Does Christian know this?»—« Ay; he has piped all hands
To quarters. They are furbishing the stands
Of arms; and we have got some guns to bear,
And scaled them. You are wanted.»—« That 's but fair;
And if it were not, mine is not the soul
To leave my comrades helpless on the shoal.
My Neuha! ah! and must my fate pursue
Not me alone, but one so sweet and true?
But whatsoe'er betide, ah, Neuha! now
Unman me not; the hour will not allow
A tear; I am thine whatever intervenes!»
« Right,» quoth Ben, « that will do for the marines.»[10]

NOTES TO CANTO II.

Note 1, page 451, line 1.

How pleasant were the songs of Toobonai, *etc.*

The first three sections are taken from an actual song of the Tonga Islanders, of which a prose translation is given in Mariner's Account of the Tonga Islands. Toobonai is *not* however one of them; but was one of those where Christian and the mutineers took refuge. I have altered and added, but have retained as much as possible of the original.

Note 2, page 457, line 21.

As Ishmael wafted on his desert-ship; *etc.*

The «ship of the desert» is the oriental figure for the camel or dromedary; and they deserve the metaphor well, the former for his endurance, the latter for his swiftness.

Note 3, page 457, line 28.

Beyond itself, and must retrace its way, *etc.*

« Lucullus, when frugality could charm,
Had wasted turnips in his Sabine farm. »—POPE.

Note 4, page 458, line 2.

Had form'd his glorious namesake's counterpart, *etc.*

The Consul Nero, who made the unequalled march which deceived Hannibal, and defeated Asdrubal; thereby accomplishing an achievement almost unrivalled in military annals. The first intelligence of his return, to Hannibal, was the sight of Asdrubal's head thrown into his camp. When Hannibal saw this, he exclaimed with a sigh, that «Rome would now be the mistress of the world.» And yet to this victory of Nero's it might be owing that his imperial namesake reigned at all! But the infamy of the one has eclipsed the glory of the other. When the name of «Nero» is heard, who thinks of the consul? But such are human things.

Note 5, page 461, line 12.

And Loch-na-gar with Ida look'd o'er Troy, *etc.*

When very young, about eight years of age, after an attack of the scarlet fever at Aberdeen, I was removed by medical advice into the highlands. Here I passed occasionally some summers, and from this period I date my love of mountainous countries. I can never forget the effect a few years afterwards in England, of the only thing I had long seen, even in miniature, of a mountain, in the Malvern Hills. After I returned to Cheltenham, I used to watch them every afternoon at sunset, with a sensation which I cannot describe. This was boyish enough; but I was then only thirteen years of age, and it was in the holidays.

Note 6, page 463, line 21.

Sung sweetly to the rose the day's farewell; *etc.*

The now well-known story of the loves of the nightingale and rose need not be more than alluded to, being sufficiently familiar to the western as to the eastern reader.

Note 7, page 465, line 11.

Than breathes his mimic murmurer in the shell, *etc.*

If the reader will apply to his ear the sea-shell on his chimney-piece, he will be aware of what is alluded to. If the text should appear obscure, he will find in «Gebir» the same idea better expressed in two lines.—The poem I never read, but have heard the lines quoted by a more recondite reader—who seems to be of a different opinion from the Editor of the Quarterly Review, who qualified it, in his answer to the Critical Reviewer of his Juvenal, as trash of the worst and most insane description. It is to Mr Landor, the author of Gebir, so qualified, and of some Latin poems, which vie with Martial or

Catullus in obscenity, that the immaculate Mr Southey addresses his declamation against impurity!

Note 8, page 466, line 23.

But deem him sailor or philosopher. *etc.*

Hobbes, the father of Locke's and other philosophy, was an inveterate smoker,—even to pipes beyond computation.

Note 9, page 467, line 13.

Flock o'er the deck, in Neptune's borrow'd car; *etc.*

This rough but jovial ceremony, used in crossing the Line, has been so often and so well described, that it need not be more than alluded to.

Note 10, page 469, line 16.

«Right» quoth Ben, «that will do for the marines.»

«That will do for the marines, but the sailors won't believe it,» is an old saying; and one of the few fragments of former jealousies which still survive (in jest only) between these gallant services.

THE ISLAND.

CANTO III.

I.

THE fight was o'er; the flashing through the gloom,
Which robes the cannon as he wings a tomb,
Had ceased; and sulphury vapours upward driven
Had left the earth, and but polluted heaven:
The rattling roar which rung in every volley
Had left the echoes to their melancholy;
No more they shriek'd their horror, boom for boom;
The strife was done, the vanquish'd had their doom;
The mutineers were crush'd, dispersed, or ta'en,
Or lived to deem the happiest were the slain.
Few, few escaped, and these were hunted o'er
The isle they loved beyond their native shore.
No further home was their's, it seem'd, on earth,
Once renegades to that which gave them birth;
Track'd like wild beasts, like them they sought the wild,
As to a mother's bosom flies the child;

But vainly wolves and lions seek their den,
And still more vainly, men escape from men.

II.

Beneath a rock whose jutting base protrudes
Far over ocean in his fiercest moods,
When, scaling his enormous crag, the wave
Is hurl'd down headlong like the foremost brave,
And falls back on the foaming crowd behind,
Which fight beneath the banners of the wind,
But now at rest, a little remnant drew
Together, bleeding, thirsty, faint and few;
But still their weapons in their hands, and still
With something of the pride of former will,
As men not all unused to meditate,
And strive much more than wonder at their fate.
Their present lot was what they had foreseen,
And dared as what was likely to have been;
Yet still the lingering hope, which deem'd their lot
Not pardon'd, but unsought for or forgot,
Or trusted that, if sought, their distant caves
Might still be miss'd amidst the world of waves,
Had wean'd their thoughts in part from what they saw
And felt, the vengeance of their country's law.
Their sea-green isle, their guilt-won paradise,
No more could shield their virtue or their vice:
Their better feelings, if such were, were thrown
Back on themselves,—their sins remain'd alone.
Proscribed even in their second country, they
Were lost; in vain the world before them lay;
All outlets seem'd secured. Their new allies
Had fought and bled in mutual sacrifice;

But what avail'd the club, and spear, and arm
Of Hercules, against the sulphury charm,
The magic of the thunder, which destroy'd
The warrior ere his strength could be employ'd?
Dug, like a spreading pestilence, the grave
No less of human bravery than the brave![1]
Their own scant numbers acted all the few
Against the many oft will dare and do;
But though the choice seems native to die free,
Even Greece can boast but one Thermopylæ,
Till *now*, when she has forged her broken chain
Back to a sword, and dies and lives again!

III.

Beside the jutting rock the few appear'd,
Like the last remnant of the red-deer 's herd;
Their eyes were feverish, and their aspect worn,
But still the hunter 's blood was on their horn.
A little stream came tumbling from the height,
And straggling into ocean as it might,
Its bounding chrystal frolick'd in the ray,
And gush'd from cleft to crag with saltless spray;
Close on the wild, wide ocean, yet as pure
And fresh as innocence and more secure,
Its silver torrent glitter'd o'er the deep,
As the shy chamois' eye o'erlooks the steep,
While far below the vast and sullen swell
Of ocean's Alpine azure rose and fell.
To this young spring they rush'd,—all feelings first
Absorb'd in passion's and in nature's thirst,—
Drank as they do who drink their last, and threw
Their arms aside to revel in its dew;

Cool'd their scorch'd throats, and wash'd the gory stains
From wounds whose only bandage might be chains;
Then, when their drought was quench'd, look'd sadly round,
As wondering how so many still were found
Alive and fetterless:—but silent all,
Each sought his fellow's eyes as if to call
On him for language, which his lips denied,
As though their voices with their cause had died.

IV.

Stern, and aloof a little from the rest,
Stood Christian, with his arms across his chest.
The ruddy, reckless, dauntless hue once spread
Along his cheek was livid now as lead;
His light brown locks so graceful in their flow
Now rose like startled vipers o'er his brow.
Still as a statue, with his lips comprest
To stifle even the breath within his breast,
Fast by the rock, all menacing but mute,
He stood; and save a slight beat of his foot,
Which deepen'd now and then the sandy dint
Beneath his heel, his form seem'd turn'd to flint.
Some paces further Torquil lean'd his head
Against a bank, and spoke not, but he bled,—
Not mortally—his worst wound was within:
His brow was pale, his blue eyes sunken in,
And blood-drops sprinkled o'er his yellow hair
Shew'd that his faintness came not from despair,
But nature's ebb. Beside him was another,
Rough as a bear, but willing as a brother,—
Ben Bunting, who essay'd to wash, and wipe,
And bind his wound—then calmly lit his pipe,

A trophy which survived an hundred fights,
A beacon which had cheer'd ten thousand nights.
The fourth and last of this deserted group
Walk'd up and down—at times would stand, then stoop
To pick a pebble up—then let it drop—
Then hurry as in haste—then quickly stop—
Then cast his eyes on his companions—then
Half whistle half a tune, and pause again—
And then his former movements would redouble,
With something between carelessness and trouble.
This is a long description, but applies
To scarce five minutes past before the eyes;
But yet *what* minutes! Moments like to these
Rend men's lives into immortalities.

V.

At length Jack Skyscrape, a mercurial man,
Who flutter'd over all things like a fan,
More brave than firm, and more disposed to dare
And die at once than wrestle with despair,
Exclaimed « G—d damn! » Those syllables intense,—
Nucleus of England's native eloquence,
As the Turk's « Allah! » or the Roman's more
Pagan « Proh Jupiter! » was wont of yore
To give their first impressions such a vent,
By way of echo to embarrassment.
Jack was embarrass'd,—never hero more,
And as he knew not what to say, he swore:
Nor swore in vain; the long congenial sound
Revived Ben Bunting from his pipe profound;
He drew it from his mouth, and look'd full wise,
But merely added to the oath, his *eyes*;

Thus rendering the imperfect phrase complete,
A peroration I need not repeat.

VI.

But Christian, of a higher order, stood
Like an extinct volcano in his mood;
Silent, and sad, and savage,—with the trace
Of passion reeking from his clouded face;
Till lifting up again his sombre eye,
It glanced on Torquil who lean'd faintly by.
« And is it thus?» he cried, « unhappy boy!
And thee too, *thee*—my madness must destroy.»
He said, and strode to where young Torquil stood,
Yet dabbled with his lately flowing blood;
Seized his hand wistfully, but did not press,
And shrunk as fearful of his own caress;
Enquired into his state; and when he heard
The wound was slighter than he deem'd or fear'd,
A moment's brightness pass'd along his brow,
As much as such a moment would allow.
« Yes,» he exclaim'd, « we are taken in the toil,
But not a coward or a common spoil;
Dearly they have bought us—dearly still may buy,—
And I must fall; but have you strength to fly?
'T would be some comfort still, could you survive;
Our dwindled band is now too few to strive.
Oh! for a sole canoe! though but a shell,
To bear you hence to where a hope may dwell!
For me, my lot is what I sought; to be,
In life or death, the fearless and the free.»

VII.

Even as he spoke, around the promontory,
Which nodded o'er the billows high and hoary,
A dark speck dotted ocean: on it flew,
Like to the shadow of a roused sea-mew;
Onward it came—and, lo! a second follow'd—
Now seen—now hid—where ocean's vale was hollow'd;
And near, and nearer, till their dusky crew
Presented well-known aspects to the view,
Till on the surf their skimming paddles play,
Buoyant as wings, and flitting through the spray;—
Now perching on the wave's high curl, and now
Dash'd downward in the thundering foam below,
Which flings it broad and boiling, sheet on sheet,
And slings its high flakes, shiver'd into sleet:
But, floating still through surf and swell, drew nigh
The barks, like small birds through a lowering sky.
Their art seem'd nature—such the skill to sweep
The wave, of these born playmates of the deep.

VIII.

And who the first that, springing on the strand,
Leap'd like a nereid from her shell to land,
With dark but brilliant skin, and dewy eye
Shining with love, and hope, and constancy?
Neuha,—the fond, the faithful, the adored,
Her heart on Torquil's like a torrent pour'd;
And smiled, and wept, and near, and nearer clasp'd,
As if to be assur'd 't was *him* she grasp'd;
Shudder'd to see his yet warm wound, and then,
To find it trivial, smiled and wept again.

She was a warrior's daughter, and could bear
Such sights, and feel, and mourn, but not despair.
Her lover lived,—nor foes nor fears could blight
That full-blown moment in its all delight:
Joy trickled in her tears, joy fill'd the sob
That rock'd her heart till almost HEARD to throb;
And paradise was breathing in the sigh
Of nature's child in nature's ecstacy.

IX.

The sterner spirits who beheld that meeting
Were not unmoved; who are, when hearts are greeting?
Even Christian gazed upon the maid and boy
With tearless eye, but yet a gloomy joy
Mix'd with those bitter thoughts the soul arrays
In hopeless visions of our better days,
When all 's gone—to the rainbow's latest ray.
« And but for me!» he said, and turn'd away;
Then gazed upon the pair, as in his den
A lion looks upon his cubs again;
And then relapsed into his sullen guise,
As heedless of his further destinies.

X.

But brief their time for good or evil thought;
The billows round the promontory brought
The plash of hostile oars—Alas! who made
That sound a dread? All round them seem'd array'd
Against them, save the bride of Toobonai:
She, as she caught the first glimpse o'er the bay
Of the arm'd boats which hurried to complete
The remnant's ruin with their flying feet,

Beckon'd the natives round her to their prows,
Embark'd their guests, and launch'd their light canoes;
In one placed Christian and his comrades twain;
But she and Torquil must not part again.
She fix'd him in her own—Away! away!
They clear the breakers, dart along the bay,
And towards a group of islets, such as bear
The sea-bird's nest and seal's surf-hollow'd lair,
They skim the blue tops of the billows; fast
They flew, and fast their fierce pursuers chased.
They gain upon them—now they lose again,—
Again make way and menace o'er the main;
And now the two canoes in chase divide,
And follow different courses o'er the tide,
To baffle the pursuit—Away! away!
As life is on each paddle's flight to-day,
And more than life or lives to Neuha: love
Freights the frail bark and urges to the cove—
And now the refuge and the foe are nigh—
Yet, yet a moment!—Fly, thou light ark, fly!

NOTE TO CANTO III.

Note 1, page 477, line 6.

No less of human bravery than the brave! *etc.*

Archidamus, King of Sparta, and son of Agesilaus, when he saw a machine invented for the casting of stones and darts, exclaimed that it was the «Grave of Valour.» The same story has been told of some knights, on the first application of gunpowder; but the original anecdote is in Plutarch.

THE ISLAND.

CANTO IV.

I.

White as a white sail on a dusky sea,
When half the horizon 's clouded and half free,
Fluttering between the dun wave and the sky,
Is hope's last gleam in man's extremity.
Her anchor parts; but still her snowy sail
Attracts our eye amidst the rudest gale:
Though every wave she climbs divides us more,
The heart still follows from the loneliest shore.

II.

Not distant from the isle of Toobonai,
A black rock rears its bosom o'er the spray,
The haunt of birds, a desert to mankind,
Where the rough seal reposes from the wind,
And sleeps unwieldy in his cavern dun,
Or gambols with huge frolic in the sun:

There shrilly to the passing oar is heard
The startled echo of the ocean bird,
Who rears on its bare breast her callow brood,
The feather'd fishers of the solitude.
A narrow segment of the yellow sand
On one side forms the outline of a strand;
Here the young turtle, crawling from his shell,
Steals to the deep wherein his parents dwell;
Chipp'd by the beam, a nursling of the day,
But hatch'd for ocean by the fostering ray;
The rest was one bleak precipice, as e'er
Gave mariners a shelter and despair,
A spot to make the saved regret the deck
Which late went down, and envy the lost wreck.
Such was the stern asylum Neuha chose
To shield her lover from his following foes;
But all its secret was not told; she knew
In this a treasure hidden from the view.

III.

Ere the canoes divided, near the spot,
The men that mann'd what held her Torquil's lot,
By her command removed, to strengthen more
The skiff which wafted Christian from the shore.
This he would have opposed; but with a smile
She pointed calmly to the craggy isle,
And bade him « speed and prosper. » *She* would take
The rest upon herself for Torquil's sake.
They parted with this added aid; afar
The proa darted like a shooting star,
And gain'd on the pursuers, who now steer'd
Right on the rock which she and Torquil near'd.

They pull'd; her arm, though delicate, was free
And firm as ever grappled with the sea,
And yielded scarce to Torquil's manlier strength.
The prow now almost lay within its length
Of the crag's steep, inexorable face,
With nought but soundless waters for its base;
Within an hundred boats' length was the foe,
And now what refuge but their frail canoe?
This Torquil ask'd with half-upbraiding eye,
Which said—« Has Neuha brought me here to die!
Is this a place of safety, or a grave,
And yon huge rock the tombstone of the wave?»

IV.

They rested on their paddles, and uprose
Neuha, and pointing to the approaching foes,
Cried, « Torquil, follow me, and fearless follow!»
Then plunged at once into the ocean's hollow.
There was no time to pause—the foes were near—
Chains in his eye and menace in his ear;
With vigour they pull'd on, and as they came,
Hail'd him to yield, and by his forfeit name.
Headlong he leapt—to him the swimmer's skill
Was native, and now all his hope from ill;
But how or where? He dived, and rose no more;
The boat's crew look'd amazed o'er sea and shore.
There was no landing on that precipice,
Steep, harsh, and slippery as a berg of ice.
They watch'd awhile to see him float again,
But not a trace rebubbled from the main:
The wave roll'd on, no ripple on its face,
Since their first plunge recall'd a single trace;

The little whirl which eddied, and slight foam,
That whiten'd o'er what seem'd their latest home,
White as a sepulchre above the pair
Who left no marble (mournful as an heir),
The quiet proa wavering o'er the tide
Was all that told of Torquil and his bride;
And but for this alone the whole might seem
The vanish'd phantom of a seaman's dream.
They paused and search'd in vain, then pull'd away,
Even superstition now forbade their stay.
Some said he had not plunged into the wave,
But vanish'd like a corpse-light from a grave;
Others, that something supernatural
Glared in his figure, more than mortal tall;
While all agreed, that in his cheek and eye
There was the dead hue of eternity.
Still as their oars receded from the crag,
Round every weed a moment would they lag,
Expectant of some token of their prey;
But no—he had melted from them like the spray.

V.

And where was he, the pilgrim of the deep,
Following the nereid? Had they ceased to weep
For ever? or, received in coral caves,
Wrung life and pity from the softening waves?
Did they with ocean's hidden sovereigns dwell,
And sound with mermen the fantastic shell?
Did Neuha with the mermaids comb her hair,
Flowing o'er ocean as it stream'd in air?
Or had they perish'd, and in silence slept
Beneath the gulph wherein they boldly leapt?

VI.

Young Neuha plunged into the deep, and he
Follow'd: her track beneath her native sea
Was as a native's of the element,
So smoothly, bravely, brilliantly she went,
Leaving a streak of light behind her heel,
Which struck and flash'd like an amphibious steel.
Closely, and scarcely less expert to trace
The depths where divers hold the pearl in chase,
Torquil, the nursling of the northern seas,
Pursued her liquid steps with art and ease.
Deep—deeper for an instant Neuha led
The way—then upward soar'd—and as she spread
Her arms, and flung the foam from off her locks,
Laugh'd, and the sound was answer'd by the rocks.
They had gain'd a central realm of earth again,
But look'd for tree, and field, and sky, in vain.
Around she pointed to a spacious cave,
Whose only portal was the keyless wave,[1]
(A hollow archway by the sun unseen,
Save through the billows glassy veil of green,
In some transparent ocean holiday,
When all the finny people are at play)
Wiped with her hair the brine from Torquil's eyes,
And clapp'd her hands with joy at his surprise;
Led him to where the rock appear'd to jut
And form a something like a triton's hut;
For all was darkness for a space, till day
Through clefts above let in a sober'd ray;
As in some old cathedral's glimmering aisle
The dusty monuments from light recoil,

Thus sadly in their refuge submarine
The vault drew half her shadow from the scene.

VII.

Forth from her bosom the young savage drew
A pine torch, strongly girded with gnatoo;
A plantain leaf o'er all, the more to keep
Its latent sparkle from the sapping deep.
This mantle kept it dry; then from a nook
Of the same plantain leaf a flint she took,
A few shrunk wither'd twigs, and from the blade
Of Torquil 's knife struck fire, and thus array'd
The grot with torchlight. Wide it was and high,
And show'd a self-born gothic canopy;
The arch uprear'd by nature's architect,
The architrave some earthquake might erect;
The buttress from some mountain's bosom hurl'd,
When the poles crash'd and water was the world;
Or harden'd from some earth-absorbing fire
While yet the globe reek'd from its funeral pyre;
The fretted pinnacle, the aisle, the nave,[2]
Were there, all scoop'd by darkness from her cave.
There, with a little tinge of phantasy,
Fantastic faces moped and moved on high,
And then a mitre or a shrine would fix
The eye upon its seeming crucifix.
Thus nature play'd with the stalactites,
And built herself a chapel of the seas.

VIII.

And Neuha took her Torquil by the hand,
And waved along the vault her kindled brand,

And led him into each recess, and show'd
The secret places of their new abode.
Nor these alone, for all had been prepared
Before, to soothe the lover's lot she shared;
The mat for rest; for dress the fresh gnatoo,
And sandal oil to fence against the dew;
For food the cocoa-nut, the yam, the bread
Born of the fruit; for board the plantain spread
With its broad leaf, or turtle-shell which bore
A banquet in the flesh it cover'd o'er;
The gourd with water recent from the rill,
The ripe banana from the mellow hill;
A pine-torch pile to keep undying light,
And she herself, as beautiful as night,
To fling her shadowy spirit o'er the scene,
And make their subterranean world serene.
She had foreseen, since first the stranger's sail
Drew to their isle, that force or flight might fail,
And form'd a refuge of the rocky den
For Torquil's safety from his countrymen.
Each dawn had wafted there her light canoe,
Laden with all the golden fruits that grew;
Each eve had seen her gliding through the hour
With all could cheer or deck their sparry bower;
And now she spread her little store with smiles,
The happiest daughter of the loving isles.

IX.

She, as he gazed with grateful wonder, press'd
Her shelter'd love to her impassion'd breast;
And suited to her soft caresses, told
An elden tale of love,—for love is old,

Old as eternity, but not outworn
With each new being born or to be born:[3]
How a young chief, a thousand moons ago,
Diving for turtle in the depths below,
Had risen, in tracking fast his ocean prey,
Into the cave which round and o'er them lay;
How, in some desperate feud of after time,
He shelter'd there a daughter of the clime,
A foe beloved, and offspring of a foe,
Saved by his tribe but for a captive's woe;
How, when the storm of war was still'd, he led
His island clan to where the waters spread
Their deep green shadow o'er the rocky door,
Then dived—it seem'd as if to rise no more:
His wondering mates, amazed within their bark,
Or deem'd him mad, or prey to the blue shark;
Row'd round in sorrow the sea-girded rock,
Then paused upon their paddles from the shock,
When, fresh and springing from the deep, they saw
A goddess rise—so deem'd they in their awe;
And their companion, glorious by her side,
Proud and exulting in his mermaid bride;
And how, when undeceived, the pair they bore
With sounding conchs and joyous shouts to shore;
How they had gladly lived and calmly died,
And why not also Torquil and his bride?
Not mine to tell the rapturous caress
Which follow'd wildly in that wild recess
This tale; enough that all within that cave
Was love, though buried strong as in the grave
Where Abelard, through twenty years of death,
When Eloisa's form was lower'd beneath

Their nuptial vault, his arms outstretch'd, and prest
The kindling ashes to his kindled breast.[4]
The waves without sang round their couch, their roar
As much unheeded as if life were o'er;
Within, their hearts made all their harmony,
Love's broken murmur and more broken sigh.

X.

And they, the cause and sharers of the shock
Which left them exiles of the hollow rock,
Where were they? O'er the sea for life they plied,
To seek from heaven the shelter men denied.
Another course had been their choice—but where?
The wave which bore them still, their foes would bear,
Who, disappointed of their former chase,
In search of Christian now renew'd their race.
Eager with anger, their strong arms made way,
Like vultures baffled of their previous prey.
They gain'd upon them, all whose safety lay
In some bleak crag or deeply hidden bay:
No further chance or choice remain'd; and right
For the first further rock which met their sight
They steer'd, to take their latest view of land,
And yield as victims, or die sword in hand;
Dismiss'd the natives and their shallop, who
Would still have battled for that scanty crew;
But Christian bade them seek their shore again,
Nor add a sacrifice which were in vain;
For what were simple bow and savage spear
Against the arms which must be wielded here?

XI.

They landed on a wild but narrow scene,
Where few but nature's footsteps yet had been;
Prepared their arms, and with that gloomy eye,
Stern and sustain'd, of man's extremity,
When hope is gone, nor glory's self remains
To cheer resistance against death or chains,—
They stood, the three, as the three hundred stood
Who dyed Thermopylæ with holy blood.
But, ah! how different! 't is the *cause* makes all,
Degrades or hallows courage in its fall.
O'er them no fame, eternal and intense,
Blazed through the clouds of death and beckon'd hence;
No grateful country, smiling through her tears,
Begun the praises of a thousand years;
No nation's eyes would on their tomb be bent,
No heroes envy them their monument;
However boldly their warm blood was spilt,
Their life was shame, their epitaph was guilt.
And this they knew and felt, at least the one,
The leader of the band he had undone;
Who, born perchance for better things, had set
His life upon a cast which linger'd yet:
But now the die was to be thrown, and all
The chances were in favour of his fall:
And such a fall! But still he faced the shock,
Obdurate as a portion of the rock
Whereon he stood, and fix'd his levell'd gun,
Dark as a sullen cloud before the sun,

XII.

The boat drew nigh, well arm'd, and firm the crew
To act whatever duty bade them do;
Careless of danger, as the onward wind
Is of the leaves it strews, nor looks behind,
And yet perhaps they rather wish'd to go
Against a nation's than a native foe,
And felt that this poor victim of self-will,
Briton no more, had once been Britain's still.
They hail'd him to surrender—no reply;
Their arms were poised, and glitter'd in the sky.
They hail'd again—no answer; yet once more
They offer'd quarter louder than before.
The echoes only, from the rock's rebound,
Took their last farewell of the dying sound.
Then flash'd the flint, and blazed the volleying flame,
And the smoke rose between them and their aim,
While the rock rattled with the bullets' knell,
Which peal'd in vain, and flatten'd as they fell;
Then flew the only answer to be given
By those who had lost all hope in earth or heaven.
After the first fierce peal, as they pull'd nigher,
They heard the voice of Christian shout, « Now fire! »
And ere the word upon the echo died,
Two fell; the rest assail'd the rock's rough side,
And, furious at the madness of their foes,
Disdain'd all further efforts, save to close.
But steep the crag, and all without a path,
Each step opposed a bastion to their wrath;
While, placed midst clefts the least accessible,
Which Christian's eye was train'd to mark full well,

The three maintain'd a strife which must not yield,
In spots where eagles might have chosen to build.
Their every shot told; while the assailant fell,
Dash'd on the shingles like the limpet shell;
But still enough survived, and mounted still,
Scattering their numbers here and there, until
Surrounded and commanded, though not nigh
Enough for seizure, near enough to die,
The desperate trio held aloof their fate
But by a thread, like sharks who 've gorged the bait;
Yet to the very last they battled well,
And not a groan inform'd their foes *who* fell.
Christian died last—twice wounded; and once more
Mercy was offer'd when they saw his gore;
Too late for life, but not too late to die,
With though a hostile hand to close his eye.
A limb was broken, and he droop'd along
The crag, as doth a falcon reft of young.
The sound revived him, or appear'd to wake
Some passion which a weakly gesture spake;
He beckon'd to the foremost who drew nigh,
But, as they near'd, he rear'd his weapon high—
His last ball had been aim'd, but from his breast
He tore the topmost button of his vest,[5]
Down the tube dash'd it, levell'd, fired, and smiled
As his foe fell; then, like a serpent, coil'd
His wounded, weary form, to where the steep
Look'd desperate as himself along the deep;
Cast one glance back, and clench'd his hand, and shook
His last rage 'gainst the earth which he forsook;
Then plunged: the rock below received like glass
His body crush'd into one gory mass,

With scarce a shred to tell of human form,
Or fragment for the sea-bird or the worm;
A fair-hair'd scalp, besmear'd with blood and weeds,
Yet reek'd, the remnant of himself and deeds;
Some splinters of his weapons (to the last,
As long as hand could hold, he held them fast)
Yet glitter'd, but at distance—hurl'd away
To rust beneath the dew and dashing spray.
The rest was nothing—save a life mispent,
And soul—but who shall answer where it went?
'T is ours to bear, not judge the dead; and they
Who doom to hell, themselves are on the way,
Unless these bullies of eternal pains
Are pardon'd their bad hearts for their worse brains.

XIII.

The deed was over! All were gone or ta'en,
The fugitive, the captive, or the slain.
Chain'd on the deck, where once, a gallant crew,
They stood with honour, were the wretched few
Survivors of the skirmish on the isle;
But the last rock left no surviving spoil.
Cold lay they where they fell, and weltering,
While o'er them flapp'd the sea-bird's dewy wing,
Now wheeling nearer from the neighbouring surge,
And screaming high their harsh and hungry dirge:
But calm and careless heaved the wave below,
Eternal with unsympathetic flow;
Far o'er its face the dolphins sported on,
And sprung the flying fish against the sun,
Till its dried wing relapsed from its brief height,
To gather moisture for another flight.

XIV.

'T was morn; and Neuha, who by dawn of day
Swam smoothly forth to catch the rising ray,
And watch if aught approach'd the amphibious lair
Where lay her lover, saw a sail in air:
It flapp'd, it fill'd, and to the growing gale
Bent its broad arch: her breath began to fail
With fluttering fear, her heart beat thick and high,
While yet a doubt sprung where its course might lie:
But no! it came not; fast and far away
The shadow lessen'd as it clear'd the bay.
She gazed and flung the sea-foam from her eyes,
To watch as for a rainbow in the skies.
On the horizon verged the distant deck,
Diminish'd, dwindled to a very speck—
Then vanish'd. All was ocean, all was joy!
Down plunged she through the cave to rouse her boy;
Told all she had seen, and all she hoped, and all
That happy love could augur or recall;
Sprung forth again, with Torquil following free
His bounding nereid over the broad sea;
Swam round the rock, to where a shallow cleft
Hid the canoe that Neuha there had left
Drifting along the tide, without an oar,
That eve the strangers chaced them from the shore;
But when these vanish'd, she pursued her prow,
Regain'd, and urged to where they found it now:
Nor ever did more love and joy embark,
Than now was wafted in that slender ark.

XV.

Again their own shore rises on the view,
No more polluted with a hostile hue;
No sullen ship lay bristling o'er the foam,
A floating dungeon:—all was hope and home!
A thousand proas darted o'er the bay,
With sounding shells, and heralded their way;
The chiefs came down, around the people pour'd,
And welcomed Torquil as a son restored;
The women throng'd, embracing and embraced
By Neuha, asking where they had been chaced,
And how escaped? The tale was told; and then
One acclamation rent the sky again;
And from that hour a new tradition gave
Their sanctuary the name of «Neuha's Cave.»
An hundred fires, far flickering from the height,
Blazed o'er the general revel of the night,
The feast in honour of the guest, return'd
To peace and pleasure, perilously earn'd;
A night succeeded by such happy days
As only the yet infant world displays.

NOTES TO CANTO IV.

Note 1, page 491, line 19.

Whose only portal was the keyless wave, *etc*.

Of this cave (which is no fiction) the original will be found in the 9th chapter of « Mariner's Account of the Tonga Islands. » I have taken the poetical liberty to transplant it to Toobonai, the last island where any distinct account is left of Christian and his comrades.

Note 2, page 492, line 20,

The fretted pinnacle, the aisle, the nave, *etc*.

This may seem too minute for the general outline (in Mariner's Account) from which it is taken. But few men have travelled without seeing something of the kind—on *land*, that is. Without adverting to Ellora, in Mungo Park's last journal (if my memory do not err, for there are eight years since I read the book) he mentions having met with a rock or mountain so exactly resembling a Gothic cathedral, that only minute inspection could convince him that it was a work of nature.

Note 3, page 494, line 2.

With each new being born or to be born, *etc*

The reader will recollect the epigram of the Greek Anthology, or its translation into most of the modern languages:—

> « Whoe'er thou art, thy master see,
> He was, or is, or is to be. »

Note 4, page 495, line 2.

The kindling ashes to his kindled breast.

The tradition is attached to the story of Eloisa, that when her body was lowered into the grave of Abelard (who had been buried twenty years) he opened his arms to receive her.

Note 5, page 498, line 24.

He tore the topmost button of his vest, *etc.*

In Thibault's account of Frederic the Second of Prussia, there is a singular relation of a young Frenchman, who with his mistress appeared to be of some rank. He enlisted and deserted at Scweid-nitz; and after a desperate resistance was retaken, having killed an officer, who attempted to seize him after he was wounded, by the discharge of his musket loaded with a *button* of his uniform. Some circumstances on his court-martial raised a great interest amongst his judges, who wished to discover his real situation in life, which he offered to disclose, but to the *king* only, to whom he requested permission to write. This was refused, and Frederic was filled with the greatest indignation, from baffled curiosity or some other motive, when he understood that his request had been denied.—See THIBAULT's *Work*, vol. ii.—(I quote from memory.)

APPENDIX.

Extract from the Voyage by Captain Bligh.

On the 27th of December it blew a severe storm of wind from the eastward, in the course of which we suffered greatly. One sea broke away the spare-yards and spars out of the starboard main-chains; another broke into the ship and stove all the boats. Several casks of beer that had been lashed on deck broke loose, and were washed overboard; and it was not without great risk and difficulty that we were able to secure the boats from being washed away entirely. A great quantity of our bread was also damaged and rendered useless, for the sea had stove in our stern, and filled the cabin with water.

On the 5th of January, 1788, we saw the island of Teneriffe about twelve leagues distant, and next day, being Sunday, came to an anchor in the road of Santa Cruz. There we took in the necessary supplies, and, having finished our business, sailed on the 10th.

I now divided the people into three watches, and gave the charge of the third watch to Mr Fletcher Christian, one of the mates. I have always considered this a desirable regulation when circumstances will admit of it, and I am persuaded that unbroken rest not only contributes much towards the health of the ship's company, but enables them more readily to exert themselves in cases of sudden emergency.

As I wished to proceed to Otaheite without stopping, I reduced the allowance of bread to two-thirds, and caused the water for drinking to be filtered through drip-stones, bought at Teneriffe for that purpose. I now acquainted the ship's company of the object of the voyage, and gave assurances of certain promotion to every one whose endeavours should merit it.

On Tuesday the 26th of February, being in south latitude 29° 38′, and 44° 44′ west longitude, we bent new sails, and made other necessary preparations for encountering the weather that was to be expected in a high latitude. Our distance from the coast of Brazil was about one hundred leagues.

On the forenoon of Sunday the 2nd of March, after seeing that every person was clean, divine service was performed, according to my usual custom on this day. I gave to Mr Fletcher Christian, whom I had before directed to take charge of the third watch, a written order to act as lieutenant.

The change of temperature soon began to be sensibly felt, and, that the people might not suffer from their own negligence, I supplied them with thicker clothing, as better suited to the climate. A great number of whales of an immenze size, with two spout-holes on the back of the head, were seen on the 11th.

On a complaint made to me by the master, I found it necessary to punish Matthew Quintal, one of the seamen, with two dozen of lashes, for insolence and mutinous behaviour, which was the first time that there was any occasion for punishment on board.

We were off Cape St Diego, the eastern part of the Terra de Fuego, and, the wind being unfavourable, I thought it more advisable to go round to the eastward of Staten-land than to attempt passing through Straits le Maire. We passed New-year's Harbour and Cape St John, and on Monday the 31st were in latitude 60° 1′ south. But the wind became variable, and we had bad weather.

Storms, attended with a great sea, prevailed until the 12th of April. The ship began to leak, and required pumping every hour, which was no more than we had reason to expect from such a continuance of gales of wind and high seas. The decks also became so leaky that it was necessary to allot the great cabin, of which I made little use except in fine weather, to those people who had not births to hang their hammocks in, and by this means the space between decks was less crowded.

With all this bad weather, we had the additional mortification to find, at the end of every day, that we were losing ground; for, notwithstanding our utmost exertions, and keeping on the most advantageous tacks, we did little better than drift before the wind. On Tuesday the 22nd of April, we had eight down on the sick list, and the rest of the people, though in good health, were greatly fatigued; but I saw, with much concern, that it was impossible to make a passage this way to the Society Islands, for we had now been thirty days in a tempestuous ocean. Thus the season was too far advanced for us to expect better weather to enable us to double Cape Horn; and, from these and other considerations, I ordered the helm to be put a-weather, and bore away for the Cape of Good Hope, to the great joy of every one on board.

We came to an anchor on Friday the 23rd of May, in Simon's Bay, at the Cape, after a tolerable run. The ship required complete caulking, for she had become so leaky, that we were obliged to pump hourly in our passage from Cape Horn. The sails and rigging also required repair, and, on examining the provisions, a considerable quantity was found damaged.

Having remained thirty-eight days at this place, and my people having received all the advantage that could be derived from refreshments of every kind that could be met with, we sailed on the 1st of July.

A gale of wind blew on the 20th, with a high sea; it increased after noon with such violence, that the ship was driven almost forecastle under before we could get the sails clewed up. The lower yards were lowered, and the top-gallant-mast got down upon deck, which relieved her much. We lay to all night, and in the morning bore away under a reefed foresail. The sea still running high, in the afternoon it became very unsafe to stand on; we therefore lay to all night, without any accident, excepting that a man at the steerage was thrown over the wheel and much bruised. Towards noon the violence of the storm abated, and we again bore away under the reefed foresail.

In a few days we passed the Island of St Paul, where there is good fresh water, as I was informed by a Dutch captain, and also a hot spring which boils fish as completely as if done by a fire. Approaching to Van Dieman's land, we had much bad weather, with snow and hail, but nothing was seen to indicate our vicinity, on the 13th of August, except a seal, which appeared at the distance of twenty leagues from it. We anchored in Adventure Bay on Wednesday the 20th.

In our passage hither from the Cape of Good Hope, the winds were chiefly from the westward, with very boisterous weather. The approach of strong southerly winds is announced by many birds of the albatross or peterel tribe; and the abatement of the gale, or a shift of wind to the northward, by their keeping away. The thermometer also varies five or six degrees in its height, when a change of these winds may be expected.

In the land surrounding Adventure Bay are many forest trees one hundred and fifty feet high; we saw one which measured above thirty-three feet in girth. We observed several eagles, some beautiful blue-plumaged herons, and paroquets in great variety.

The natives not appearing, we went in search of them towards Cape Frederic Henry. Soon after, coming to a grapnel close to the shore, for it was impossible to land, we heard their voices, like the cackling of geese, and twenty persons came out of the woods. We threw trinkets ashore tied up in parcels, which they would not open out until I made an appearance of leaving them; they then did so, and, taking the articles out, put them on their heads. On first coming in sight, they made a prodigious clattering in their speech, and held their arms over their heads. They spoke so quick, that it was impossible to catch one single word they uttered. Their colour is of a dull black; their skin scarified about the breast and shoulders. One was distinguished by his body being coloured with red ochre, but all the others were painted black, with a kind of soot, so thickly laid over their faces and shoulders, that it was difficult to ascertain what they were like.

On Thursday, the 4th of September, we sailed out of Adventure Bay, steering first towards the east-south-east, and then to the northward of east, when, on the 19th, we came in sight of a cluster of small rocky islands, which I named Bounty Isles. Soon afterwards we frequently observed the sea, in the night-time, to be covered by luminous spots, caused by amazing quantities of small blubbers, or medusæ, which emit a light, like the blaze of a candle, from the strings or filaments extending from them, while the rest of the body continues perfectly dark.

We discovered the island of Otaheite on the 25th, and, before casting anchor next morning in Matavai Bay, such numbers of canoes had come off, that, after the natives ascertained we were friends, they came on board, and crowded the deck so much, that in ten minutes I could scarce find my own people. The whole distance which the ship had run, in direct and contrary courses, from the time of leaving

England until reaching Otaheite, was twenty-seven thousand and eighty-six miles, which, on an average, was one hundred and eight miles each twenty-four hours.

Here we lost our surgeon on the 9th of December. Of late he had scarcely ever stirred out of the cabin, though not apprehended to be in a dangerous state. Nevertheless, appearing worse than usual in the evening, he was removed where he could obtain more air, but without any benefit, for he died in an hour afterwards. This unfortunate man drank very hard, and was so averse to exercise, that he would never be prevailed on to take half a dozen turns on deck at a time, during all the course of the voyage. He was buried on shore.

On Monday the 5th of January, the small cutter was missed, of which I was immediately apprised. The ship's company being mustered, we found three men absent, who had carried it off. They had taken with them eight stand of arms and ammunition; but with regard to their plan, every one on board seemed to be quite ignorant. I therefore went on shore, and engaged all the chiefs to assist in recovering both the boat and the deserters. Accordingly, the former was brought back in the course of the day, by five of the natives; but the men were not taken until nearly three weeks afterwards. Learning the place where they were, in a different quarter of the island of Otaheite, I went thither in the cutter, thinking there would be no great difficulty in securing them with the assistance of the natives. However, they heard of my arrival; and when I was near a house in which they were, they came out, wanting their fire-arms, and delivered themselves up. Some of the chiefs had formerly seized and bound these deserters; but had been prevailed on, by fair promises of returning peaceably to the ship, to release them But finding an opportunity again to get possession of their arms, they set the natives at defiance.

The object of the voyage being now completed, all the bread-fruit plants, to the number of one thousand and fifteen, were got on board on Tuesday the 31st of March. Besides these, we had collected many other plants, some of them bearing the finest fruits in the world; and valuable, from affording brilliant dyes, and for various properties besides. At sunset of the 4th of April, we made sail from Otaheite, bidding farewell to an island where for twenty-three weeks we had been treated with the utmost affection and regard, and which seemed to increase in proportion to our stay. That we were not insensible to their kindness, the succeeding circumstances sufficiently proved; for to the friendly and endearing behaviour of these people may be ascribed the motives inciting an event that effected the ruin of our expedition, which there was every reason to believe would have been attended with the most favourable issue.

Next morning we got sight of the island Huaheine; and a double canoe soon coming alongside, containing ten natives, I saw among them a young man who recollected me, and called me by my name. I had been here in the year 1780, with Captain Cook, in the Resolution. A few days after sailing from this island, the weather became squally, and a thick body of black clouds collected in the east. A water-spout was in a short time seen at no great distance from us, which appeared to great advantage from the darkness of the clouds behind it. As nearly as I could judge, the upper part was about two feet in diameter, and the lower about eight inches. Scarcely had I made these remarks, when I observed that it was rapidly advancing towards the ship. We immediately altered our course, and took in all the sails except the foresail; soon after which it passed within ten yards of the stern, with a rustling noise, but without our feeling the least effect from its being so near. It seemed to be travelling at the rate of about ten miles an hour, in the direction of the wind, and it dispersed in a quarter of an hour after passing us. It is impossible to say what injury we should have received, had it passed directly over us. Masts, I imagine, might have been carried away, but I do not apprehend that it would have endangered the loss of the ship.

Passing several islands on the way; we anchored at Annamooka, on the 23d of April; and an old lame man called Tepa, whom I had known here in 1777, and immediately recollected, came on board, along with others, from different islands in the vicinity. They were desirous to see the ship, and on being taken below, where the bread-fruit plants were arranged, they testified great surprise, A few of these being decayed, we went on shore to procure some in their place.

The natives exhibited numerous marks of the peculiar mourning which they express on losing their relatives; such as bloody temples, their heads being deprived of most of the hair, and, what was worse, almost the whole of them had lost some of their fingers. Several fine boys, not above six years old, had lost both their little fingers; and several of the men, besides these, had parted with the middle finger of the right hand.

The chiefs went off with me to dinner, and we carried on a brisk trade for yams; we also got plantains and bread fruit. But the yams were in great abundance, and very fine and large. One of them weighed above forty-five pounds. Sailing canoes came, some of which contained not less than ninety passengers. Such a number of them gradually arrived from different islands, that it was impossible to get any thing done, the multitude became so great, and there was no chief of sufficient authority to command the whole. I therefore ordered a watering party, then employed, to come on board, and sailed on Sunday the 26th of April.

We kept near the island of Kotoo all the afternoon of Monday, in hopes that some canoes would come off to the ship, but in this we were disappointed. The wind being northerly, we steered to the westward in the evening, to pass south of Tofoa; and I gave directions for this course to be continued during the night. The master had the first-watch, the gunner the middle-watch, and Mr Christian the morning-watch. This was the turn of duty for the night.

Hitherto the voyage had advanced in a course of uninterrupted prosperity, and had been attended with circumstances equally pleasing and satisfactory. But a very different scene was now to be disclosed; a conspiracy had been formed, which was to render all our past labour productive only of misery and distress; and it had been concerted with so much secrecy and circumspection, that no one circumstance escaped to betray the impending calamity.

On the night of Monday, the watch was set as I have described. Just before sunrise, on Tuesday morning, while I was yet asleep, Mr Christian, with the master at arms, gunner's mate, and Thomas Burkitt, seaman, came into my cabin, and, seizing me, tied my hands with a cord behind my back; threatening me with instant death if I spoke or made the least noise. I nevertheless called out as loud as I could, in hopes of assistance; but the officers not of their party were already secured by sentinels at their doors. At my own cabin door were three men, besides the four within; all except Christian had muskets and bayonets; he had only a cutlass. I was dragged out of bed, and forced on deck in my shirt, suffering great pain in the mean time from the tightness with which my hands were tied. On demanding the reason of such violence, the only answer was abuse for not holding my tongue. The master, the gunner, surgeon, master's mate, and Nelson the gardener, were kept confined below, and the fore hatchway was guarded by sentinels. The boatswain, and carpenter, and also the clerk, were allowed to come on deck, where they saw me standing abaft the mizen-mast, with my hands tied behind my back, under a guard, with Christian at their head. The boatswain was then ordered to hoist out the launch, accompanied by a threat, if he did not do it instantly, TO TAKE CARE OF HIMSELF.

The boat being hoisted out, Mr Hayward and Mr Hallet, two of the midshipmen, and Mr Samuel, the clerk, were ordered into it. I demanded the intention of giving this order, and endeavoured to persuade the people near me not to persist in such acts of violence; but it was to no effect; for the constant answer was, « Hold your tongue, sir, or you are dead this moment. »

The master had by this time sent, requesting that he might come on deck, which was permitted; but he was soon ordered back again to his cabin. My exertions to turn the tide of affairs were continued; when Christian, changing the cutlass he held for a bayonet, and holding me by the cord about my hands with a strong gripe, threatened me with immediate death, if I would not be quiet; and the villains around me had their pieces cocked and bayonets fixed.

Certain individuals were called on to get into the boat, and were hurried over the ship's side; whence I concluded, that along with them I was to be set adrift. Another effort to bring about a change produced nothing but menaces of having my brains blown out.

The boatswain and those seamen who were to be put into the boat were allowed to collect twine, canvass, lines, sails, cordage, an eight-and-twenty gallon cask of water; and Mr Samuel got one hundred and fifty pounds of bread, with a small quantity of rum and wine; also a quadrant and compass; but he was prohibited, on pain of death, to touch any map or astronomical book, and any instrument, or any of my surveys and drawings.

The mutineers having thus forced those of the seamen whom they wished to get rid of into the boat, Christian directed a dram to be served to each of his crew. I then unhappily saw that nothing could be done to recover the ship. The officers were next called on deck, and forced over the ship's side into the boat, while I was kept apart from every one abaft the mizen-mast. Christian, armed with a bayonet, held the cord fastening my hands, and the guard around me stood with their pieces cocked; but on my daring the ungrateful wretches to fire, they uncocked them. Isaac Martin, one of them, I saw, had an inclination to assist me; and as he fed me with shaddock, my lips being quite parched, we explained each other's sentiments by looks. But this was observed, and he was removed. He then got into the boat, attempting to leave the ship; however, he was compelled to return. Some others were also kept contrary to their inclination.

It appeared to me, that Christian was some time in doubt whether he should keep the carpenter or his mates. At length he determined on the latter, and the carpenter was ordered into the boat. He was permitted, though not without opposition, to take his tool-chest.

Mr Samuel secured my journals and commission, with some important ship papers; this he did with great resolution, though strictly watched. He attempted to save the time-keeper, and a box with my surveys, drawings, and remarks, for fifteen years past, which were very numerous, when he was hurried away with—« Damn your eyes, you are well off to get what you have. »

Much altercation took place among the mutinous crew during the transaction of this whole affair. Some swore, « I 'll be damned if he does not find his way home, if he gets any thing with him, » meaning me; and when the carpenter's chest was carrying away, « Damn my eyes, he will have a vessel built in a month; » while others ridiculed the helpless situation of the boat, which was very deep in the water, and had so little room for those who were in her. As for Christian, he seemed as if meditating destruction on himself and every one else.

I asked for arms, but the mutineers laughed at me, and said I was well acquainted with the people among whom I was going; four cutlasses, however, were thrown into the boat, after we were veered astern.

The officers and men being in the boat, they only waited for me, of which the master-at-arms informed Christian, who then said, « Come, Captain Bligh, your officers and men are now in the boat, and you must go with them; if you attempt to make the least resistance, you will instantly be put to death; » and, without further ceremony, I was forced over the side by a tribe of armed ruffians, where they untied my hands. Being in the boat, we were veered astern by a rope. A few pieces of pork were thrown to us, also the four cutlasses. The armourer and carpenter's mate then called out to me to remember that they had no hand in the transaction. After having been kept some time to make sport for these unfeeling wretches, and having undergone much ridicule, we were at length cast adrift in the open ocean.

Eighteen persons were with me in the boat,—the master, acting surgeon, botanist, gunner, boatswain, carpenter, master, and quarter-master's mate, two quarter-masters, the sail maker, two cooks, my clerk, the butcher, and a boy. There remained on board, Fletcher Christian, the master's mate; Peter Haywood, Edward Young, George

Stewart, midshipmen; the master-at-arms, gunner's mate, boatsman's mate, gardener, armourer, carpenter's mate, carpenter's crew, and fourteen seamen, being altogether the most able men of the ship's company.

Having little or no wind, we rowed pretty fast towards the island of Tofoa, which bore north-east about ten leagues distant. The ship while in sight steered west-north-west, but this I considered only as a feint, for when we were sent away, « Huzza for Otaheite! » was frequently heard among the mutineers.

Christian, the chief of them, was of a respectable family in the north of England. This was the third voyage he had made with me. Notwithstanding the roughness with which I was treated, the remembrance of past kindnesses produced some remorse in him. While they were forcing me out of the ship, I asked him whether this was a proper return for the many instances he had experienced of my friendship? He appeared disturbed at the question, and answered with much emotion, « That—Captain Bligh—that is the thing—I am in hell—I am in hell. » His abilities to take charge of the third watch, as I had so divided the ship's company, were fully equal to the task.

Haywood was also of a respectable family in the north of England, and a young man of abilities, as well as Christian. These two had been objects of my particular regard and attention, and I had taken great pains to instruct them, having entertained hopes that, as professional men, they would have become a credit to their country. Young was well recommended; and Stewart of creditable parents in the Orkneys, at which place, on the return of the Resolution from the South Seas, in 1780, we received so many civilities, that in consideration of these alone I should gladly have taken him with me. But he had always borne a good character.

When I had time to reflect, an inward satisfaction prevented the depression of my spirits. Yet, a few hours before, my situation had been peculiarly flattering; I had a ship in the most perfect order, stored with every necessary, both for health and service; the object of the voyage was attained, and two-thirds of it now completed. The remaining part had every prospect of success.

It will naturally be asked, what could be the cause of such a revolt? In answer, I can only conjecture that the mutineers had flattered themselves with the hope of a happier life among the Otaheitans than they could possibly enjoy in England; which, joined to some female connexions, most probably occasioned the whole transaction.

The women of Otaheite are handsome, mild, and cheerful in manners and conversation; possessed of great sensibility, and have sufficient delicacy to make them be admired and beloved. The chiefs were so much attached to our people, that they rather encouraged their stay among them than otherwise, and even made them promises of large possessions. Under these, and many other concomitant circumstances, it ought hardly to be the subject of surprise that a set of sailors, most of them void of connexions, should be led away, where they had the power of fixing themselves in the midst of plenty, in one of the finest islands in the world, where there was no necessity to labour, and where the allurements of dissipation are beyond any conception that can be formed of it. The utmost, however, that a commander could have expected, was desertions, such as have already happened, more or less in the South Seas, and not an act of open mutiny.

But the secrecy of this mutiny surpasses belief. Thirteen of the party who were now with me had always lived forward among the seamen; yet neither they, nor the messmates of Christian, Stewart, Haywood, and Young, had ever observed any circumstance to excite suspicion of what was plotting; and it is not wonderful if I fell a sacrifice to it, my mind being entirely free from suspicion. Perhaps, had marines been on board, a sentinel at my cabin-door might have prevented it; for I constantly slept with the door open, that the officer of the watch might have access to me on all occasions. If the mutiny had been occasioned by any grievances, either real or imaginary, I must have discovered symptoms of discontent, which would have put me on my guard; but it was far otherwise. With Christian, in particular, I was on the most friendly terms; that very day he was engaged to have dined with me; and the preceding night he excused himself from supping with me on pretence of indisposition, for which I felt concerned, having no suspicion of his honour or integrity.

THE

LAMENT OF TASSO.

ADVERTISEMENT.

At Ferrara (in the library) are preserved the original MSS. of Tasso's Gierusalemme and of Guarini's Pastor Fido, with letters of Tasso, one from Titian to Ariosto; and the inkstand and chair, the tomb and the house of the latter. But as misfortune has a greater interest for posterity, and little or none for the cotemporary, the cell where Tasso was confined in the hospital of St Anna attracts a more fixed attention than the residence or the monument of Ariosto—at least it had this effect on me. There are two inscriptions, one on the outer gate, the second over the cell itself, inviting, unnecessarily, the wonder and the indignation of the spectator. Ferrara is much decayed, and depopulated; the castle still exists entire; and I saw the court where Parisina and Hugo were beheaded, according to the annal of Gibbon.

THE

LAMENT OF TASSO.

I.

Long years!—It tries the thrilling frame to bear,
And eagle-spirit of a child of song—
Long years of outrage, calumny, and wrong;
Imputed madness, prison'd solitude,
And the mind's canker in its savage mood,
When the impatient thirst of light and air
Parches the heart; and the abhorred grate,
Marring the sunbeams with its hideous shade,
Works through the throbbing eyeball to the brain
With a hot sense of heaviness and pain;
And bare, at once, captivity display'd
Stands scoffing through the never-open'd gate,
Which nothing through its bars admits, save day
And tasteless food, which I have eat alone
Till its unsocial bitterness is gone;
And I can banquet like a beast of prey,

Sullen and lonely, couching in the cave
Which is my lair, and—it may be—my grave.
All this hath somewhat worn me, and may wear,
But must be borne. I stoop not to despair;
For I have battled with mine agony,
And made me wings wherewith to overfly
The narrow circus of my dungeon wall,
And freed the Holy Sepulchre from thrall;
And revell'd among men and things divine,
And pour'd my spirit over Palestine,
In honour of the sacred war for him,
The God who was on earth and is in heaven,
For he hath strengthen'd me in heart and limb.
That through this sufferance I might be forgiven,
I have employ'd my penance to record
How Salem's shrine was won, and how adored.

II.

But this is o'er—my pleasant task is done:—
My long-sustaining friend of many years!
If I do blot thy final page with tears,
Know, that my sorrows have wrung from me none.
But thou, my young creation! my soul's child!
Which ever playing round me came and smiled,
And woo'd me from myself with thy sweet sight,
Thou too art gone—and so is my delight:
And therefore do I weep and inly bleed
With this last bruise upon a broken reed.
Thou too art ended—what is left me now?
For I have anguish yet to bear—and how?
I know not that—but in the innate force
Of my own spirit shall be found resource.

I have not sunk, for I had no remorse,
Nor cause for such : they call'd me mad—and why!
Oh Leonora! wilt not *thou* reply?
I was indeed delirious in my heart
To lift my love so lofty as thou art;
But still my frenzy was not of the mind;
I knew my fault, and feel my punishment
Not less because I suffer it unbent.
That thou wert beautiful, and I not blind,
Hath been the sin which shuts me from mankind;
But let them go, or torture as they will,
My heart can multiply thine image still;
Successful love may sate itself away,
The wretched are the faithful; 't is their fate
To have all feeling save the one decay,
And every passion into one dilate,
As rapid rivers into ocean pour;
But ours is fathomless, and hath no shore.

III.

Above me, hark! the long and maniac cry
Of minds and bodies in captivity.
And hark! the lash and the increasing howl,
And the half-inarticulate blasphemy!
There be some here with worse than frenzy foul,
Some who do still goad on the o'er-labour'd mind,
And dim the little light that's left behind
With needless torture, as their tyrant will
Is wound up to the lust of doing ill:
With these and with their victims am I class'd,
'Mid sounds and sights like these long years have pass'd;

'Mid sights and sounds like these my life may close:
So let it be—for then I shall repose.

IV.

I have been patient, let me be so yet;
I had forgotten half I would forget,
But it revives—oh! would it were my lot
To be forgetful as I am forgot!
Feel I not wroth with those who bade me dwell
In this vast lazar-house of many woes?
Where laughter is not mirth, nor thought the mind,
Nor words a language, nor ev'n men mankind;
Where cries reply to curses, shrieks to blows,
And each is tortured in his separate hell—
For we are crowded in our solitudes—
Many, but each divided by the wall
Which echoes madness in her babbling moods;—
While all can hear, none heed his neighbour's call—
None! save that one, the veriest wretch of all,
Who was not made to be the mate of these,
Nor bound between distraction and disease.
Feel I not wroth with those who placed me here?
Who have debased me in the minds of men,
Debarring me the usage of my own,
Blighting my life in best of its career,
Branding my thoughts as things to shun and fear?
Would I not pay them back these pangs again,
And teach them inward sorrow's stifled groan?
The struggle to be calm, and cold distress,
Which undermines our stoical success?
No!—still too proud to be vindictive—I
Have pardon'd princes' insults, and would die.

Yes, sister of my sovereign! for thy sake
I weed all bitterness from out my breast,
It hath no business where *thou* art a guest;
Thy brother hates—but I can not detest;
Thou pitiest not—but I can not forsake.

V.

Look on a love which knows not to despair,
But all unquench'd is still my better part,
Dwelling deep in my shut and silent heart
As dwells the gather'd lightning in its cloud,
Encompass'd with its dark and rolling shroud,
Till struck,—forth flies the all-ethereal dart!
And thus at the collision of thy name
The vivid thought still flashes through my frame,
And for a moment all things as they were
Flit by me;—they are gone—I am the same.
And yet my love without ambition grew;
I knew thy state, my station, and I knew
A princess was no love-mate for a bard;
I told it not, I breathed it not, it was
Sufficient to itself, its own reward;
And if my eyes reveal'd it, they, alas!
Were punish'd by the silentness of thine,
And yet I did not venture to repine.
Thou wert to me a crystal-girded shrine,
Worshipp'd at holy distance, and around
Hallow'd and meekly kiss'd the saintly ground;
Not for thou wert a princess, but that love
Had robed thee with a glory, and array'd
Thy lineaments in beauty that dismay'd—
Oh! not dismay'd—but awed, like One above;

And in that sweet severity there was
A something which all softness did surpass—
I know not how—thy genius master'd mine—
My star stood still before thee:—if it were
Presumptuous thus to love without design,
That sad fatality hath cost me dear;
But thou art dearest still, and I should be
Fit for this cell, which wrongs me, but for *thee*.
The very love which lock'd me to my chain
Hath lighten'd half its weight; and for the rest,
Though heavy, lent me vigour to sustain,
And look to thee with undivided breast,
And foil the ingenuity of pain.

VI.

It is no marvel—from my very birth
My soul was drunk with love, which did pervade
And mingle with whate'er I saw on earth;
Of objects all inanimate I made
Idols, and out of wild and lonely flowers,
And rocks, whereby they grew, a paradise,
Where I did lay me down within the shade
Of waving trees, and dream'd uncounted hours,
Though I was chid for wandering: and the wise
Shook their white aged heads o'er me, and said
Of such materials wretched men were made,
And such a truant boy would end in woe,
And that the only lesson was a blow;
And then they smote me, and I did not weep,
But cursed them in my heart, and to my haunt
Return'd and wept alone, and dream'd again
The visions which arise without a sleep.

And with my years my soul began to pant
With feelings of strange tumult and soft pain;
And the whole heart exhalèd into one want,
But undefined and wandering, till the day
I found the thing I sought—and that was thee;
And then I lost my being all to be
Absorb'd in thine—the world was past away—
Thou didst annihilate the earth to me!

VII.

I loved all solitude—but little thought
To spend I know not what of life, remote
From all communion with existence, save
The maniac and his tyrant; had I been
Their fellow, many years ere this had seen
My mind like theirs corrupted to its grave,
But who hath seen me writhe, or heard me rave?
Perchance in such a cell we suffer more
Than the wreck'd sailor on his desert shore;
The world is all before him—*mine* is *here*,
Scarce twice the space they must accord my bier.
What though *he* perish, he may lift his eye
And with a dying glance upbraid the sky—
I will not raise my own in such reproof,
Although 't is clouded by my dungeon roof.

VIII.

Yet do I feel at times my mind decline,
But with a sense of its decay:—I see
Unwonted lights along my prison shine,
And a strange demon, who is vexing me
With pilfering pranks and petty pains, below

The feeling of the healthful and the free;
But much to one, who long hath suffer'd so,
Sickness of heart, and narrowness of place,
And all that may be borne, or can debase.
I thought mine enemies had been but man,
But spirits may be leagued with them—all earth
Abandons—Heaven forgets me;—in the dearth
Of such defence the powers of evil can,
It may be, tempt me further, and prevail
Against the outworn creature they assail.
Why in this furnace is my spirit proved
Like steel in tempering fire? because I loved!
Because I loved what not to love, and see,
Was more or less than mortal, and than me.

IX.

I once was quick in feeling—that is o'er;—
My scars are callous, or I should have dash'd
My brain against these bars as the sun flash'd
In mockery through them;—if I bear and bore
The much I have recounted, and the more
Which hath no words, 't is that I would not die
And sanction with self-slaughter the dull lie
Which snared me here, and with the brand of shame
Stamp madness deep into my memory,
And woo compassion to a blighted name,
Sealing the sentence which my foes proclaim.
No—it shall be immortal!—and I make
A future temple of my present cell,
Which nations yet shall visit for my sake.
While thou, Ferrara! when no longer dwell

The ducal chiefs within thee, shalt fall down,
And crumbling piecemeal view thy hearthless halls,
A poet's wreath shall be thine only crown,
A poet's dungeon thy most far renown,
While strangers wonder o'er thy unpeopled walls!
And thou, Leonora! thou—who wert ashamed
That such as I could love—who blush'd to hear
To less than monarchs that thou couldst be dear,
Go! tell thy brother that my heart, untamed
By grief, years, weariness—and it may be
A taint of that he would impute to me—
From long infection of a den like this,
Where the mind rots congenial with the abyss,
Adores thee still;—and add—that when the towers
And battlements which guard his joyous hours
Of banquet, dance, and revel, are forgot,
Or left untended in a dull repose,
This—this shall be a consecrated spot!
But Thou—when all that birth and beauty throws
Of magic round thee is extinct—shalt have
One half the laurel which o'ershades my grave.
No power in death can tear our names apart,
As none in life could rend thee from my heart.
Yes, Leonora! it shall be our fate
To be entwined for ever—but too late!

END OF VOL. VI.

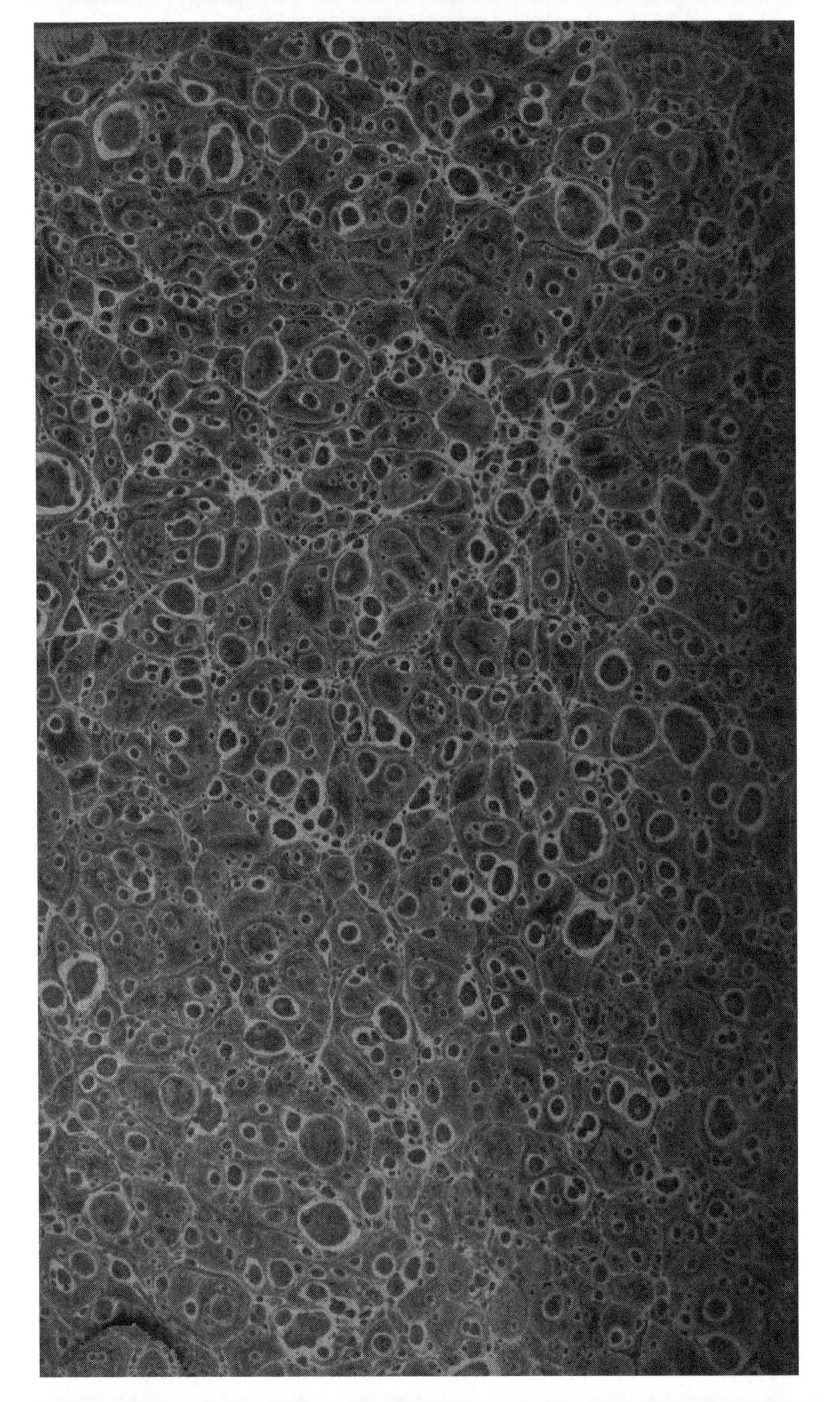

Lightning Source UK Ltd.
Milton Keynes UK
UKHW031330060121
376525UK00009B/566